To Jim & Jane
my friendly neighbours

JR 29/09/01

THE LIFE AND TIMES OF A FALL GUY

THE LIFE AND TIMES
OF A FALL GUY

Joe Powell

Book Guild Publishing
Sussex, England

First published in Great Britain in 2007 by
The Book Guild Ltd
Pavilion View
19 New Road
Brighton, BN1 1UF

Typesetting in Times by
Acorn Bookwork Ltd, Salisbury, Wiltshire

Printed in Great Britain by
Athenaeum Press Ltd, Gateshead

A catalogue record for this book is available from
The British Library.

ISBN 978 1 84624 110 9

He either fears his fate too much,
or his deserts are small.
Who fails to put it to the touch,
to win or lose it all.

To my family

It was my wife, Julie, who first suggested then encouraged me to write these memoirs. Then it was two of my sons, Nicholas and Julian, plus Julian's wife Emma, who provided and updated my computer. They also gave me instruction in its use.

Then Shelley, my eldest daughter, and Penelope, my youngest, kept me up to the bit, as they say, after I had wiped 40 pages of script off the computer. Several months passed however before I again restarted.

Alex, my youngest son, rekindled the effort by putting all the stills on disc. After all their help and encouragement, I was duty bound to complete it. Without all this help and cajoling, it would never have seen the light of day.

It is to my family, therefore, that this book is dedicated.

Contents

Preface

This is the story of Joe Powell, one of the first professional stuntmen in the British film industry.

At the age of seventeen he enlisted in the Grenadier Guards, then transferred to the Special Service unit (which later became No. 4 Commando). During his service he took part in several reconnaissances in France and Holland, raids on Dieppe and Boulogne, the D-Day Landings at Ouistreham, and the attack and capture of Flushing.

After the War, Joe found work as an extra on both British and American movies being produced in the UK. He realised that with his military background he could bring realism into the mass of war films currently being made and could also offer his services for the action stunt scenes. He met up with a captain from the SAS, Captain Jock Easton, MC, and together they gate-crashed the movie industry and formed the first professional stunt team in the UK.

During a quiet period in film work, both men volunteered for service to fight in the Korean War with the 21st SAS Artists' Rifles. After six months' training at Aldershot a telegram was received from General MacArthur saying, 'Home for Christmas', and the operation was cancelled.

When Joe returned to Civvy Street again, his efforts won the right for British stuntmen to be taken abroad on location for the first time, on the film *The Crimson Pirate*. This opened the doors for stuntmen to also be employed on future films being produced around the world.

Joe's career lasted over forty years, during which time he worked in many countries around the world and with many international stars. In his book he reveals how he performed some of the most daring and memorable stunts ever seen.

1

My Early Years

I was born in March 1922 at the Shepherd and Flock public house, Shepherds Bush, London. Three sisters had preceded me and my father evidently went wild with excitement when I arrived. That initial elation, however, gradually diminished as time went by.

We were at the Shepherd and Flock for a number of years although I can't remember much about it. One day the police called at a builder's yard nearby to borrow a ladder to enable them to look into the bar, where my father was entertaining some of his friends after hours. Prosecution followed and Dad lost his licence. Before Dad married he had served in the Life Guards and during the First World War was promoted to quartermaster sergeant. As such he acquired some knowledge of catering, which was to stand him in good stead in future years.

The Life Guards was at that time solely a horse regiment, so his past riding experience helped him find his first job after losing his licence. He was employed in a theatre as an extra, riding a horse on stage as part of a cavalcade. The cavalcade would enter stage left, ride across the stage and exit right. Dad and the other riders then rode around the back of the stage to reappear once more and repeat the performance. This continued over a period, during which the actors carried on with their dialogue. After several circuits of the stage, however, the audience gave Dad a cheer each time he reappeared. The fact was that his horse had a limp and was immediately recognisable. The actors found this too distracting, and Dad, along with the horse, was sacked. Thus Dad's brief theatrical career came to an abrupt end.

Dad fortunately had beautiful copperplate handwriting and was next employed by firms of solicitors to write out wills and conveyances. From these contacts he gained sufficient knowledge of the law to help him to find a way round reapplying for another pub licence. This enabled him to obtain a new licence to take over the tenancy of a pub in Camden Town named the Camden Head. The pub was rather notorious, as it was frequented by the local tearaways, known as the Sabini Mob. But with his knowledge of catering and the help of my mother, who was a marvellous cook, he started high-class lunches and turned the pub into a meeting place for local businessmen. It became a great success.

It was here that I spent the first part of my life. Work in a pub is for three hundred and sixty-five days a year; there is no time off for Christmas and other special occasions. The long hours of work my parents spent in running the pub meant I was left for long periods after school, or at weekends, with little to keep me occupied. I was encouraged to join the Cubs, which certainly took up some of my time. I also attended camp and was taught the rudimentary art of boxing. Instead of progressing to the Scouts, however, I joined the 1st Battalion Royal Fusiliers Cadet Corps. More camps followed and between camps we were drilled by a sergeant major from the Coldstream Guards. The drill I learned was to stand me in good stead, as some years later I was to join the Grenadier Guards.

Cadets only occupied me two days a week, and as a restless boy I was soon looking for new outlets. This was around the time of the home-built Flying Flea, a single-seated aircraft. This caught my interest, and I bought the magazine *Flight*, to learn more about flying. I soon convinced myself that I could build my own version of the Flying Flea. Had I ever been allowed to finish it, it would of course never have flown but it illustrates the measure of my ambition at the age of around twelve.

Using the beer cellar as a workshop, I set about building this contraption. I was convinced that what I was creating would release me from this earthbound existence. From *Flight* I obtained the address of one of the aircraft manufacturers to whom I wrote regarding the tail wheel of an aircraft featured in the magazine. This brought forth a surprising result. The Air Ministry sent round an inspector, who descended on my father, who had the same initials as me. He was accosted in the bar, and taken to one side to be interrogated about this request for details of the tail wheel for an aircraft which was still on the secret list. My father was not amused.

Finding the money to build this so-called aircraft was difficult. Nearly opposite the pub was Pratt Mews, where there was a whole-sale fruiterer who supplied all the local barrow boys with their produce. As they loaded their barrows, they emptied out the apples, tomatoes and oranges from the boxes, which were then discarded. The fruit boxes made excellent firewood. I obtained a set of four worn-out ball bearings from Moy's, a local engineering firm, and built a cart like nearly all the local boys had in those days. I then went into business. The wood was dry and thin, and easily chopped up into firewood bundles. Nearly all domestic fires then were coal fires and I soon had regular customers.

Domestic washing machines were unheard of in those days. If not washed by hand, the week's washing was put into a hessian sack and delivered to a laundry. I never found out whether the whole sack and the contents were washed in one go, or whether the articles inside were washed individually. Whatever the case, my firewood clients gave me extra money to take their bag wash to the laundry and return it after it had been washed. This, of course, boosted my earnings.

To help me further, I was allowed to do odd jobs at a garage in the mews. At times this included helping break up old T-Type Fords for scrap or spares. As a result, I frequently returned home – sometimes late at night – filthy dirty, and covered with grease. On reaching the pub, I used to open the door just far enough to see when my father's back was turned while serving a customer, then rush in through the bar and through the door leading to our living quarters. After this had become a regular feature, the customers used to spot me and shout, 'There he goes!' It was then a question of whether I could move fast enough around the tables and chairs and escape through the door to avoid a clip around the ear from my father. The customers thought this great entertainment, and part of their evening's enjoyment, but I thought the practice very unsporting.

Eventually the scruffy pursuits of the publican's son were bought to an end and Pratt Mews was declared off-limits. This brought to an end my earnings as a firewood supplier and carrier of bag-wash deliveries. About this time, Bill Johnson, our cellar man, complained about the mess I was making trying to build the aircraft in his cellar. His complaints were heeded, and I was banned from the cellar.

I was at this time the only child in the family not playing a musical instrument. As my three sisters played the piano, it was decided that I should play the violin to accompany them. The lessons were held at school. Probably due to the help I received from my sister Ethel, who also played the violin, I quickly picked up the basic technique. Soon I was accompanying her while she played the piano. This was a regular feature on Sundays, the only day on which the whole family could sit down to a meal together. The routine was that, during the meal, one of us was designated to wind up the gramophone and play classical music. Once the meal was finished, everything was cleared away, and the children were expected to supply the musical entertainment.

I remember well the last occasion on which I was to play. I was accompanying my sister as usual when my attention was drawn to some kids playing in the street below. As I knew the piece, I didn't need to concentrate too much on the written music. This resulted in me not always keeping strict time, and I found myself constantly falling behind. I quickly caught up once I realised, but this must have happened several times, and I was unaware of the danger signals my sister was giving me. Things reached a point where my father could not tolerate the uncoordinated music any longer. He bounded across the room, snatched the violin from my grasp, and hit me with it. The instrument smashed to smithereens. It was a great pity really, because in fact I was just beginning to enjoy playing. It was, however, the end to my musical career, though my mother kept the pieces for a number of years.

My father then made another attempt to reform me. He decided to find work for idle hands, and have me where he could keep an eye on me. Attached to the main saloon bar was a small cigarette store. It had two doors, one from our living quarters and the other leading to the bar. In the bar, Dad installed a gramophone, which it became my duty to wind up and play records to the customers, classical records that we normally only played on Sunday afternoons. The customers often showed their appreciation by handing lemonade and Smith's Crisps round the door. I shared this duty with my sisters, and once one of them took over I would sometimes sit upstairs at an open window, looking out on the street below.

There was always something interesting going on. The pub was on the corner of Pratt Street and Camden High Street. The corner was a favourite meeting place for street orators. In those days, as there was no television, politicians had to go to the people to state their case. On this corner on different occasions one could listen to ex-criminals relating their experiences in prison. One in particular used to end his speech by taking off his shirt to reveal scars on his back, left, he assured us, by being flogged while in jail. He would then pass around his hat for his listeners to show their appreciation for the entertainment that he had provided.

From the political side, we had speakers such as Sir Oswald Mosley, leader of the British Fascists, and William Joyce, who later became known as Lord Haw-haw when he broadcast German propaganda over the radio to Britain during the Second World War. At other times we had speakers from the Communist Party. At each meeting, members of the opposing political parties would turn up to heckle. Feelings used to run high. A few years earlier, there had been the Spanish Civil war, in which the Germans and Italians took part. A large number of men from Britain had joined an international brigade to fight for the Spanish Republican Government against General Franco. This was all fresh in people's minds and frequently there was fighting in which the police joined as they tried to separate the opposing factions. At other times, fights would break out between the barrow boys who frequented our pub and Irish customers from the Brighton pub opposite.

Camden Town was an exciting place for a small boy in many ways. The place was all noise and bustle. The trams used to screech up and down the High Street. On the corner of Pratt Mews, the Dowset brothers carried out their illegal betting and were frequently raided by the police, who arrested bookmakers and punters alike. Just below our window, the local fishmonger had his stall, which was illuminated at night by a pressurised paraffin lamp. He sold whelks, mussels and cockles, which customers from the pub would come out to enjoy as a break from their serious drinking.

Across the road was the Bedford Music Hall from where, during intervals between performances, the artists would rush into the pub, knock back a few glasses of their favourite tipple, then tear back to perform. From the music hall, we had musicians, singers, conjurers, tap dancers, bandspeople and performers of all sorts who toured all over the country all the year round. A little further down the High Street was the Hippodrome. Here, for a few coppers, you could sit in the gallery – known as the gods, being the highest place in the theatre – and listen to the most talented artists and watch acts as good as any you can see in today's London Palladium – and in many cases better.

In those days, a shilling (twelve old pennies) would buy a packet of five Woodbine cigarettes, a box of matches, half pint of beer, and a visit to the gods. It should be remembered that there were 240 old pennies to the pound. During this period, a brand new Ford Ten could be bought for a hundred pounds, as could a four square Ariel motorcycle. You could get a second-hand Austin with a gate change gearbox in full running order for ten pounds. A gallon of ROP (Russian Oil Products) petrol cost ten old pence a gallon.

At the other end of the High Street was the Gaumont Cinema. Each performance included a second feature film, a Disney cartoon, a newsreel showing the world news and an organ recital. The organ used to rise from the orchestra pits on hydraulics, under the glare of spotlights, and play for fifteen minutes. And then you would have a stage show. Sometimes this featured what were known as Carroll Levis's Discoveries, young entertainers trying to get their feet on the first rung of the professional performer's ladder. The entrance fee was less than a shilling.

Other free entertainment consisted of street buskers, of which there were a great number. Most of them were ex-servicemen, formerly from regimental bands in the First World War. As long as buskers kept moving, the police didn't interfere with them. As a result, the musicians paraded along one side of Camden High Street, then crossed over and continued playing on the opposite pavement. There were men on either side of the road with collection boxes. All of them had their campaign medals pinned to their jackets.

Also moving up and down shouting their wares were the coster-mongers. Often you would see a man playing a barrel organ, with the proverbial monkey sitting on top. At least twice a week there was an escapologist's act on the corner of Pratt Street. All of them in their own way scraped a living. I can't remember seeing many beggars then, but today they are a common sight. In those days quite a big percentage of the transport was horse drawn and brewers' drays delivered beer. As we had no refrigeration, blocks of ice were delivered and stored in lead-lined wooden boxes. All household coal was delivered by horse and cart. There was a spin-off from all this horse-drawn traffic: horse droppings were never long left on the street. Housewives used to appear with bucket and shovel to scoop up the manure for either their window boxes or, if they were lucky, their gardens.

The roads were surfaced with wooden tar blocks, laid to absorb the noise of the horses' steel-clad hooves. At times when the roads were repaired, boys used to collect the worn blocks, find two ball bearings and, with four screw eyes, construct scooters. It was a familiar sight to see fifteen or twenty boys on these scooters racing each other around the streets. It wasn't uncommon for the nails holding the tar block to come out and for a boy to be sent flying. As this was one of the hazards of scooting, it was vital to carry a hammer to cater for this eventuality by knocking the tar block back into place.

Sometimes as a diversion on a Saturday night we would go to Pages Stores, a butcher's shop in Chalk Farm Road. Because there was no refrigeration and the meat could not be stored, any meat left unsold after five o'clock at night would be auctioned off. The dialogue between the auctioneer and the housewives prior to the bidding was like a pantomime in itself; the wives in the know wouldn't start bidding for the Sunday joint until the breakfast sausages were also included!

2

Getting into Shape

As I got a little older, I combined regular trips to the Prince of Wales swimming baths with work-outs at the Primrose Hill open-air gymnasium. By now I had become pals with Albert Smith, the son of a local fireman. Albert's father was a keen keep-fit enthusiast, a passion which he had passed on to Albert. Although there were no gym instructors at the gym, there was always help to be found from other enthusiasts.

It was from the top of Primrose Hill that we watched Crystal Palace burn and from where we saw the airships R100 and R101 fly over London. The ill-fated R101 crashed in France due, it was said, to all the alterations in the construction stipulated by the air transport body. The remaining airship, which had been designed by Barnes Wallis, was then broken up, as it was maintained that this particular means of air transport was unsafe.

Sunday mornings at Primrose Hill attracted quite large crowds to watch the amateur gymnast performers, a number of whom eventually became professionals. There wasn't a great deal of equipment there; mostly it consisted of rings, trapeze bars, hanging ropes, and parallel and horizontal bars. There were also, however, balancing acts, with three or four men, and a large number of acrobats.

Among the characters that turned up at the gym on Sundays was Peggy Bernard, a one-legged man who earned his living performing high diving acts around the country and was also a good gymnast. Then there was Max Martin Schultz of Baden, Germany, an all-in wrestler with a huge physique. Whether that was his true name or if he was indeed from German stock I never did find out. He certainly didn't have a German accent. The name was probably for the benefit of the fly posters announcing the various venues for wrestling matches around the country. At that time it became fashionable for wrestlers to take Italian or German names.

The other venue for the keep-fit enthusiasts was Highgate Ponds where, in addition to the types using the Primrose Hill gym, you would find boxers and wrestlers, plus yoga devotees, along with members of the Highgate High Diving Club. To young boys like me, these were the men we wished to emulate when we grew up. The high-diving board at Highgate was thirty feet high, which to me at the time seemed an enormous height. Little did I think that later in life I would be throwing myself off heights over three times as high. Nor did I realise that all this background would provide the preparatory training for my future life and career as a stuntman.

On leaving school at fourteen I worked for a firm called Cox's, a subsidiary of Lucas, the electrical company. Here I learned to wind electrical armatures for magnets and retrieve lead plates from batteries, which was pretty uninteresting work. As the job appeared to hold no future prospects, Albert Smith and I took a job in a firm named Sulzer Bros. They made speedometer cables for cars and supplied steam pipes for power stations and swimming pools. Quite a lot of the work was very heavy, which gave the two of us a further opportunity to develop and exercise our muscles – our number one priority at that time. For additional exercise we used to cycle to the Finchley open-air lido, have a swim, then bike home for breakfast and still be at work by 8 a.m.

In 1938 excitement gripped the country with the threatened war with Germany. Britain was mobilised, with all the Territorial Army, Auxiliary Navy and Air Force personnel called to the colours. At the barracks in Albany Street, Camden Town, the Army Territorials reported for duty, mostly accompanied by tearful families, friends and sweethearts. Dispatch riders and staff cars arrived and departed with seemingly increased regularity; hourly updates on the situation were given on the radio; daily newspapers went as soon as they were printed, while the evening newspapers sold as fast as the vendor could collect the money. All this seemed an anti-climax when the Prime Minister, Neville Chamberlain, arrived back from Munich waving the now famous piece of paper signed by Adolf Hitler, which he held aloft as he left the aircraft, saying, 'Peace in our time.'

In 1938 my father died and Mum carried on with the pub, assisted by my sister Ethel and two barmaids. The brewers decided the pub was too big for a woman to handle and efforts were made to get us out. Mum refused to move until the brewers came up with alternative premises with accommodation. There were six children in the family for my mother to raise. After months of haggling, eventually another pub was found by the brewers – the Princess of Wales in Dovehouse Street, Chelsea. This turned out in time to be a much bigger handful than the Camden Head, as during the bombing of London some five thousand Irish workers were housed in Onslow Square just around the corner from us. Talk about out of the frying pan into the fire!

The Princess of Wales was an interesting pub. Opposite us in Dovehouse Street was the Chelsea Women's Hospital and further along the street was the Brompton Hospital. On the same side as the pub, running down to Kings Road, were one-storey houses. They were all rather dilapidated, and their appearance was not improved by the subsequent bomb damage suffered during the Blitz. They remained like this until after the war, when they were replaced by high-quality and expensive luxury housing.

The public bar at the Princess of Wales was frequented mainly by working-class men and women, while the saloon bar was used by doctors from the hospitals, local artists, actors and a sprinkling of film people.

3

Preparing for War

A year passed and once again the possibility of war was looming. During this second scare, I joined countless others digging trenches in Primrose Hill which were intended to shelter people from the threatened air raids if hostilities broke out. In September 1939, the inevitable happened and a state of war was declared. I never found out whether the trenches were ever used by civilians, but I do know that an anti-aircraft battery was positioned there.

I duly went to the recruiting office in Whitehall, but the sergeant in charge, suspecting quite rightly that I was under age, turned me away. A month later I reported to another recruiting office in Malden and was accepted as a recruit for the Grenadier Guards. Soon after joining up I was ordered to report to Chelsea Barracks to undergo initial training. The training consisted of the old peace-time drill based upon forming fours armed with the old Lee Enfield rifle and its eighteen-inch bayonet. None of this was new to me, as I had done it all before in the Army Cadets.

The day began with the bugler sounding Reveille. Recruits had to jump out of bed, wash and shave, clean up the barrack room and make up their beds ready for breakfast parade. After inspection we were released for breakfast. As far as I can remember, the day was broken up into five training periods – three before lunch, and two in the afternoon. These periods consisted of drill, small arms and Bren gun instruction, PT, and bayonet fighting which, while no doubt necessary, didn't fill me with great confidence when I thought of the great number of German troops armed with Schmeissers for close quarter fighting. The British Army hadn't yet received supplies of any American Tommy guns at this time.

After afternoon tea we had to return to the barrack room where, sitting astride our beds, we spent an hour cleaning our equipment and polishing our boots. No talking was allowed and during this period the trained soldier or platoon corporal would walk up and

13

down asking questions about the regiment's history, which we had to learn by heart. At the end of the period the equipment would be inspected. If it was passed, you could go to supper. If the equipment didn't come up to scratch, the unfortunate squaddie concerned would return after supper and start all over again, sometimes failing a second inspection and finishing up in the wash house after 'lights out' still blanching by candlelight.

This was the routine for the first six weeks, following which we were transferred to Windsor Barracks. Here we had much more freedom, but the training was much more rigorous. It consisted of route marches, firing on the range, field manoeuvres, cross-country running and, of course, the inevitable drill on the square.

At Windsor, as at Chelsea, there were a small number of officer cadets, who were forced to spend the first six months of their training in the ranks before being sent to Sandhurst. They were treated exactly the same as us and slept in the same barrack rooms. All NCOs, however, had to call them 'Mister'. On one occasion we were drilling on the square after it had been raining. One of the potential officers, named Purvis, marched slightly out of line each time he approached a puddle. The drill sergeant halted the squad opposite the puddle, but Purvis was now out of line. We were then turned to face the sergeant. Standing in front of Purvis, he told him: 'Mr Purvis, when I give the order, you will take one short sharp pace to the rear into the puddle. When I say, 'One step forward', you will step out of the puddle. This order is for Mister Purvis alone. Right then, in the puddle, out of the puddle!' The order was given three or four times, much to the amusement of the rest of the squad. It must sound very childish now, but it provided light relief to what was becoming a bit of a chore – we had all volunteered to fight a war, not to spend the duration drilling. When we resumed drilling marching up and down, Purvis no longer avoided the puddle.

While at Windsor I remember reading in one of the national newspapers about a demonstration at Trafalgar Square being addressed by the darling of the Labour left, Ellen Wilkinson. A picture of the assembled crowd, among whom I could see only one man in uniform, accompanied the article. The theme of the speech was 'Britain Blancos while Russia Bleeds'. 'Open the Second Front now' was the demand. At this time some regiments were training with wooden Bren guns, and squaddies would jump out from behind cover with cardboard cut-outs of a tank. The troops then had to take appropriate action. Had the demand been acted upon and the Second Front opened, the British Army would have been decimated.

After two months' training at Windsor we were transferred to Wellington Barracks in London. During the time we spent there I was never detailed to do guard duty at Buckingham Palace, although we were all drilled in case we were. However, I did several guards on the War Office. Apart from our normal training, which included a run around Green Park before breakfast, we spent weeks filling sandbags to construct machine-gun posts to protect government offices in Whitehall and the Houses of Parliament in case of an invasion. Here again I was fortunate, as in my free time I could get home. Finally we were posted to an active battalion, and I was sent to the 3rd Battalion Grenadier Guards in Lincolnshire.

Here the training became even more rigorous and realistic in preparation for war. We undertook long route marches followed by three- or seven-day manoeuvres against other troops, sometimes in battalion and other times brigade strength. These were interspersed with seven-mile cross-country runs. I thoroughly enjoyed this side of army life. To add realism to the situation, on no less than three occasions the whole command was stood to as a German invasion was deemed imminent. Subsequently we were moved to Castle Douglas in Scotland. Here we trained in the hills and again participated in three- and seven-day schemes against other regiments.

While in the Scottish hills I learned to love the area and appreciate the physical demands made on us. But I was getting rather restless – it seemed that my mother and sister were seeing more action in London during the bombing than I was experiencing stationed in Scotland. We still carried on with our drill parades. It seemed to me that whenever the training officers ran out of ideas they held a drill parade. At this time I had become pals with a tough Londoner named Johnny Bowers. We both yearned for action and became rather bolshie when we didn't get any. The dreary routine was relieved a little when I joined the battalion boxing team. I escaped several parades while in training under Corporal Ship, who had been an ABA light-heavyweight champion. I won a novice heavyweight boxing match within the Guards Brigade which was staged while we were stationed in Scotland.

15

Bowers and I continued in our uncooperative ways and as a result fell foul of the company sergeants and Foster, the company sergeant major. Foster had a peculiar long neck that earned him the nickname of 'Swannie'. Troops used to sing on the march in those days as a way to relieve the monotony, and this gave Bowers and me the opportunity to start the song, 'Way down Upon the Swannee River', with us both of course laying loud emphasis on 'Swannee'. This obviously annoyed the sergeant major, but gave great amusement to the rest of the company, who wondered how far we would go to annoy Foster. Swannie solved the problem by making us both stretcher-bearers and transferring us to the HQ Company, where we were attached to the RAP (Regimental Aid Post).

While with the RAP we had to undergo a course of first aid instruction, and when on exercises travelled in the ambulance. We soon turned this to our advantage, so that while the battalion marched we stretched out on the stretcher bunks in the ambulance, emerging only when we stopped for a brew up or meal. One day as we lay sleeping on the bunks we were rudely awakened by the ambulance suddenly increasing speed, leaving the road and driving over very rough ground, throwing us all over the place. It came to a halt abruptly and guess who threw open the rear doors – Foster! Outside the rain was pelting down and Foster was up to his eyes in mud. He gave a roar of rage as he saw Bowers and me completely warm and dry inside. He screamed at us to get out, throwing out all our jackets and equipment; we were wearing only shirts, trousers, socks and boots. We scrabbled around in the pouring rain trying to sort ourselves out. What had happened was that a dispatch rider had skidded and come off his motorbike, injuring his legs. The ambulance was needed to take him to hospital.

We were in full view of two companies. The spectacle of Bowers and me grovelling in the mud and rain, soaked to the skin and trying to get dressed, must have been hilarious. The couple of hundred guardsmen viewing this scene were falling about in hysterics. It was Swannie's revenge. Naturally Bowers and I were both put on a charge and given several punishment drills. These punishment parades in full marching order lasted one hour each and were taken by the duty sergeant. There were two each afternoon after all other duties had been finished.

On one of these parades, Swannie appeared, dismissed the duty

16

sergeant and proceeded to chase the arse off us for the full hour. He then reappeared on the second parade, during which one guardsman fell out with severe cramp. Two officers' batmen, unused to this sort of treatment, also collapsed. The sweat was running off us and we were breathing hard. Swannie halted the squad and turned us to face him. Some of the other men were swaying on their feet, but Bowers and I were among the fittest men in the battalion and relatively unaffected. Coming up to me, Swannie pushed his face close to mine. 'Well, Powell, how do you like that medicine?'

'Oh, it was great, sergeant major. But can we keep going? I've a bit of a sweat on and don't want to catch cold,' I answered. He erupted with rage and chased us even harder and another two squaddies fell by the wayside. He screamed louder and louder, and then quite suddenly lost his voice. Both Bowers and I burst out laughing and were promptly marched to the guardroom and placed under close arrest. The charge was: 'Laughing on the 3.30 punishment parade'. Between us we had a whole list of punishment parades to fulfil, with little chance of completing them all. Fortunately fate came to our rescue, as the whole battalion was drafted to join a ship at Inverary to be trained in landing exercises in preparation for the reoccupation of France.

The ship was the *Karanger*. She was a converted passenger ship, with LCAs (landing assault craft) hanging in the davits where her lifeboats had formerly been. I believe that she had come from the Far East. The ship was awash with cans of tinned fruit, which we hadn't seen for a very long time. As we were allowed to buy them, we all made pigs of ourselves. I also laid in a good stock to take home with me on leave.

We spent three weeks aboard the *Karanger* practising landings, most of which were wet ones, with us wading to the beach. The training culminated in a three-day scheme against a Special Service (SS) unit. On the morning of the exercise we were awakened by a bugle sounding Reveille. I thought this very odd, as it was obvious the sound would reverberate around the hills and give advance notice of our arrival. The next event was even more incredible: we were lined up on deck in the dark and the sergeant major came along the ranks feeling our chins to ensure that we had all shaved.

We duly embarked in the landing craft, leaving the ship's side and making way to our appointed landing spot in formation.

Again the landing was a wet one, and at that time of the year the water was extremely cold. Twenty-four hours later several men were suffering from hypothermia. The landing was unopposed and we trudged off up into the hills. During the whole of the three days' scheme we didn't lay eyes on any of the SS unit. However, there was no doubt at all that they had seen us, as we were continuously sniped at over the whole period. I had been lumbered with a Boys 18 anti-tank rifle, which, with its five foot barrel, was quite cumbersome. To keep moving and taking cover from snipers over a three-day exercise proved to be a frustrating and exhausting experience.

Worse was to come. The lorry carrying our greatcoats was captured by the SS unit, so without them we were left wet and cold over the whole of the three days. Our problems didn't finish there. One of our fifteen-hundredweight trucks had been captured by the SS and its driver interrogated. He was given a note stating he had been captured and could no longer participate on the scheme. He was told that if he were seen again he would be on a charge and was ordered to give this note to his CO confirming this. The driver promptly returned to his headquarters and delivered the note. It was a good ruse. A number of SS men jumped out of the back of the truck as it arrived back and shot up our headquarters. Of course this couldn't have happened in action, but somewhere in the back of my mind I was beginning to get a message.

The scheme came to an end and we were marched back to the edge of the loch to re-embark on the landing craft and return to the ship. The road we followed ran parallel to the loch. LCAs were flat-bottomed boats which, with the right beach, could get close in so that hopefully you could embark without even getting your boots wet. But presently there came an order to 'right wheel'. All three companies marched into the loch until everyone was almost up to their armpits in water before being halted and stood at ease to wait until the LCAs arrived to pick us up.

After that we were disembarked at Glasgow, put into lorries and driven back to Castle Douglas. The message forming in my mind was getting through to me. On that return journey the realisation came to me loud and clear: I was in the wrong mob!

4

On Special Service

The punishment parades continued. We weren't alone at Castle Douglas. Also stationed there was an SS unit who had a black hackle in their caps, and several other troops, one of which was later to become known as No. 9 Commando. I decided to try to see their commanding officer to volunteer for a transfer into one of the SS units. The duty sergeant went off to make enquiries, and in due course I was ushered in front of his CO. Questions were asked and my rank and number taken. Next day I was hauled in front of my own CO and charged with improperly approaching an officer, and confined to billets for seven days.

Two days later I was ordered to report to Wellington Barracks, London, for an interview with Major Vaughan for possible enlistment into the SS, after which I had to return to my unit. Within two days I was informed that I had been selected and was posted to a SS unit in Troon, Ayrshire.

When leaving Castle Douglas in a fifteen-hundredweight truck we passed Swannie Foster. 'Cheerio, Swannie,' I shouted. 'I'm off to join a real fighting mob now!' Swannie grimaced and shook his fist, but then his face broke into a huge grin.

My jibe about a fighting mob was of course unfair. The 3rd Battalion Grenadier Guards had fought a rearguard action at Dunkirk. The battalion further distinguished itself much later in North Africa at a place called Long Stop Hill, where it threw the Germans off and handed it over to another unit, only having to retake the hill after it had been recaptured by the enemy.

I arrived in Troon to find that No. 4 Special Service Unit was commanded by a Colonel Lister. At first I was far from impressed. This volunteer force had been drawn from more than sixty different regiments. Although all were in battle dress, each man had the name of his parent regiment on his shoulder flashes and wore his own regimental headgear and badge. There were guardsmen's hats, tank berets and a variety of Scottish headgear with red and black hackles, plus peaked caps known as cheese cutters worn by front-line infantry. The height of the men varied greatly, unlike the standard in the Guards. When on parade as a unit they really looked a ragtag-and-bobtail lot. I began to wonder what sort of unit I had joined and let myself in for. As far as the drill was concerned, all I can say is that it was just about adequate and no comparison to that of the Guards.

I was told Lister was an ex-university boxing light-heavyweight. He was known as 'Fighting Knife Lister'. He got the name from his innovative way of keeping the troops on their toes. All the men at that time carried a fighting knife strapped to their right leg. Anyone falling behind in some in some particular aspect of his training had the fighting knife taken away from him. It was not returned until he regained the required standard. It may now all seem rather childish, but the men took it very seriously. As we all lived among the civilian population, all the locals were well aware of the situation. A man dispossessed of his knife would choose to walk down the road on the side which prevented his right side from being seen by anyone he met. It was all psychological, but it worked. We were all proud of our prowess and could not face the shame of being made an example of as someone who had failed to keep up with the physical or disciplinary demands required by the service.

This type of discipline suited me down to the ground, while the imminent possibility of getting into action made me mature into a real fighting man. This was serious soldiering. All the schoolboy pranks I had become associated with in the Guards came to an end. Colonel Lister left our unit to become CO of the Allied Unit, which eventually became No. 10 Commando. Our new CO was Lord Lovat, the last man in Great Britain to head his own private army, the Lovat Scouts.

The difference between the Guards and the SS units was immediately obvious. After a short lecture by the regimental sergeant major, we were allocated civilian digs. Our landlady was paid the princely sum of six shillings and eight pence a day for our food and accommodation. The reason for billeting us out instead of housing us in conventional barracks soon became apparent. The SS units were formed to reconnoitre the German-held coastline, land and harry the enemy's lines of communication, keep them guessing and obtain information for the eventual landing of the Second Front. These raids could be made anywhere in Europe. Landing conditions could vary greatly, so this necessitated the use of different types of landing craft and training areas similar to the area where a raid was to take place. Raids could involve numbers ranging from just a handful of men in a small dory to a whole unit. Constantly moving to new training areas meant that army barracks would seldom ever be available and therefore civilian accommodation was used. Troon, however, became our operating base to which we always returned.

From Troon we constantly carried out mock raids against other regiments or to test Home Guard readiness. We were continuously training in the use of a wide variety of landing craft. There were cross-channel passenger ships adapted to carry LCAs and we also landed from tank landing craft, dories, Eurekas (American boats) and Yorkshire cobles, we even used Royal Engineers' bridging pontoons. With all this training, however, only about one in five of the planned raids ever materialised. This was due to a number of factors. It could depend upon the weather, amount of moonlight or available landing craft (in the early days these were in short supply). Sometimes it was a question of the availability of motor gun boats which often took us most of the way. Raids were often made, too, in the light of the latest intelligence reports and we were frequently briefed by British spies who had just returned to the UK from occupied Europe.

All this gives some idea of the vigorous training undertaken by the SS units. All the men were volunteers who, before joining, had already undergone at least two years' training with their parent units. This previous training meant that there was always specialist knowledge of every branch of the Army available to be called upon if required. The unit was divided into six troops, plus a headquarters troop. Each troop had its own specialist know-how, but also acquired a working knowledge of the other troops' expertise, in areas such as demolitions, mountaineering, parachuting, direct and indirect machine-gun fire, mortars, and a variety of landing craft. All were trained in assault landings.

As I had already received some training with LCAs in the Guards, I was accepted straight into an active service unit. Once in the unit, however, training never ceased and was completely varied. It included lectures on the conditions existing in areas we were to raid and the study of oblique photos that low-flying unarmed Beaufighters had obtained for us. Members of the SOE (Special Operations Europe) also gave lectures. In this way everybody felt intimately involved in the war and all the training became immediately relevant to us. Sometimes we would go to the docks or steel works to be instructed in sabotage. I enjoyed a parachuting course at Ringway, but in fact never did jump on an operation. Another course was in mountain warfare, spread over six weeks at Braemar. Colonel John Hunt and Squadron Leader Smyth had devised part of the course. Prior to the war, Smyth had been the man who had reached the highest point on Everest without the use of oxygen. John Hunt, of course, led the successful conquest of Everest. Both gave interesting lectures on mountaineering in various parts of the world.

Braemar was our base camp. There were six other camps within a six- to eight-mile radius of Braemar, each of which we visited in turn. We set out for one of them on a Monday, carrying all the food and ammunition we needed for the week's training. The camp consisted of Arctic-type tents, cooking facilities provided by a small Primus in each tent, with the food cooked in our mess tins. Before breaking camp in the morning, there was a meal of beans and bacon, plus hard tack biscuits and tea. During the day we munched dry biscuits, ate some bully beef, sucked glucose sweets, and drank from our water bottles. After marching all day and taking part in mock battles against other regiments we returned to our camp for the night, unless we were training during the night by attacking some other unit. The reason for this way of feeding was that we could keep moving and never climb or march on a full stomach. It enabled us to cover long distances in a remarkably short time.

Throughout all the exercises, everyone was briefed. If you didn't pay attention it was easy to get caught out. At any time during a scheme or manoeuvre an officer would suddenly say to one of the men, 'Your troop sergeant and corporal have been killed. Now you must lead the rest of the men. You are in sole charge and responsible for completing this mission.' The man now in command would then issue orders and instruct the other privates as if he was the NCO. At all times you had to exercise self-discipline. If you weren't capable of doing so, you could be RTUed – returned to your parent unit – obviously in disgrace. High standards were expected, but not enforced, if you couldn't accept this you were regarded as useless to the SS.

On returning to the Arctic tents, we used to prepare an evening meal consisting mainly of bully beef, hard tack biscuits and pemmican, which was lean fresh meat dried, pounded and mixed with other ingredients. Our compo rations had all sorts of goodies to augment these meals, such as chocolate and cigarettes. No bread was supplied except on the weekends when we returned to base camp – it then tasted as good as cake.

Saturday mornings we arrived back at the base camp around noon. Afternoons and evenings were free, so we were able go to the pub or local dance. At the end of the six weeks we returned to Troon, lean as greyhounds. We had, however, been taught a great deal. Whether marching up hill or down, we were trained to keep the same length of step as far as possible and a constant pace so that one's heartbeat, respiration and muscular effort were at all times synchronised. Once you achieved this rhythm you could keep going for hours on end, covering vast distances in a very short time. It was an experience that I thoroughly enjoyed. At the same time I came to appreciate the wonderful scenery of the Highlands.

5

Down to Serious Business

In 1943 we were sent on one of our schemes to Cornwall, where the terrain approximated an area in France where a raid was planned. We needed to demonstrate that a landing on such a rugged coast-line was feasible, although at that time of the year it was thought to be next to impossible due to the huge swells and high cliffs. The Navy refused to take part in the exercise, apart from taking us by tank landing craft to within a quarter of a mile of the selected landing spot on the Lizard. Instead of boats, it was decided to use the Royal Engineers' bridging pontoons, as these were thought to be strong enough to stand up to a battering against the rocks.

The plan was to paddle in, and when close enough, drop anchor. Once the anchor had taken hold it would allow the pontoon to be held, while the line was gradually paid out to get us close enough to jump for the rocks and ascend the cliffs. The swell was such that one moment you were on the crest of a wave and then, as the sea dropped, a rock would be uncovered rising at least fourteen feet above you. While the swell was at its highest you had to jump for it. Once everyone was ashore, the climbing started. Two men were left on each pontoon to haul back out to sea to await our return. They kept their fingers crossed that the anchor would remain firm. If it didn't, with only two men to man it the pontoon risked being smashed against the rocks.

The exercise was watched by a whole lot of top brass from the War Office. To make the attack seem more effective, our colonel, Colonel Dawson, had sent a number of men down the cliff to hide. Once we had landed, they were to ascend the cliffs with us to put in a mock attack, after which we were all lined up to be inspected. One of the groups of high-ranking officers present included Admiral Cowen. While some of the top brass may have been deceived by Dawson's ploy, the admiral obviously wasn't. He stopped in front of the ranks, and with a twinkle in his eye and a very knowing look, said, 'I would have thought that far more of you would have received a soaking.' There was no doubt that he had realised what had happened.

After the exercise we returned to Troon to await the order to carry out the raid, but it was, however, cancelled. The next assignment was a planned attack on Holland, where a hotel had been taken over by the German Army as a rest camp for their officers recuperating from the Russian Front. There was a great deal of surf at this new proposed landing area, so we were sent to train at Great Yarmouth, where similar conditions existed. It was decided to use Yorkshire cobles, as these craft were considered to give us the best chance of landing and getting off the beach for the return. At Yarmouth we trained every day for three weeks. The plan was to land, go inland straight to the hotel, shoot up anyone on the ground floor and place a large explosive charge in the lift and send it up to the top floor where it would be detonated to cut off any chance of escape. We were then to pull back after setting fire to the ground floor and shoot any Germans trying to escape. No doubt if reviewed in the way war is looked at today, such action would have qualified for trial before a War Crimes Tribunal! Let's not forget, however, that these were desperate times and should be viewed in that light. For example, the Germans were trying to burn down London, and their U-boat crews were machine-gunning allied sailors escaping from their torpedoed ships.

However, the planned attack was one of those that never materialised. We went out on the MTB (motor torpedo boat) several times, but were recalled for a variety of reasons, last-minute intelligence concerning German troop movements or the presence of E-boat packs in the area. Whether the Germans got wind of our intentions or not we shall never know, but one night they were waiting for us and a tremendous battle took place. Although their E-boats were faster, they couldn't outgun our MTBs, whose skippers would happily take on a larger number without a second thought. One MTB rammed an E-boat amidships and left her sinking, but as a result had to return to England going astern all the way. Fortunately it wasn't the boat I was on, because we were crowded in the forepeak and would have all bought it. As it was, the gunner on our foredeck was killed in the fighting. There was a pom-pom gun directly above our heads, and the empty casings spewing out onto the deck along with the actual firing created a hell of a din. It was interesting to see every commando's first reaction as soon as battle commenced. To a man, without a word of command, we all started to blow up our inflatable Mae West lifejackets.

On our return the raid was cancelled, as it was decided that we had been rumbled by the Germans. Although there had been great attention to detail in all these proposed raids, our lack of navigational skill soon became apparent. On one of the raids we were taken to within two miles of the French coast, where we embarked in our dory. There were eight of us, including a lieutenant and a captain. The captain was crouched in the bows with his compass, holding his hand in the air just visible to the coxswain so that he would know whether to steer to port or starboard. After about forty minutes, through the mist we saw the outline of what appeared to be an E-boat. The hurried whisper was passed back: 'Cut the motor!' The hope was that nobody on board had seen us. But it was too late. Gun turrets were being trained in our direction. I had a new type of grenade that held a heavy charge of Nobel's 808, which I was ordered to throw at the other boat as soon as we were close enough. We had no chance whatsoever – I was expecting to be blown out of the water at any second. Fortunately suddenly it dawned on everyone that we had in fact sailed in a complete circle and arrived back on our own MTB. Our irate captain immediately gave the order to shove off and make a second attempt. We never found out what the MTB crew thought of us 'pongos', as they called us.

Our captain then made a very sensible decision: he handed the navigation over to Corporal Phillips, who had served in the Merchant Navy. After about another hour, however, we still hadn't reached the coast, the mist was lifting, and it was becoming lighter. It became obvious that if we had landed, it would have been full daylight before we re-embarked, taking into account the time required ashore. Phillips was therefore ordered to turn 180 degrees and return to our MTB. After a further hour's sailing we still hadn't spotted our MTB, which was fitted with an infrared light on the top of her mast. We had been issued with specially adapted binoculars to pick up this light, but still couldn't see anything (we were in touch with her crew by radio, however). To help us locate them, they decided to fire off one of their guns so that we could sail towards the sound. We heard nothing through the mist. Eventually they fired every gun on board, but we still didn't hear a sound. The MTB skipper radioed that he couldn't risk hanging about any longer and was returning to England. We had no option but to do the same.

We were now completely dependent upon Corporal Phillips. Having sailed on our motor all day, we suddenly ran out of petrol. That night half of us paddled while the others tried to snatch some sleep. Four hours later we changed over. There were two walkie-talkies in the boat and every hour it was the duty of one of us to see if we could raise some assistance. During the second day we received an answer – but realised that we were talking to ourselves. The man in the bow was conversing with the man in the stern, with half of us crowded around one of the walkie-talkies, and the others around the other. Looking back it's hard to understand how eventually we won the war!

During the second night we sighted a convoy and signalled to them by flashlight. The naval escort flashed back to us in Morse so fast that we couldn't read the message. They soon disappeared. On the third day, at about eleven o'clock in the morning, we sighted a buoy. I was certain that there would be something on the buoy of use although I didn't know what. I persuaded everyone to pull for it. The tide at this point was very strong and we were all getting very tired after paddling for so long. But we made a huge effort and got very close to the buoy, whereupon Sergeant Coxall made a tremendous leap on to it and tied up. On the buoy were two water bottles and water-purifying tablets, some Horlicks tablets, plus a Very light flare and several cartridges. It had been well worth our efforts and we now felt greatly encouraged. We also reasoned that the buoy must only lie a few miles off the English coast. I noticed that the petrol tank was slung at a slight angle. I suggested to the captain that if we all settled near the bow and levelled it out there might be a little more petrol we could use. This proved to be the case, and we steamed happily for perhaps another hour, after which it was back to paddling.

Some hours later, six gunboats appeared on the horizon bearing down in our direction. We didn't know whether they were ours or German. I couldn't believe the next order, which was, 'Stand to your guns!' Personally I felt very silly standing in a tiny boat pointing a Tommy gun at six gunboats bristling with light artillery and machine-guns. As they came closer, however, we found to our utter relief that they were British gunboats. Feeling extremely stupid we hid our weapons, hoping that our brave attempt had not been noticed. As one of the gunboats came alongside, our lieutenant said to the captain, 'Let's ask them for some petrol, and we'll complete the journey without them.' Nobody said a word, but as soon as a line had been secured, everybody jumped for it, and was aboard and down below deck, drinking hot cocoa in a flash. In any case our little dory would never have run on the high-octane fuel which powered the three aircraft engines of the gunboats.

The drill for landing from either MGBs (motor gun boats) or MTBs (motor torpedo boats) was for the MGBs to leave England in line astern. With three leading, we would be fourth, with the remaining three in line astern behind us. This formation was kept until we were about three miles from our landing point. Our MTB would then approach the coast on a silenced engine. A mile off the coast we transferred into our assault boats and three of the MGBs would then roar off to starboard and three to port, opening up their engines to create maximum distraction. Our MTB awaited our return a mile off the coast while we went ashore for the task allotted us. Two men were left in our dory. After we had landed, they in turn pulled offshore a few hundred yards, dropped anchor and awaited a signal from the landing party to come back in to pick us up. The object of the exercise was that our presence would not be revealed should the Germans be patrolling the beach. As an extra precaution, the landing party also took ashore with them an inflatable dinghy, so that if something happened to the dory, they could still leave the beach and head for home.

On one occasion, returning from a reconnaissance in France, where we had landed on the longest and broadest beach we had ever seen, we couldn't attract the attention of our dory crew. We flashed them several times and waited, but as there was no sign of them we decided to inflate the dinghy and paddle out to sea. These dinghies were pumped up by compressed air bottles activated by pulling on a string. On this particular occasion, due to the improper seating of the valve, half the air was escaping and emitting a very loud squealing noise. We all hit the deck and remained motionless and prayed that there were no German patrols close at hand. Lying very still, we waited for the bottle to exhaust itself. Quite suddenly a searchlight started to sweep the sea and then, to our utter horror, the beach. We lay there holding our breath, expecting machine-guns to open up at any moment. We had no cover whatsoever and would have had no possible chance of survival. After what seemed forever, the beam was switched off. It was decided to wade out to sea holding the half-inflated dinghy, which seemed a better option than lying on the beach. When the water came up to our armpits, our boat suddenly appeared, and we thankfully clambered aboard. Once sufficiently far enough out to sea, we turned on the boat party to ask what had kept them. Evidently they had had difficulty in starting the engine, and had lain in the bottom of the boat while the searchlight was sweeping the sea. We were thankful we had escaped with our lives – the odds had certainly been against us.

Once again we returned to Troon, where we took part in schemes against other regiments. On one occasion we landed at night to attack a Home Guard position on the island of Arran. For some reason we were late in embarking. While waiting for the order to board the TLC (tank landing craft) that was to ferry us over, we were all lounging around sitting on whatever we could find. Suddenly we heard an almighty bellow: 'Commando!' Apart from all heads turning in the direction of the roar nobody moved, except for one chap who asked, 'Who the fuck's that?' It was in fact our new second-in-command, Major Mills Roberts, seconded to our unit from the Irish Guards. He had obviously expected the whole unit to jump to its feet upon his command. He must have been severely shocked by the lack of reaction. No doubt he thought the reason for his secondment must have been to instil some discipline into this unruly mob. His late arrival on the scene may in fact have been the reason for our delay in setting off. We were now ordered to embark on the tank landing craft for Arran.

It was very dark by the time we arrived at Arran. Although TLCs draw very little water, ours hit a sandbank some yards from the beach and we had to swim for it. We were soaked through and it was bitterly cold. We now faced a twenty-mile hike across hilly country to arrive at the point from which to launch our mock attack. We had just taken up our positions for the assault when a line of trucks full of Home Guard appeared. 'Sorry, boys, but we can't wait any longer. We've got to milk the cows,' they shouted to us. We immediately set off back to re-cross the island to rendezvous with the TLC to return to Troon, arriving back at our embarkation point without any halts. We had therefore covered some forty miles without a break, except for the time taken in preparing for the mock assault. By the time we reached the embarkation point, Major Mills Roberts was on his knees. I'm sure that his opinion of his new unit had radically changed from his first impression of us on the Troon quayside. At a later date Mills Roberts left No. 4 Commando to become CO of No. 6, where he distinguished himself in action in North Africa.

On one scheme in Scotland, we were to attack a regiment trained in mountain warfare. We had already occupied the high ground and, remaining out of sight all day, tracked the regiment making their way along the valley. They halted in late afternoon and set up camp for the night. The camp was well laid out, with bivouacs erected, but no defensive positions were dug. This was the first day of a three-day exercise. By 5 p.m. the camp settled down, food was prepared and meal times observed. They then posted guards, while we just watched and observed. One of our men, an artist, sketched the whole camp layout. He located the cookhouse, CO's tent, and so on. In complete contrast we travelled light without the paraphernalia accompanying regular troops, carrying all our own individual rations and ammunition. Our gas capes served as tents.

At about one o'clock in the morning, we made our way down the mountainside, and took up positions just outside the perimeter of the camp. There was no doubt that they had thought that they would not be attacked on the very first night of the scheme. Some of our men were detailed to stalk and silence the guards, which was soon achieved. Still we remained undetected. Then it started to rain and without doubt the pattering of the raindrops on the bivouacs helped us. Suddenly whistles were blown and we rushed the camp, firing blanks and throwing thunder flashes. Tents and bivouacs were collapsed on their occupants. The whole camp was left in utter chaos and by the time they had untangled themselves we were gone. They didn't know what had hit them. It reminded me of what had happened at Loch Fyne when we in the Guards were on the receiving end of an SS raid.

This particular unit had been training in Scotland for two years before being called into action. We didn't see them again until later in the war when they landed in support of us in the attack on Flushing. Equipped with mountain guns, their first shot fired in the action was at a dockside crane, in the cabin of which a German

31

sniper had taken up position. The crane cabin was blown off completely with that one shot.

One of the raids which did materialise was at Boulogne. On this raid we crossed to France on one of the converted Channel ferries. A few miles off the coast, we transferred to LCAs (landing assault craft) which were manned by the Royal Navy. As usual the job of the crew was to land the men then pull back some distance from the shore to await the signal at the end of the operation. They then came back to re-embark the men and return to the mother ship, which would be a few further miles off the coast. The raiding party was under the command of Lord Lovat.

I wasn't in the landing party, but was left on board with a Boys five foot anti-tank gun as LCA protection, along with one other with a Bren gun. When I tried to sight the gun on an object ashore I soon realised that it was useless, as the movement of the LCA made it impossible to keep the sights on target. Fortunately the LCA had on board a stripped Lewis machine-gun, which had 100 round magazines. One in five of the bullets was a tracer. Although I hadn't seen one before, it proved to be ideal for the job.

The landing party had been ashore for about ten minutes when the Germans discovered them. Heavy machine-gun fire opened up, which was returned with tracer bullets lighting up the sky and augmented by mortar fire from both sides. A searchlight was turned on and started sweeping the beach, but as nothing was found it was directed seawards and soon located us. We were fully caught in its beam and machine-gun fire was directed at us, but fortunately it was inaccurate. I opened up with the stripped Lewis gun. The tracer bullets meant I didn't have to sight the gun, just hose pipe the tracer straight into the beam. It was extremely lucky that I had taken the Lewis, because the Bren gun of the other chap with me instantly jammed. The skipper had immediately opened the throttle and kept moving our position. The searchlight went out, but I sprayed the area for good luck before turning my attention to the area from which the enemy fire had come and silencing the machine-gun. Meanwhile the skipper of the LCA continued changing our position pretty rapidly, but staying close enough to get inshore quickly to pick up the landing party.

I don't think the Boulogne raid achieved very much, except that it allowed our military command to estimate the strength of the enemy in that particular area. These were probing raids to keep the

Germans harassed, and to provide information for our planners. They also kept the Germans guessing as to the intentions of the raid. None of the landing party was killed or wounded, but the Germans were certainly rattled. They kept up a heavy rate of fire with both machine-guns and mortars long after we were well out to sea.

Between raids, training never stopped. We were taken to steel works, to be shown how to sabotage similar installations. During visits to docks we were instructed on how to destroy dockside cranes. I liked the variety of training and found it stimulating.

I had persuaded my friend Peter O'Kelly to come on the Ringway parachuting course with me. Like a number of Irishmen, Peter had fatalistic ideas about certain situations. In the early days of the war, parachutists had to exit through an aperture in the floor of the aircraft. We used to jump in a stick of ten men, so five men would sit one side of the aperture and five opposite. On the word 'Go', the first man would throw his legs over the aperture and jump, followed by the second from the other side and so on. The sixth man to jump would shout 'Container, container, container!' and then jump followed by the remaining men. The reason for this was that the three containers would be dropped so that they landed in the middle of the stick, enabling all the men to get quickly to their supplies and equipment.

O'Kelly was always fearful that he would one day be the sixth man and that he would collide with the containers. The inevitable happened and O'Kelly became number six. During take-off Peter didn't look at me because he knew that I would be laughing. When it became time for him to jump, he shouted, 'Container ... Container ... Container ...' so slowly that there were five parachutists in the air, followed by three containers, then a huge gap in the sky followed by the remaining five men.

Originally when the call came for volunteers for the parachute course, I said to O'Kelly, 'Come on, Peter. This is where we separate the men from the boys.' After the jump, Peter looked mighty relieved that a container hadn't hit him. He then said in a very flat voice, 'Sod you on separating the men from the boys.'

33

6

The Raid on Dieppe

The Raid on Dieppe and Objectives as we Understood to be at the Time

The objective of the Dieppe raid was to carry out a full-scale landing, hit the enemy and withdraw. The lessons learned were then to be evaluated, and incorporated into the future D-Day landings. Canadian troops formed the main force, which would make the major assault on the town itself. The task of the Special Forces was to silence the gun batteries ranged on the beaches, which could have made the Canadians' assault impossible. No. 3 Special Services were to take the battery on the left and No. 4 the guns on the right. The batteries were so sited that they couldn't be hit by the Navy from the sea owing to the trajectory of their fire. They were also protected by heavy anti-aircraft guns, making it difficult for the RAF to deal with them, so it became our job to take them out.

Unfortunately, No. 3's LCAs ran into an E-boat and were scattered, with only about twenty men getting ashore. As a result of this engagement the Germans were fully alerted. No. 4 came under fire from machine-guns and mortar. Two men immediately in front of me were killed and I was knocked out. One of the men who died was Corporal John Whattley. Prior to the landing John was wearing a very valuable watch. 'If I buy it, take my watch. I don't want the Germans to have it,' he told me. I always regret that I didn't remember his last words, as I'm sure his family would have treasured it.

When I came to, everybody had left the beach and was pressing on inland. I couldn't have been unconscious for long as I soon caught up with the tail end of the group before they reached the battery. To give you some idea of the odds, the estimated strength of the enemy was three hundred men in both the batteries we were attacking. No. 3 Special Services, pinned down their complete battery with only twenty men. The German gunners were forced to turn their guns inland for protection against No. 3's sniping, which was kept up during the whole of the operation. Although they therefore had insufficient men to attack the battery, their presence prevented the German guns being turned on the beaches.

A later German report spoke highly of these men. It singled out the courage and devotion to duty of one man of No. 3 Commando in particular. When his body was found it was evident from the marks he had made in the grass before dying that he had been dragging himself towards the battery in spite of his wounds.

We of No. 4 had breached the defences of our battery and several Bren gunners had taken up positions firing at the battery's perimeter defences, keeping the Germans' heads down. All of us carried spare Bren gun magazines, which we dropped off to our allocated gunners to keep them supplied with ammunition to maintain a heavy rate of fire. Gunner Burrows and Corporal Waddington were directing such a heavy fire that both barrels were red hot. Waddington had the brilliant idea of pissing down one of the barrels to cool it. Unfortunately the urine turned to steam and scalded his penis. He spent the rest of the time with his penis tied up in his white handkerchief, which I thought at the time would probably make an ideal target for the Germans.

Once the group I was with had dropped the extra magazines, we fanned out and took up positions facing inland to fire on the enemy's perimeter defences to prevent them turning their guns on our attacking forces. The attack was successful and the German guns were spiked. In this action Major Porteous, who led the attack and was wounded, received the Victoria Cross.

Having completed our task, we returned to the beaches to re-embark. On the way back we came across a number of dead and wounded Germans in a cornfield. They had obviously been caught in our crossfire while escaping from the battery. Once back in our LCAs our next task was to take up position in front of Dieppe beach, ready to go to the assistance of the Canadians. It was while we were waiting offshore that we heard over the radio that unfortunately our military intelligence had failed to receive information that some time before the landing a German armoured division had moved into the outskirts of Dieppe. Completely outgunned and outnumbered, the Canadians had suffered very heavy casualties.

The position ashore became untenable. It was obvious that our small number could in no way assist in trying to extricate them and we were forced to retire. Although we in No. 4 were the only force to achieve our objective and knock out a battery, this in no way detracts from the magnificent operation of the twenty men from No. 3 facing an impossible task or that of the Canadians, pockets of whom were still fighting on long after we had returned to England.

To an extent the operation was a disaster, with so many dead, wounded and taken prisoner. There can be no doubt, however, that the lessons learned from this operation undoubtedly saved thousands of lives when eventually the invasion of Europe took place. Due to the numbers of casualties involved, many people thought that Dieppe had been a D-Day failure. German propaganda also claimed that it was a real landing that had been repulsed. Dieppe, though, was just a dress rehearsal for the eventual liberation of Europe.

Shortly after we returned from Dieppe, Brigadier Lucky Laycock of Combined Operations inspected us. About this time, it had been decided that the Special Services designation should be changed to that of Commando. We were issued with green berets, and while we retained our parent regimental badge, shoulder flashes were replaced by Commando ones. This did have the effect of smartening us up, but to my mind things changed from that moment on.

Reflections on Dieppe Lord Louis Mountbatten's Deception & Responsibility.

An amazing story about the Dieppe Raid has emerged some sixty years after the battle I had always understood that the raid was a D-Day rehearsal. An exclusive article in the *Daily Express* by John Hughes-Wilson, a retired British Military Intelligence Officer, however, painted an entirely different story – one which seemed completely unbelievable.

It emerged that the Dieppe Raid was the brainchild solely of Lord Louis Mountbatten. The article states that it was Mountbatten's power-crazed quest for glory that led to the massacre at Dieppe.

The second Canadian Division, which had been based in Sussex, led the main assault on the coastal town. A frontal attack over open beach against German pillboxes. Many were slaughtered before they had even managed to clear the beach. Over one thousand were massacred, nearly two and a half thousand maimed or captured, and only a thousand managed to return to England.

Mountbatten's incompetent staff had failed to get even the most basic intelligence on the state of the beaches. Fifty tanks were destroyed, most stuck in the shingle. The RAF suffered its biggest defeat of the war, losing 150 planes to the Luftwaffe's 46. A German commander wrote of the attack, 'This reckless affair mocked all the rules of military strategy and logic'.

A previous attack was planned in July, when the Germans spotted the landing craft and bombed them, but several thousand Canadian soldiers flooded back ashore and the attack was cancelled.

Mountbatten then carried out the most breathtaking deception of the Second World War. He decided to plan a new raid on Dieppe without clearing it with his bosses, the Chiefs of Staff. It would appear that his sole purpose was to prove that he should be the Allied Commander-in-Chief of the D-Day landings.

Churchill was in Moscow with Stalin, and knew nothing of the planned raid. The truth was that Mountbatten had mounted the raid in total defiance of the Chiefs of Staff.

In 1942 the acting Chairman of the Chiefs of Staff, General Nye, had not been informed of the pending raid. On his return, General Alan Brook, who had been away with Churchill, came into the situation room and exploded saying, 'What the bloody hell is Mountbatten up to in the Channel?'

Mountbatten repeatedly lied about where the responsibility for this disaster lay. It was stated that Mountbatten swore his own Combined Operation Staff to secrecy, by telling them that the raid had been ordered by the Prime Minister.

After the war, Mountbatten claimed that the Dieppe raid had provided valuable lessons for D-Day. Pat Porteous, one of the two VCs of the raid, retorted, 'Nonsense, we could have learned as much in Weymouth Bay'.

Lord Lovat stated that Mountbatten had only ordered the operation through vanity and conceit, and a desire to steal the glory.

Mountbatten's biographer said, 'Mountbatten rewrote history with a cavalier indifference to fact.'

A later Prime Minister, Anthony Eden, who knew him well, called him 'a pathological liar'.

Field Marshall Gerald Templer went one better, saying to Mountbatten, 'Dickie you're so twisted that if you swallowed a nail, it would come out as a cork screw'.

Mountbatten was later blown up by the IRA.

Some time later we were posted to Winchester. Although we still did the occasional speed march, the training was in no way as rigorous as in Scotland. We also received an intake of police volunteers. They had not been recruited from regular army units, but had gone straight to Achnacarry, the Commando training camp. Although they had seen no action, a percentage of them were soon promoted to NCOs. This caused some disillusion in the unit. We started to have drill parades, with emphasis placed upon smart turnout. The unit was becoming like an ordinary line regiment, the likes of which I had joined the SS to escape.

A unit boxing team was started, which I joined as a heavyweight. As a result I was excused some of the drill parades in order to train, which relieved some of the boredom beginning to creep in. I shared a billet with two men from another unit, as accommodation at Winchester barracks was not available. One of them was Tom, a cross-country runner, and I started to train with him in the evenings. Life took on a regular pattern. If there were no guard duties and we were not in training, most evenings were spent in the pub or at a local dance.

As a result of boxing, my nose became bent and as I was having difficulty breathing an operation became necessary. It was carried out at Winchester Hospital. Here I became very fond of a nurse and even met her after the war. But there was no future in the relationship, as I had no job or even a trade to go back to. I had no idea of how I was going to earn my living in Civvy Street. She eventually left me to take a job in South Africa.

After a period at Winchester, during which time we had also carried out a few reconnaissances in France and Holland, we were moved to a camp near Chichester, West Sussex, in preparation for the D-Day landings. While at the camp we took part in night schemes against other units. This was a relief after all the spit and polish and square bashing at Winchester. On the way to Chichester we passed thousands upon thousands of troops, armoured cars, tanks and all the paraphernalia of the war machine. There was no doubt that the invasion was definitely on.

The new camp was colossal and housed several other units apart from our own. There was an amusing incident involving Peter O'Kelly, the mad Irishman I had befriended and whom I persuaded to go on the Ringway parachute course with me. Peter had been at an Officers Training Unit, preparatory to taking a commission in the Irish Guards – or at least that was the idea. What happened in fact was that he had been given the option of volunteering for the Commandos or being court-martialled for hitting a Guards drill sergeant.

Peter and I had returned very hot and sweaty from a speed march and went for a shower. Unfortunately all the showers set up in the camp were full, with long queues of men waiting their turn. Peter, however, had noticed an officers' shower in another part of the camp. On investigation we found it was empty, so we duly took possession and started to shower. We hadn't been there long before a lieutenant looked in and demanded to know what we were doing in there. With great presence of mind Peter, who was six feet five and had retained an air of authority from his OCTU (Officer Cadet Training Unit) days, tore the officer off a strip in his cultured voice delivered with a military clip. He ordered him to stand to attention when addressing a superior officer, shouting that if he didn't get to hell out of there in double quick time he would put him on a charge and march him before his CO. The lieutenant concluded that he had made a ghastly mistake, apologised and beat a hasty retreat. I don't know what punishment Peter would have received for impersonating an officer, or what I would have got as his accomplice, but we didn't wait around to find out. I nearly burst out laughing while Peter was giving the officer a dressing down and it was as much as I could do to contain myself. But once we had reached the safety of our own lines, we both fell about laughing.

7

D-Day Dawns

Eventually we were embarked for D-Day. I can't now remember
how many days we were aboard waiting due to bad weather, but
eventually, it was all systems go. It was a glorious sight as we left
Southampton. Thousands and thousands of craft of all shapes and
sizes were steaming towards the French coast and Normandy.

During the trip we were fully occupied priming grenades, filling
magazines and being brought up to date with the latest photographs taken at various levels by the RAF's Beaufighters. Stripped
of armament to keep down their weight and increase their speed,
these aircraft were used solely for reconnaissance purposes and
piloted by tremendously courageous and dedicated airmen. Thanks
to the photographs and the thoroughness of the planners, every
member of our unit was able to identify on the ground the roads,
houses and other features we would pass en route to the enemy
battery that was to be our target.

Dawn was beginning to break when we embarked into our LCAs,
and set off for the Ouistreham beach. The plan was for a line
regiment to take the beach for us, so that we could go all out for the
six-inch gun battery that we were to silence. After this we were to go
hell for leather inland to take up position on the extreme left flank
of the Allied army. When we got to the beach, however, although
the line regiment had landed and taken up firing positions, they
were pinned down without making any progress. No one could
blame them, it was their first time in action and the machine-gun
and mortar fire was very heavy. But experience had taught us long
ago that the last place to be caught was the beach. The Germans
had had plenty of time during their occupation to organise defensive
fire, but we went through them like a dose of salts. However, we still
suffered forty casualties. On reaching the road leading to the battery
we pushed on as fast as we could. It was here that one of the many
personal tragedies of war happened. Half our unit was made up of

Free French and one of them was shot and killed just a few yards from his home, where the family was still living.

Just as at Dieppe, Bren gunners took up positions firing into the battery to keep the German gunners pinned down, while the main assault group stormed the battery to capture and spike the guns. The group Peter O'Kelly and I were in was to take up positions facing inland to hold off any counter attack. The operation worked like clockwork. After a while O'Kelly and I were called to help carry out some of the wounded to a place were they could be picked up and evacuated back to England.

Having achieved our first objective, we pushed inland to cross over the River Orn via the Pegasus Bridge, which had been captured by the airborne forces, but was still under heavy machine-gun fire from the Germans. On the way to the bridge we had to use a road that at the time seemed to go on for ever. It was under constant machine-gun fire, which meant we had to constantly drop into a ditch for cover, then get up and run for it – short distances at a time – when the fire was directed elsewhere. This of course slowed our progress towards the Pegasus Bridge and put the airborne troops under additional pressure in holding it for us. One machine-gun position in particular was bringing down very heavy fire on us. Fortunately a tank had now got ashore and was rumbling up the road to support us. Someone fired a Very pistol in the direction of the machine-gun, but it needed a second flare before the tank located the slit trench from where the fire was coming. The tank revved up and charged straight for the position. One of its tracks ran over the trench and locked. The tank then rotated rapidly on its other track in circles until it had completely demolished the trench and filled it in, burying its occupants. In all probability they are still there. The silencing of the machine-gun post allowed us to make better progress and reach the bridge.

Coming under fire from other directions, we still had to dodge from cover to cover and wait for breaks in the firing before making a final sprint to the bridge itself. Once we were on the bridge its steel sides afforded us cover, providing we kept our heads down. On arriving at the far end of the bridge it was again a question of waiting for a lull in the firing to make a dash for safety on the other side of the road. I started to run and had covered only a short distance when my Tommy gun magazine fell off. I immediately stopped and turned, kicked the magazine back on to the bridge and sought cover there while I replaced it. That move saved my life. As I stopped, a burst of fire hit the road a few paces in front of me. Had I run on I would certainly have run into it.

Once we had cleared the bridge, we made our way inland to Le Plein, a little village on the extreme left flank of the Allied armies. Our position was astride the road leading to Salenelles, a town held by the Germans. Between us lay Dives. This area was infested with mosquitoes attracted by the dampness of the area and the bodies of dead men and animals lying there. The animals, mostly cows, had been killed in artillery bombardments and cross fire from machine-guns. Our unit was very thin on the ground, and with no anti-tank guns we felt vulnerable to possible armoured vehicle attack. We didn't even have enough men to cover the whole area. Whenever the Germans attacked to our left, we had to dispatch a number of men there to keep moving from cover to cover to give the impression that the whole area from Le Plein to the sea was occupied by a large force. Fortunately for us the ground from Salenelles to the sea was open ground, which afforded no cover to the attacking forces, and we were able to maintain the position.

One day, while patrolling the area, we became careless and found ourselves in an exposed position. Undetected by us a German patrol had advanced and taken up position in woods the other side of the Salenelles road, from where they opened up with very heavy fire. We managed to find cover but were effectively pinned down. In front of us was a barbed wire fence, with another alongside the road, which was at least 100 yards to our right. Across the road itself was another barbed wire fence, and then an open space across to the wood from where the well-concealed Germans were firing. After a break in the firing everything went quiet. No doubt the Germans believed that they had got us all. Our officer suddenly commanded, 'Fix bayonets!' Nobody moved. There was an incredulous shout in a cockney voice from someone in the patrol: 'Fix fucking bayonets?' He didn't follow this up with what we were all thinking at that moment – along the lines of 'Get stuffed' or words to that effect. Had we made a bayonet charge, there would have been no way in which we would have survived getting over the first fence, let alone have reached the Germans. No doubt the officer in command had been completely flummoxed by our predicament, felt that he had to shout something and said the first thing that entered his head. Given time to reflect, I'm sure that he would not have given such an order.

We managed eventually to extricate ourselves and only on one occasion did the Germans reach our position in any strength of force, but then were thrown back with very heavy losses.

After we had knocked out the battery at Ouistreham and taken up position at Le Plein, the plan was for us to be relieved after ten days and return to England. There we were to re-form and then land at various points behind German lines to cut their communications, generally probe their defences and keep them guessing as to where the next attack was likely to be. What actually happened was that due to bad flying weather, the main Airborne re-enforcement didn't arrive for several days. When they did, it was the most fantastic sight, with thousands of aircraft carrying paratroopers and towing gliders with troops and supplies. As the gliders cast off and started to descend, they were given a very hot reception. Once on the ground, the German artillery opened up on their landing areas and we were convinced that they must have received many casualties.

A few days later we were at last relieved and withdrew behind the front line under cover of darkness, two miles from our former position. We had just settled down for the night when we were aroused and ordered to go back to Le Plein. The troops who had replaced us had come from the Western Desert and had no experience of close-quarter fighting in wooded areas, so it was decided to withdraw them and give them retraining. Thus, instead of returning to England prior to re-forming and then raiding behind German lines for which we had been trained, for the next sixty-four days we just became front-line troops. This had several disadvantages: we had no anti-tank guns and no cookhouse, and we lived on compo rations which contained no bread, only hard biscuits.

From here we used to probe the German front line practically every night. Half a dozen Jews who spoke German joined the unit and one of them always came on patrol with us. The idea was to get as close to the German lines as we could without being detected. A loud hailer with a spike was then pushed into the ground. After withdrawing to what we considered was a safe distance, the German-speaking Jew would then start broadcasting propaganda to the enemy and invite them to surrender. The Germans were certainly rattled by these tactics, and fired off thousands of machine-gun and rifle rounds and mortared the whole area. They certainly didn't get much sleep, and this was achieved with half a dozen men and a German-speaking Jew.

Our biggest problem was the millions of mosquitoes. We used to console ourselves with the thought that if we had it bad then the Germans would have it worse. It wasn't until we broke through their lines, however, that we found for some reason their areas were free from the insects.

One night, O'Kelly and I were leading a patrol close to the German lines when the platform of my Tommy gun fell off and the rounds spilled out with a tremendous clatter. This alerted the enemy, who immediately opened up with machine-guns. This fire was very heavy and we took cover in a ditch where we stayed for some time even after it stopped. We turned back to rejoin the patrol, only to find that they had all disappeared.

Worse was to follow, as the Germans had sent out a patrol to intercept ours. They were working round between us and our own lines. We moved off parallel to our own lines and ahead of the Germans. Once we thought that we were far enough ahead of them, we turned towards our own lines. But we realised we had moved too far off our own lines, and were approaching those of another regiment. The danger now was that we stood the chance of being shot by another patrol. It was still quite dark when we came across a lookout post. Fortunately the squaddie manning it was fast asleep. Thank God he was. He awoke with a start as we shook him and looked likely to die of shock. By the time we reached our own lines, our patrol had long since returned and it had been assumed that O'Kelly and I had bought it.

After we had spent sixty-four days in the line a number of NCOs and officers were summoned to meet our brigadier. We all expected to be told that we would now be returning to England to resume our original plans of harassment, and also to be congratulated on what we had achieved so far. How mistaken we were! He looked round at us and said, 'Well, you've had an easy time until now, but now you're going to harry the Hun.' This was a prelude to a forty-mile advance on our part.

Our first move was to relieve some paratroopers at Bois de Bavant. This had evidently been a comparatively quiet part of the front line. Airborne had taken advantage of the quiet period to reconnoitre the German positions, which they had outlined on the maps. They had also accumulated a large quantity of two-inch mortar shells and as we had no transport there was no way in which we could carry this arsenal when the proposed advance commenced. One of our officers thought that it would be a good idea to range the German positions using this spare ammunition. The Germans weren't a bit pleased when the firing started. They started mortaring us back and in no time at all a complete battle was raging before the Paras had got clear, so they weren't pleased either. 'What's the matter with you stupid bastards? This was a quiet area before you lot arrived!' they shouted.

The patrolling continued over the next two weeks, as did the mortaring, which got heavier and heavier. Of course the Germans had also reconnoitred the Airborne positions during the so-called quiet period and as a result their fire was also very accurate. It was therefore decided that we should pull back some fifty yards and reposition our trenches there. The ground was very hard and O'Kelly and Corporal Maybury, both ex-Guardsmen, had to have their trenches deeper than most of us due to their height. We employed the sandbags and tree logs the Paras had used on their trenches to reinforce our new positions. As the mortaring was spasmodic, we placed a lookout some distance in front of our old positions, and it was his job to blow a whistle when he heard the German mortars hit the base plate. This meant that we only had a few seconds to dive for cover before the mortar shells started to explode around us.

Sometimes when the whistle blew we were halfway between our old slit trenches and the new ones. When O'Kelly was caught like this he dropped the sandbags he was carrying and ran for his new trench, but as it was the deepest, a number of men close by had already dived in it to take cover. O'Kelly was only able to get partially into the crowded trench and was hit in the legs by shrapnel. When the mortaring stopped, O'Kelly asked Corporal Maybury to look at the wounds. 'They're not bad, Peter – only flesh wounds.' Peter's six-foot-five frame was very lean to say the least. He raised himself painfully on one elbow. 'Flesh wounds be fucked! I'm only skin and bone.' O'Kelly was evacuated back to Blighty. After his recovery in England, however, he didn't return to No. 4 Special Services but was sent to India. I didn't see him again until after the war.

During our stay at Bois de Bavant I was promoted to sergeant, having been made up to corporal at Le Plein. It was from Bois de Bavant that the main advance started. As we advanced, most of the contact with the Germans consisted of artillery and mortar exchanges. At the end of a forty-mile push we were up near Le Havre, where we halted and were told that we were returning to England. As most of France had now been liberated, we wondered where our next theatre of operation would be. We were returned to a camp in southern England to await our next posting.

Once the big push started in France the lines of communication were being extended, as all supplies were being transported from Cherbourg and the distance increased as the advance proceeded. Although the port of Antwerp had been captured, it couldn't be used, as the entrance via the Schelt was blocked by the German occupation of Flushing on the island of Walcheren. Belgium on the south side of the Schelt had been freed, but Flushing was heavily fortified, with huge pillbox emplacements housing heavy guns and machine-gun posts. Here, then, was our next objective.

8

The Attack on Flushing

Military intelligence had estimated that Flushing could only be taken by a division. The main defences were stretched out along a thin strip of land line parallel to the Schelt. The strip was festooned with concrete pillbox emplacements. The RAF had bombed this strip so heavily, leaving huge craters, that it had become known as the 'poxy cock'. The pillboxes were so strongly constructed, however, that they had remained virtually unscathed.

In the period after our arrival at Breskins, the Belgium town opposite Flushing, was a relatively quiet one. It didn't entail much training, but we spent a lot of time studying RAF aerial photographs of the Flushing fortifications.

It was decided that the attack was to be by night and carried out not by a division but solely by a Marine Commando brigade to which we had been seconded. This was a vast reduction in the numbers that military experts had originally estimated necessary to carry out the operation. The plan was for heavy artillery to shell the pillboxes in order to make the Germans keep their heads down. This wouldn't have worried the occupants of the pillboxes unduly because they were well sheltered, but the artillery could obviously achieve greater accuracy than the RAF. In any case, we didn't want to land during an aerial bombardment.

Some time after the shelling started, under cover of darkness, we crossed the Schelt as fast as our boats would take us. We were relying solely upon surprise and speed for the success of our attack. Thanks to the complacency of the German defenders we remained undetected. Had we been seen, most likely we would have not even survived half the journey across. The artillery was allocated areas of shelling. As we got close to our landing point, we radioed back to the gunners to lift the shelling in that area and rushed ashore. As we reached other areas in turn we used the same procedure, so we were therefore advancing under a lifting barrage. The Germans were obviously used to bombing and shelling, which they treated with contempt. Probably they were also aware that there had been no big Allied military build-up in the Breskins area, and therefore no likelihood of any real attack against Flushing. They must have felt very secure in emplacements impervious to both shelling and bombing. Their lack of observation reflected this and we were among them before they realised it.

We had now penetrated behind their fortifications. So confident were they of their seemingly impregnable positions that nearly all their guns faced across the Schelt in order to fire upon any shipping attempting to reach Antwerp. Because we were very lightly armed, we were able to move at great speed. Running down the backs of the pillboxes, we threw No. 77 phosphorus smoke grenades into them. When we saw smoke coming out of the firing apertures we doubled around and threw in thirty six grenades. The Germans inside could not breathe or see. Those who had not been killed had no option but to surrender, which they did in great numbers. Further inside the docks we met with fierce resistance. All the fortifications overlooking the Schelt, however, had been put out of action within two hours of our landing. Within the next few days, the whole of the island was captured, which allowed the port of Antwerp to be opened and thus shortened the lines of supply to all the front line troops, which up to that time had had to come all the way from Cherbourg. This greatly assisted in bringing the war to an end.

We then bypassed the next island, South Beveland, and occupied North Beveland where we met no resistance. The Germans now realised the danger facing them and rushed eleven thousand marines on to the next island, Schouwen. Here the war virtually ended for us, apart from reconnaissance and patrols we made on Schouwen to keep the Germans guessing as to whether a further Allied push north was imminent. We were far too small a force to attempt to take Schouwen against such odds, as the brigade was now spread out over three islands, with just No. 4 on North Beveland. The German presence posed a serious threat, because if they mounted a counter-attack and retook Walcheron all Allied supplies would once again have to reach the front line via Cherbourg. The Germans were very aware of this and started amassing landing craft at Schouwen.

This build-up on Schouwen meant we were very exposed. We

50

were again very thin on the ground, as had been the case at Le Plein in France. There was nothing for it but to continue keeping the Germans guessing about a possible push north by constantly reconnoitring Schouwen by night. We also sometimes acted as observers on Schouwen for the artillery to bombard German positions during the day. While there was always the possibility that the enemy would attempt to retake North Beveland, they were in a way at a disadvantage despite their superiority of numbers. They had no aerial observation and therefore hadn't a true idea of our strength. Had they known the position, there is no doubt that they would have attacked. As it was, they limited their actions to raids from Schouwen on to North Beveland on a number of occasions.

We established look-out posts along the north coast of North Beveland, opposite Schouwen. During the day only a few of them were manned (as the whole of Schouwen's coastline could be observed). In this situation neither we nor the Germans would attempt to cross. At night these additional posts were manned and from them patrols were sent out along the dykes to make contact halfway with men from the next post along and then return. There were not enough of us to man the whole coastline. On one patrol we came under fire. Some instinct told me that we had run into another of our own patrols. I ordered my section to hold their fire. My call stopped the firing. I then shouted the password and received the correct reply. I stood up cautiously, as did a person from the direction in which the shooting had come. Telling the section to keep me covered I started to walk towards the man opposite, who also came towards me. It turned out to be a Dutch resistance group, formed from the islanders to augment our numbers. Luckily their fire was inaccurate, and we hadn't returned it. After greeting our opposite numbers we went back to our respective posts.

On another occasion while resting at our post, we heard heavy machine-gun and rifle fire and immediately set out in the direction we judged it to have come from. By the time we arrived at the area the firing had stopped. We met Sergeant Miles from the next post who told us he and his men had run into a German raiding party. They had exchanged fire and driven the Germans off. Together we searched the area and found a number of machine-gun barrels and belts of cartridges which had obviously been dumped in panic.

There was also evidence that at least one man had been hit, as we saw where the grass had been flattened as the Germans dragged his body back to their boat. Our respective patrols went back to their posts to await dawn and daylight, when our patrols would return to the main post for food.

When this particular morning dawned a heavy mist was lying between the two islands. As it started lifting, it was only a matter of time before the transport arrived to take us back to the main post. I decided not to wait for transport, but out of curiosity walked back alone to have one more look at the area where Sergeant Miles had exchanged fire with the German patrol. As I reached the approximate spot, I heard muffled voices coming from the seaward side of the dyke. Peering over the top of the dyke, I could see a boat, with dimly outlined figures standing about the deck. It was in all probability the area where the Germans had landed. I heard an engine start. Determined not to allow them to escape, I shouted to them to surrender in the few words of German we had been taught and fired a warning burst over their heads. The volume of fire I received in return from what appeared to be a small wooden boat was unbelievable. Ducking down, I ran along to another point from which to fire. I had been told that in certain light it's possible to see your rounds going towards a target, but I had never believed it until now. In the prevailing light conditions I had the satisfaction of being able to hosepipe the bullets on to the boat. The firing brought the patrols from both posts rushing to join me and take up positions all along the dyke. The alert had gone back to headquarters and the artillery had opened up on Schouwen in the vicinity from where the attacking Germans would have embarked. A radio message was sent to a small naval unit which provided us with support requesting them to come round to a given point and cut off the enemy patrol. The unit replied that their exact position was unknown as they had lost their bearings in the mist, but they were somewhere between Schouwen and North Beveland, adding they had come under heavy fire.

The Royal Navy had in fact come under friendly fire – from me! The naval unit had been patrolling between the two islands, but had neglected to inform anyone of either their position or their intentions. In the fog they had dropped anchor in the area where the Germans had landed the night before. Once the information

Cornwall landings, 1943.

Cornwall landings, 1943.

No. 4 Special Service assault team.

Return to Boulogne with the stripped Lewis.

Return from Dieppe under Lord Lovat, 1943.

Photograph courtesy of the Imperial War Museum, London. H22584.

Buckingham Palace. Major Porteous receives his VC.

En route to Normandy, 1944.   Photograph courtesy of the Imperial War Museum, London. B5099.

D-Day, en route to Pegasus bridge, 1944.

Photograph courtesy of the Imperial War Museum, London. B5221.

D-Day; returning from the Battery, Ouistreham.

Photograph courtesy of the Imperial War Museum, London. BU1190.

Occupation of North Beveland, 1944.

No. 4 Commando Memorial, Scotland.

BANDIT-SMASHERS FLY TO JUNGLE

By Daily Graphic Reporter

THREE of Britain's toughest terrorist-smashers will fly from England to Malaya to-day. They will lead a team of Special Air Service fighting men which will follow them in a few months.

As soon as they arrive the three officers will lay the groundwork for training Britain's jungle army in new tactics to beat the bandits.

The three are Major Anthony Greville-Bell, of Ascot; Captain Jock Easton, and Captain Alastair MacGregor, both of London.

Major Greville-Bell and Captain MacGregor were awarded the D.S.O. in Italy, and all three won the M.C. with the Maquis in France.

They served with Major Roy Farran in Palestine.

FILM STUNT MAN

Major Greville-Bell got into the news from Spain in 1949, when he began to train as a matador pending the return of his yacht, held up by Customs. Captain Easton runs a London film agency and has taken part in 58 British films since the war, mainly as a stunt man. He "doubles" for American film actor Gregory Peck.

Volunteer for action in Malaya

Tough man for a tough job ... Captain Jock Easton is shown in this exclusive "Daily Graphic" picture leaving London after giving up his job as a film stunt man and volunteering for Malaya.

And the ribbons? They are (left to right) the M.C., 1939-45 Star, Africa Star, Italy Star, France and Germany Star, Defence Medal and Victory Medal. Story on Page 2.

February 1951. Jock leaves for Malaya with a group to form the 22nd SAS Malayan Scouts.

Capt Jock Easton, MC, before a tobacco run, Tangier, Spain.

With Burt Lancaster in *The Crimson Pirate*, 1952.

In 1952 Tex Ritter appeared at our Harringay Rodeo.

Some of the boys with the Hispano Suiza in Spain in 1956.

got through, the artillery stopped firing and we hastened back to our main post, which was by a small harbour, to borrow a foghorn and guide the boat in. When she had tied up, I noted with satisfaction the flattened bullets, which showed how accurately I had hit the boat. Had she been of wood as I had thought at the time, none of the crew would have escaped. Thank God it was steel. The vessel was much larger than I had supposed, with quite heavy armament. Everyone had had a narrow escape, without any casualties.

Apart from this incident, and the occasional patrols on Schouwen, life again became boring. We were being used purely as line troops, which was not our true role. One of our other duties while on observation during the night was to take bearings on the launchings of V2 rockets. These were the rockets, which were hitting London and the Home Counties. Details were passed to the RAF who subsequently bombed the launching sites.

Things became so quiet that boxing matches were arranged within the Commando Brigade, of whom we were the only army unit, the rest being Marines. I represented No. 4 as the British heavyweight and another heavyweight was chosen from the French half of the Commando. From the ringside the two of us witnessed a rather large Marine dispatch his opponent in a first-round knockout. The Frenchman and I had been drawn to fight one another. He had a proposition to put to me: 'We will fight flat out for the first round to decide which of us is best suited to fight the Marine. We then coast through the next two rounds, so that whoever fights him will not have had a tough previous fight and be the fitter to meet him.'

It seemed a sensible idea to me and I agreed. For the first round we went at it hammer and tongs. Towards the end of the round the Frenchman whispered, 'OK, you take him.' For the next two rounds we took heavy swings at each other, some of which missed or we pulled. Towards the end of the last round as one of his wild punches caught me flush on the chin, he nearly gave the game away by standing back and saying, 'Pardon.' I was awarded the fight, and met the Marine in the final, which I won on points. Apart from this, life again became exceedingly boring. We were disappointed being where we were. We were not allowed to rejoin our Army Commando brigade, which meant that we would not take part in the Rhine crossing. The fighting, as far as we were concerned, finished on North Beveland.

When the war in Europe ended we were sent to Germany, to Recklinghausen on the Rhine. The next few months were spent patrolling the area to prevent ex-concentration-camp inmates pillaging and looting from German civilians. Although this was understandable on their part after all they had been through, it was still against the law. We also had to contend with young Germans known as Werewolves, who were determined to continue the fight against the Allied forces. They were, I suppose, the product of the German Youth Movement. Another of our duties was to mount guard on a prisoner-of-war camp housing ex-guards from concentration camps who were waiting to be tried by the Allied Control Commission. Once more we had been relegated to become line troops carrying out garrison duties

A notice was pinned on our daily order board asking for volunteers to fight in the Far East. I thought this would be preferable to what we were doing, so I volunteered. Later the order was retracted to include only those volunteers prepared to sign on for another three years. I withdrew my application because I could see that the war in the Far East wouldn't last much longer and by signing on I would again finish up doing garrison duties. In any case, from Germany we were beginning to become eligible for home leave in the UK.

9

Entering the Film World

One day while on leave from Germany, I was standing in uniform at a bus stop in Chelsea waiting for a bus to the West End, when a man approached me and asked if I could ride a horse. As this seemed a rather unusual question in the circumstances I looked hard at him, wondering if he was some kind of nut. He then explained that he had booked two horses for a ride in Rotten Row with a friend, but his companion was now unable to come. As he had to pay for both horses anyway and I appeared to be on leave, he wondered whether I would like to accompany him. One of my pastimes in Germany had been learning to ride, so I readily agreed.

We trotted around Rotten Row for about an hour, which I found rather tame but still better than wandering aimlessly around the West End. Afterwards we went to a pub for a pint and he asked me what I would be doing after I was demobbed. I didn't know, I said, but as I had no trade I would probably take up professional boxing for a living. I asked him what he did. He told me that he was an actor working at Shepherds Bush Studios, very close in fact to where I was born. 'That sounds interesting. Is there any possibility of me seeing inside the studio during some shooting?' I asked. 'Certainly, just come to the studios and ask for me, and I'll fix it,' he said.

'Why don't you go?' said my mother when I told her of the meeting. I said that the actor appeared to be particularly scruffy, and if I asked for him I doubted that anyone would have heard of him. I'd probably be thrown out on my ear, I added. 'They can only say no,' my mother said, 'and Shepherds Bush is not far from here.' So I decided to give it a go. With great trepidation I went to the main entrance of Shepherds Bush Studios and asked for Dennis Price. I expected to be asked, 'Who's Dennis Price?' Instead a company runner was called to escort me to him. It turned out that he was by now quite a well-established actor in British films.

He was rigged out in a Napoleonic French officer's uniform, with lots of gold braid and a sword. He told me that I had come at the right time, as he had just been called on the set. This was a mock-up of the interior of a Spanish theatre in Madrid. He was playing opposite Stewart Granger in a film entitled *The Magic Bow*. Granger was playing the lead role as Paganini, the violin virtuoso. Before the shooting started a third assistant explained the scene to me: Paganini is in the middle of a performance when members of the audience start to become restless and agitated. Suddenly they appear fearful as the doors burst open and in marches an officer leading Napoleon's crack soldiers, who have captured Madrid. They were supposed to strike terror into the audience, but when the troops burst in I couldn't stop laughing.

'Cut!' shouted the director. Coming over to me he demanded to know what I found so amusing. This was a very dramatic point in the film and the last thing he wanted was the audience to laugh, he said. I was terribly embarrassed, especially as everybody was now looking in my direction. 'Don't apologise – just tell me what you were laughing at,' the director said.

I explained that I had understood that the soldiers were supposed to strike terror into the hearts of the audience. 'But just look at them,' I said. 'They all made an entrance like untrained ballet dancers, with half of them carrying their rifles incorrectly.' He went quiet for a moment before explaining that they were the only extras he could get – men unfit for the armed forces or for working down the mines, or too old to be given any heavy work under a control of engagement government order. He turned away with a sigh and continued directing. I didn't wait around to thank Dennis Price for letting me in to the studios, as I thought that he would be furious at me messing up his scene. I hurriedly left the studio and went home. Leave finished two days later and I returned to Germany to await my demob.

One night in the sergeants' mess everybody was talking about their impending return to Civvy Street and the jobs they were going back to. Someone asked me what I was going to do. I had no idea and so said the first thing that came into my head. 'I'm going into the film industry, to bring realism into action films,' I replied. This resulted in gales of laughter and expressions of disbelief. Who did I know in the film industry? they asked. 'Well there's Dennis Price and Stewart Granger,' I said. Of course I hadn't even spoken to

Granger, but I went on, 'There's always someone mentioned in the newspapers who I know. For a start, a great many actors, producers and other film people used to come into my mother's pub.' While a small number did in fact come in, I hadn't spoken to them either.

Someone produced a newspaper brought back from leave and said, 'All right, show us.' I flicked through the pages. There in an article on the film industry I came across the name of George Archibald, manager of Independent Producers. I had of course never heard of him, but said, 'There you are. There's a man I know quite well. When I get home I'll just drop him a line and he'll give me all the introductions I'll need to set the whole thing up.' Why waste time – why didn't I drop him a line now? they asked me. 'What a good idea. I will,' I agreed. Paper and pen were produced and put in front of me. With amused faces lined up watching me, I wrote:

Dear George Archibald,
While on leave a short time ago I visited Gainsborough Studios at Shepherds Bush. I was shocked by the calibre of the men portraying Napoleonic soldiers. As the Commandos are about to be demobbed they could be suitably employed in the film industry to bring realism to such scenes as those required in The Magic Bow *production. I would therefore be grateful if you would arrange an introduction to the person who is most likely to want to take advantage of using these most highly trained and super fit men before they disappear into the commercial world and become unavailable,*
Yours sincerely,
Sgt J. A. Powell

The letter was snatched out of my hand, put in an envelope bearing an address contained in the article and posted. Of course I did not expect a reply. I considered that even if it did reach George Archibald, it would be destined for the waste-paper basket.

I was demobbed and forgot all about the incident. A couple of weeks passed before a letter arrived, which had been re-directed from Germany. It was from George Archibald, telling me that he found my letter most interesting. If I phoned Dennis Van Thal at Pinewood Studios for an appointment, he would discuss the matter with me. He ended by wishing me good luck. My letter to him had been written as pure bravado, but now having received this letter of introduction I decided to give it some thought. A few days later, again after being prompted by my mother, I decided to phone Dennis Van Thal. He agreed to meet me and I was invited down to Pinewood Studios. At this stage, of course, I had no idea where Pinewood was or anything about the film industry.

Having found my way to Pinewood Studios I was directed to Van Thal's office. I explained to him how I had been at Gainsborough Studios during the shooting of *The Magic Bow* and related my conversation with the director. Van Thal seemed quite interested. He said that I should speak to Gerry Dearham at Denham Studios, which was just down the road from Pinewood, and made an appointment for me through Dearham's secretary.

As I had had the opportunity to rehearse my story with Van Thal, I gave Dearham the same account with more confidence and extra embellishments. Dearham, however, was unimpressed. He gave the impression that he thought I had a ruddy cheek expecting to come straight out of the Army into the film industry. I suppose he was probably right. Just as he was obviously about to terminate the interview I told him that I couldn't understand what he had against the idea when it had been so well received by both Dennis Van Thal and, more importantly, by George Archibald, who had thought the idea contained great merit. At the mention of Archibald's name, Dearham's jaw dropped. And without more ado he wrote a letter of introduction for three ex-Commandos, Jimmy Spearman, Cliff Waddington and myself, which I had to take to Captain Cricket, who was the union secretary of the Film Artistes Association, the crowd artistes union. The surname of the woman running the office was Bacon, and inevitably she was known as Streaky. I received three union cards on behalf of two other ex-Commandos and myself in due course and I was told to register with an agent named Archie Woof.

When I met him, it was soon apparent that he was aptly named. His office was above a shop in Charing Cross Road. I went up the stairs and knocked at the door immediately in front of me. Archie opened it himself and somewhat tersely asked me what I wanted. When I told him I wanted to register with him, he seemed even more impatient and directed me through another door to my right which he closed behind me. I found myself in a room crowded with people waiting to see him. Suddenly the door opened again and Archie called me in. During my brief conversation with Archie, I had been spotted while the door was open by Muriel Cole, a casting woman from Ealing Studios.

'He'll do for one of my farmer types,' she said. She was casting for the film *The Loves of Joanna Godden*. The open-air life I had been living had given me a fresh complexion that was in keeping with the farming folk she was looking for. I had therefore obtained a job on my very first day of registration, and was booked for a day at Ealing Studios.

The scene was set in a farmhouse dining room, where a number of us were seated around a table with the two principals, Googie Withers and John McCallum. I had nothing to do except pretend to be eating and occasionally engage in 'silent conversation' with other crowd artistes sitting either side of me. The scene lasted for ten days, for which I received the princely sum of twenty-seven shillings and sixpence, plus overtime. I was beginning to think that it was money for old rope. I never saw the film, or ever heard whether I appeared in it. It was, however, my start in the film industry.

For the next six months, I was fortunate enough to get several crowd jobs. It was good experience, because I found out where all the studios were located and the rates of pay and, more importantly, got to know several assistants and crowd casting people. One of my first jobs was at the First National Studios at Borehamwood. I was a sedan chair carrier, dressed in trousers secured at the knees, stockings, shoes with buckles and a cocked hat. The film was entitled *Three Weird Sisters*. As a crowd artiste you are virtually an animated prop and I was thankful that none of my former comrades from the Commandos could see me. I was soon getting fed up with being a crowd extra. It seemed an aimless existence with its early morning calls. There were tea breaks twice a day, which I looked forward to, not because I was hungry, but because it helped pass the day. I drank the tea and ate the buns purely out of boredom. The airless atmosphere on the set and the hot lamps all day left me lethargic and more tired than if I'd done a hard day's work. Also once a fortnight I was meeting ex-Commandos in a pub off Covent Garden, where we consumed black and tans. It was not long under these conditions that my weight shot up from thirteen and a half stone to seventeen and a half.

I decided that I had to find some physical activity, so I joined the Polytechnic Boxing Club in Regent Street. Over a period of time I was able to bring my weight down to fourteen and a half stones. The trouble here was that there were very few heavyweights with whom I could train. If you sparred with a light-heavyweight or middleweight and threw some heavy punches, you were accused of taking liberties. On the other hand, your opponents felt free to punch their weight, which didn't exactly please me.

I struck up a friendship with one man named McClusky. He was sparring partner to Freddie Mills, who was the World Light-Heavyweight Champion at the time.

After training one night, we were sitting in the Poly canteen talking when he asked me what I did for a living. When I told him, he said that the casual work would suit him down to the ground. I said that if he was prepared to change his name to Jimmy Spearman, I had a union card he could use. All he had to do was to register with Archie Woof and he could obtain work. Both my mates from the Commando had turned down my offer of joining me in the industry. The real Jimmy Spearman had gone to the Far East as a sniper, while Cliff Waddington had taken a job as a London newspaper journalist. McClusky assumed the name of Spearman and as far as I am aware he is still known as such. Jimmy joined me in many screen punch-ups after the stunt team had been created. He was ideally cast as a heavy.

I had reached the stage where I had had enough of the crowd work and had decided that I had better look around to see what else I could do when I met a chap named Bob Usher. He was a Canadian, and had had several film jobs as a rider. He introduced me to Captain Jock Easton, MC, who was just out of the SAS and was starting a stunt team.

Jock was an interesting character. He had been brought up in the fairground and had ridden on the Wall of Death. He left after a number of years to join the Army, with which he served in India. When the war broke out, he was drafted to France and took part in the evacuation of Dunkirk. On his return to England he took a commission in the Royal Artillery. Later on he was in a number of actions in North Africa, where he won his Military Cross. Jock volunteered to join David Stirling when the latter formed the SAS. Parachuting into Sicily, he was wounded and taken prisoner. He escaped from a prisoner-of-war camp near Naples once he had recovered from his wounds, making his way up to the north of Italy and entering Switzerland, where he was interned. He escaped from internment and crossed into France where he joined up with the French Maquis. He stayed with them until the Allied invasion, and then returned to England. By the time I met him he was in London and starting the Jock Easton Film Stunt Team.

10

The Partnership

Jock had set himself up in the office of Sid Roy, an agent who was the brother of Harry Roy, the bandleader. To become an agent, one had to be licensed by the then London County Council. Jock hadn't registered himself as an agent, but worked through Sid Roy on a split-commission basis. The office was in a side street off the Haymarket. After I'd explained to Jock how I had got into the film business, we decided to pool our experience and join forces. It turned out to be a partnership that was to last a great number of years.

Sid Roy was rarely in his office as his engagements took him all over the country. This meant that if both Jock and I were working, we had to find some aspiring stuntman to sit in the office to take calls, most of which at that time were from members of the team we formed. On one occasion, when we left a new member in charge, Larry Taylor, one of our established team, came in to enquire whether there was anything happening. Our new recruit became very officious: 'I'll give you a call if you're needed, but don't hang around here in the office, because I'm very busy and have a lot to do.' Larry didn't take kindly to this treatment, but said nothing and left the office.

About an hour later, our office minder received a call from an American-voiced person, saying that he urgently required a rider for a stunt double. The size, hair colouring and height the caller quoted all seemed to fit the minder, who also happened to be a rider. There was only one problem: the double had to have very short hair and be clean-shaven. Although in fact he had very long hair and a moustache, the minder confirmed that he was just the man for the job. The American said that he would pick him up in two hours from the Haymarket, in front of the Paramount Cinema. He also confirmed that the daily rate would be on a standard-rate American contract, which was far in excess of anything we had ever dreamed of. He added that it was a fortnight's contract. It was important to be on time, the caller stressed, as the double had to be rushed directly to the studios to be fitted that day in his costume.

Half an hour before the appointed time Larry Taylor approached the man standing outside the cinema and casually asked if anything had come in. He received the same answer: 'I'll call you if you're needed.' Another hour passed by, and once again Larry turned up. He asked the minder was he sure there was nothing doing in the way of jobs. This time our office minder got really annoyed. If Larry wanted to be given work, he said, he shouldn't make a nuisance of himself. Of course this time our office minder was clean-shaven, minus his moustache and with a very short haircut. We never found out how long he did wait outside the Paramount Cinema, but obviously Larry's American accent had been very convincing.

As I had now got one foot into the stunt world, I decided to get rid of my union card so that no matter how tough things became I would not be tempted to go back into the crowd. As it happened, an ex-boxer friend of Jimmy Spearman had asked Jimmy how he could get into the crowd union. I gave him my union card and told him that his name was now Joe Powell and that he was to get registered with Archie Woof and several other agents who were providing crowd extras at that time. He kept the name for quite some time, but eventually approached Streaky at the crowd union office, saying that he wanted to change his name because he was being muddled up with a stuntman. He took his uncle's name – Leo Phillips. He teamed up with another ex-fighter named Arthur Mullard. The two of them were affectionately known as Big Ugly and Little Ugly. After a number of years Leo emigrated from Britain to Canada, where I heard he made a name for himself on Canadian television. Arthur, of course, became a household name on British television, in a great number of TV comedy series.

Our team was gradually becoming known and accepted within the film industry as stuntmen to be relied upon to beef up action scenes. British film directors hadn't up to now really thought of stuntmen as being a separate entity within the industry. They thought that if some action was needed, people could be found from within the ranks of the crowd artistes. As a result, there had been no stunts of any importance in British films. From now on, however, directors dreamed up stunts and screenwriters scripted them in.

I was asked to perform my first big stunt on *The Small Voice* being shot at Ealing Studios. In the film I was a motorcycle policeman chasing a car that criminals were escaping in. During the chase, one of the gang leaned out of the window and fired a revolver at me. The first part of the shot was done in the studio, with me on my motorbike held in a cradle to keep me upright. Behind me was a back screen on which was projected a winding road. In front of me was a camera, with a mirror fixed above the lens. I watched the road behind me in the mirror and reacted to the bends, which through the camera looked as if I was following a car. At a given signal from the director, a sharp shooter behind me fired a 2.2 rifle, with the bullet passing between my elbow and leg through the windscreen of the motorbike. On film, of course, one could not see from which direction the bullet had come. I had to react to this hit and there the shot was cut.

The shot was continued on location at night, the camera picking me up speeding down the road and swerving from side to side to simulate the effect of having been fired at. I then had to leave the road on the motorbike at forty miles an hour, mount a grass verge and hit a tree, supposedly dying. Of course I couldn't be seen jumping off the motorbike before it hit the tree. As there were no recognised stuntmen who had performed such a stunt, I had to work it out for myself. What I planned was to go straight for the tree and, just before the crash, jam on the front brake and at the same time pull hard on the handle bars. I hoped this would lift me out of the saddle and take me to the left of the tree. I just had to hope that I'd got it right.

In fact it worked perfectly. I still had my hands on the handlebars when the motorbike hit the tree. The scene was so realistic that a prop man thought that if I wasn't dead, then at least I was badly injured. He ran in front of the camera to get to my assistance and ruined the shot. I had to perform it again on a very bent motorbike. To give you some idea of how things were in those days, the production manager wouldn't pay me for the re-shoot and wanted to repair the motorbike instead of paying for a replacement. When eventually he did reimburse me for the motorbike, he regarded that as part of my remuneration.

Although by now we had joined Equity, the actors' union, we

weren't really recognised by them either. There was no such thing as a written stunt contract and no way in which I could get paid any more than twenty-five pounds for the night's work. At that time the top crowd pay for a smart crowd turning up in their own clothes was five guineas, which was five pounds five shillings. Equity artistes' pay started at five pounds six shillings. To put this in perspective, in 2003 the basic contracts were as follows. Basic daily contract – £399 per day, plus stunt adjustments; weekly contract – £1,595 plus stunt adjustments; stunt coordinators – daily rate; £586; weekly rate, £2,026.

Early on, while we were getting the team established, Jock sent me down to Pinewood Studios as a possible double for Griffith Jones, who was starring in *Miranda*, a film directed by Ken Annakin in 1948. It was a comedy fantasy about a mermaid played by Glynis Johns. Although the interview was at Pinewood, the interiors for the film (the tank work) were to be shot at Islington Studios, a converted power station.

Anthony Darnborough did the interviewing seated at his desk. Standing at his side was a woman I took to be his secretary. I can't remember what I was actually asked at the interview, but throughout the woman kept butting in with her own questions. I directed my answers to Darnborough. I had remembered what Jock always said: 'Go to the top of the tree – ignore the twigs.' Thinking about it now I am sure that my annoyance with the woman must have shown in my face. It was only at a later date that I found out that the 'twig' was none other than Betty Box, the producer. On reflection, I reckon I was lucky to have landed the job.

Miranda was shot at a time when the unions were beginning to feel their feet and make their presence felt. The tank where much of the film was shot was dressed with seaweed to resemble the cave where Miranda the mermaid lived. The question arose as to whether the seaweed was alive or dead. If it was alive, then it was the gardeners' responsibility. If, however, it was dead, then its maintenance was the job of the props department. As nobody could reach a decision either way, all work stopped. An expert was called from the Botanical Gardens at Kew to give judgement. I can't now remember what the verdict was.

A double for Glynis was found in the person of Edna Norris, a great swimmer. Together we had to go to Manchester for the mermaid tail to be made and tested at the local swimming baths.

Whilst most of the swimming shots were done by Edna, there were many shots where Glynis had to wear the tail in the water.

Naturally mermaids do not wear bras, and so the mermaid was to wear a long wig with the tresses stuck on to cover her modesty. Nevertheless, neither Glynis nor her double wanted to be pulled out of the tank when the water quite often had dislodged the strategically placed hair. I always had to be in the water of the tank as a lifeguard, especially at times when the tail was causing them to cramp and they needed to get out quickly. On these occasions I would swim over to them and then, when they had placed their arms around my neck, swim to the ladder with them still holding on and climb it, at which point the wardrobe department would cover them with towels and carry them to the dressing room. It wasn't the most onerous job I have ever had.

While the water in the tank was kept at a fairly high temperature, it was surprising how, after several hours' shooting, we couldn't stop shivering. We kept warm between shots in a portable heated hut that was specially erected. *Miranda* was hailed as a great success and the type of light comedy film at which British directors excel.

My next big stunt was a high fall off a ship portrayed as the *Titanic* in the film *A Night to Remember* (1958). The scene was set at the time of the sinking, showing the panic of passengers and crew fighting for room on the lifeboats. For my part, I had to be knocked backward over the side of the ship from the top deck by one of the crew trying to get past me. The ship chosen was moored at Glasgow Docks and was in the process of being scrapped. One side of the vessel had already had a considerable amount of steel removed. The reduction in weight had allowed the remainder of the hull to rise further out of the water. The higher it rose the better, as far as the film company was concerned, as the original *Titanic* had been far larger than the ship we were using. The result, however, was that the main deck was now some ninety feet above the water. At the time of accepting the job, I had never dived from a height above twenty feet. Initially I was at a loss to work out how I was to make the fall look dramatic and avoid making it look like a dive. In any case, I wasn't competent enough to dive from that height. I decided that the only way to make it look realistic was to go for real.

The shot was at night, about two o'clock in the morning. It was bitterly cold and beginning to snow. Big studio lamps illuminated the whole of the side of the ship. Other lamps were directed onto the lifeboats that were already in the water and full of passengers and crew who had escaped. Some of the lamps were shining directly into the water, which gave the impression the surface was at least ten feet lower than it was. During the first part of the fall I just didn't know where I was. After being knocked backwards I was already turning a very ungainly somersault. My main purpose had been to lose height and try to gain control in the last thirty feet, before I hit the water. In the last moments of the fall I suddenly caught a glimpse of flotsam on the water which showed its true surface. Throwing my arms about and kicking with my legs, I just managed to enter the water head first instead of hitting it flat on my back. I congratulated myself on having entered the water fairly cleanly, but when I stripped off, I found that I had a bruise swelling up from my hip right down to my ankle. The water was freezing. To show you how cold it was, some naval seamen who were paid to swim towards the lifeboats in the overall scene were asked to go back in the water for another shot from a different angle. They all refused, although the film company had offered to treble the fee, which initially the seamen had thought was tremendously generous – that is, until they actually experienced the conditions.

I learned a lot from that fall and used the experience gained as the basis for all my future falls. Most of these varied from twenty to fifty feet except for the ones I was called upon to do in two films, *The Guns of Navarone* (1961) and *The Man Who Would be King* (1975), which exceeded even the fall from the *Titanic*.

11

Our Bid for Recognition

The more films we worked on, the better known we became and the more enquiries we received. We found that we couldn't cope with having a casual office minder at Sid Roy's office, so we moved to another agent named Jack Lewis. We still retained the name the Jock Easton Film Stunt Team – we just had a different telephone number. While the office situation improved, there was still a problem in that Jack Lewis had his own stage show and was only available between performances. So we moved yet again to the Pat Larthe Agency. Pat ran her agency for small parts and mannequins. She was in attendance all the time, along with a secretary, which solved our problems for a while.

As directors came to make more use of our stunt team, so they started to think up bigger stunts in their scripts. They also became more specific in their requirements. It wasn't sufficient just to provide a stunt double. Stuntmen were expected not only to be proficient at carrying out the actual stunt, but also capable of inter-preting from the script the action required leading up to and following the stunt. They were required to make suggestions to the director and also instruct the actor for whom they were doubling. The artiste also would sometimes request particular actions he would like incorporated. All this meant that the agent had to correctly assess the capabilities of every stuntman sent to the studios. Pat Larthe was at a disadvantage because she was never on the set. She had to rely upon Jock or me regarding the suitability of a selected man for the particular stunt involved. During this period, in addition to our own engagements, Jock and I were chasing around the studios finding the work in the first place. The cost of this was coming out of our own pockets. The work generated from our efforts was producing commissions for Pat Larthe, but none of it recompensed Jock or me. We were benefiting in the long run, however, for we were providing a new facility for the British film industry, which was in turn creating a new type of employment and ensuring work for ourselves.

Many changes had been taking place in the film industry. Initially three main agents had managed crowd work engagements – Archie Woof, Ronnie Curtis and the Crowd Union, which had an agency licence and was managed by Captain Cricket and 'Streaky' Bacon. The Film Producers Association decided to eliminate the small agents and set up their own agency, the Film Casting Association (FCA). For this purpose they head-hunted Gabby Howard, who had assisted Archie Woof over a long period. The FCA was backed by no less than sixty film companies, of which the biggest was the J. Arthur Rank Organisation.

The FCA offer to the Crowd Union was that crowd artistes would no longer have to pay commission. Instead, the film companies using the crowd would pay seven and a half percent of their wages to the FCA. This also applied to American companies using British studios or, in fact, crowd artistes for any purpose. Though it may have sounded all right at the time, what this new move did was to keep down the wages, as the FCA was working for and on behalf of the employing companies. Also under the old system, if your face didn't fit with one agent, there were others from whom to gain employment. Under the new arrangement, if your face didn't fit, you were out.

Jock had never had a crowd ticket and I had given mine away, but some of the team had previously been Film Artist Association (FAA) members, or if we had brought them in, they had acquired crowd tickets, in order to supplement their stunt earnings. This led to all sorts of problems. Crowd casting directors would phone the FCA to send down certain men on a crowd call knowing that there were action scenes in the script which we were establishing as stunt work. This meant they would only receive the pay of a crowd artiste. When we first started, crowd artistes' daily pay was twenty-seven shillings and sixpence a day, with the pay of the top crowd artistes, known as smart crowd, set at five pounds five shillings a day. As an Equity artiste, the minimum daily pay was five pounds and six shillings. It therefore paid the film companies to ask for a man to take part in crowd scenes on crowd wages right up until he was required to perform some stunt, and then only increase his salary while he was actually doing a stunt. He had no stunt insurance and was required to sign an indemnity form agreeing that he

70

was performing that particular stunt at his own risk and that the extra remuneration covered that risk. As a result of this practice, we were losing work – those of us, that is, who refused to work through the FCA. Gerry Dearham, the casting man I had met at Denham Studios, was now running the FCA. He was a thorn in our side for a number of years and we crossed swords with him on a number of occasions.

I decided that I had to try to resolve this problem. I wrote to Sir Henry French, Chairman of the British Film Producers Association, suggesting that it would be in the interests of the film industry to have a basic number of stuntmen under annual contract. They would be required to undertake training of various kinds to become proficient at their craft and make their screen performances realistic. I suggested, too, that stuntmen should also be available during rehearsals to work with principal members of the cast to sharpen up their individual performances. I pointed out that having professional highly qualified stuntmen immediately available would encourage American film directors to produce films in the UK.

My idea would also mean that stuntmen, when not working on a particular film, could undertake training in other arts, which would broaden their employment possibilities. Specialising in one particular form of stunt was fine as long as that performance was currently required. The trouble is that films go in cycles, and while there may be a call for, say, horse-riding stunts over a long period, suddenly tastes change and films are being produced which require a totally different type of action.

Three weeks later I received a letter from Sir Henry stating that a large number of the artistes whose names I had submitted were available through the FCA. I was very disappointed with his reply, because such a group under continuous training would have complemented the Rank Charm School. This had been set up to train actors especially for the film industry, the equivalent of the provincial repertory companies which provided experience for stage actors who gravitated to the London theatres. A large number of artistes originally contracted through the Rank Charm School did in fact become stars in British films. A number also made their mark in America.

A film entitled *Christopher Columbus* (1949) was in the pre-production stage. The production manager, Billy Boyle, heard of the work we'd been doing, and asked to see me. He said that he would be interested in taking a number of us stuntmen under contract for a lengthy period. This was good news indeed. After our now established team had discussed this, I was asked to try and negotiate a basic fee of twenty pounds per week, plus stunt money on top negotiated prior to any stunt being performed. Subsequently Billy Boyle called me to the studio to negotiate the contract.

At our meeting we established the number of men required and that additional fees should be agreed prior to a stunt or particular action. The only sticking point was the contractual fee. I was asking twenty pounds per week, but was being offered only fifteen. Everyone said that we should all stick out for the twenty pounds per week. I approached Billy Boyle again, but he turned us down. The shooting on *Christopher Columbus* started without us.

Paddy Ryan, one of our main stuntmen at this time, knew the director, David MacDonald. He suggested we went to the studio to see him and perhaps get his support. Paddy and I were dismayed to find boys on the set who had told me that they would not work for less than twenty pounds, but then had been contracted through the FCA. Many of them were shamefaced and were trying not to be noticed. I decided that enough was enough. There was only one answer to the problem. Our agency in future would only employ men working with Equity agreement.

After a perfectly amicable discussion, I parted company with Pat Larthe by buying out my sole agreement with her. I had decided to proceed without an agent. By now I was pretty broke. Fortunately for me I lived in my mother's pub, the Princess of Wales in Chelsea, where I worked behind the bar and as a cellar man in return for my food and lodgings. In my spare time I continued to chase up film work.

Later on the same year, Paddy Ryan made contact with a London theatre production, a musical entitled *Tough at the Top*. The production called for six stunt men, plus a heavyweight boxer to fight in a ring on stage with the singing lead, George Tossi. The show was at the Adelphi Theatre in the Strand. It was being produced by the famous impresario, C. B. Cochran. As well as many stage shows, Cochran had also promoted boxing matches. Paddy had an amazing memory and could remember names, weights, and the outcome of world contests, some of which Cochran had promoted. They got on famously.

One of the highlights of the show was a boxing match for the heavyweight championship of the world. The performance opened with a backcloth painted with the figures and faces of fight fans looking out towards the auditorium as if watching a fight in progress. To add to the realism, members of the cast were in front of the backcloth also facing the audience's way and screaming encouragement at two imaginary fighters. Sounds taken from an actual fight were overlaid along with the cast dialogue. The effect was excellent and exciting. Suddenly a shout went up, 'He's down!' and all the lights went out. When they came on again, the backcloth had been lifted to reveal a boxing ring around which the cast was gathered. Lying on the canvas was George Tossi being counted out by Paddy Ryan, playing the part of the referee. Saved by the bell, George then got to his feet and sang to the fight crowd, among whom was the female lead, Maria de Tilly. She sang to George to encourage him in the fight and back he went to his corner. It was at this point that I, as the opponent, was scheduled to come to the front of the ring and sing, 'It seems unfair that he should have this aid, may I enlist the love of some sweet maid?' The fight crowd would then sing encouragement to me, after which I would return to my corner and the bell would sound for the fight to continue. We then went through a rehearsed fight routine in which I got knocked out.

During a break one day in a rehearsal, Paddy Hayes, an ex-professional fighter who had two tin ears, went with me to a cafe in the Strand near the Adelphi for a coffee. We had just received our coffees when I noticed lipstick on my cup. I said in a fairly loud voice to the waitress, 'There's lipstick on my cup.' The waitress replied in an even louder voice right on cue, 'Are you sure that it isn't your own?' I had completely forgotten that for this particular rehearsal we were all wearing make-up for the lighting set-up and stage effects. Everyone in the crowded cafe turned to look at us. Paddy and I fled.

For some days prior to the full dress rehearsal, I was sent under the stage to improve my singing, tutored by the band's pianist. All was now set for the full dress rehearsal at which Cochran himself would be present, along with Alan Herbert, who had written the score, and several backers and other invited guests. The rehearsal went like clockwork, right up until I made my singing debut, this time at the front of the ring. When I had finished singing there was an awful silence. The show came to an abrupt stop, followed by complete silence. A member of the cast, who had been holding his lips as tightly closed as he could, suddenly expelled his breath. The volume was such that it sounded rather like the liferaft that we had tried to inflate with the faulty valve on the beach in France. The whole cast, plus the invited audience, fell about in absolute hysterics. After a period of prolonged laughter, the director shouted, 'Take ten!' As the cast started to leave the stage still convulsed with laughter, I climbed down out of the ring and joined the exodus, feeling terribly embarrassed. The director, Wendy Toy, came up and put her arm around my shoulders. 'Don't worry about it, Joe. I somehow think that that scene will be taken out,' she said consolingly.

The show lasted six months. There was a heat wave at the time, which didn't encourage theatre audiences. In addition, there were several other popular musicals about at the time, such as *Annie Get Your Gun* and *Brigadoon*. During the whole time that *Tough at the Top* ran I never tired of hearing the music and I still think that it was a great show, in fact, I consider it as one of the highlights of my career as a stuntman.

During this time there had been no stunt work for Jock. He had, however, been offered a job as an engineer aboard an ex-naval gunboat making runs from North Africa to Spain smuggling cigarettes. The boat was owned by other ex-SAS officers, who hadn't found their feet in Civvy Street. After Jock joined them, I wasn't to see him for quite some time.

12

We Decide to go it Alone

Having bought out my sole agreement with the Pat Larthe Agency, I started to chase stunt work while living in the Princess of Wales pub in Chelsea. One of the calls I received was from Pinewood Studios, for a parachutist to do a parachute jump with a dummy representing the female lead in the film *Stop Press Girl* (1949). At the interview, I said that we would need three parachutes in case of more takes. It would take too long to repack one 'chute between takes. The truth of the matter was that I didn't know how to re-pack a chute. In the Army, all the re-packing was done by WAAFs (members of the Women's Auxiliary Air Force).

A fee was agreed for each jump should I be required to perform more than one. This was necessary because quite often, through a technical fault or patchy cloud, part of the jump could be missed on camera. I had learned my lesson from the time I crashed the motorcycle twice into a tree at forty miles per hour only to be paid for one stunt. I forget now where the parachutes came from; all I remember was the name of the packer – Reg Penn. The agreement was that they would be delivered to Pinewood Studios.

One of the snags was that I had never done a free drop before. All my jumps in the Army had been by static line. And I certainly hadn't dropped with a dummy. We were to take off from Elstree Aerodrome, where we had to wait several days for clear weather. It was cloudy and overcast – not particularly encouraging – but eventually the cameraman decided that there was a hole in the clouds and we could get the shot in. The first time I saw the 'chutes was when a car from the studio arrived with them. The production company expected me just to put one on and be ready to jump. I picked up a parachute and made for the lavatory. 'Why don't you leave the parachute here?' asked the production assistant. I answered that it was a matter of training: 'Once you have the 'chute you mustn't let it out of your sight.' It was pretty feeble explanation, but the best I could manage at the time. I had to get into the lavatory out of sight because I didn't know how to fit it.

This 'chute was a seat pack, and although the principle was much the same, the fitting was different. I also had to work out how I was going to jump with the dummy. All the time I was struggling, trying to work out how to fix the harness, the production assistant was knocking on the door shouting that if I didn't hurry we would lose the light. Eventually I decided that I'd got it more or less right and on emerging was rushed to the plane. It was a four-seater, single-engined Fairchild Argos. One of the front seats had been removed to allow me to exit with the dummy so I sat on the floor facing the tail plane. The Air Ministry, before authorising the jump, had insisted the door be removed, and the space covered with a sheet of three-ply. They reasoned that if the door was removed without the doorway being covered, it would affect the aerodynamics of the plane for take-off. They hadn't thought about how I was to get rid of the plywood sheet prior to jumping.

I tied the hands of the dummy so that I could place its arms around my neck and dive out of the plane dragging the dummy with one hand around its waist and the other on the ripcord. My plane was due to reach a height of six thousand feet, while another plane carrying the camera crew on board would be below at three thousand feet. The signal for me to jump was to be a green light flashed at us from the camera plane. Around four thousand feet there was a tremendous bang as the three ply was sucked out of the plane. I thought for a moment that the tail plane had been knocked off, particularly as the plane bounced about as the pilot struggled to regain control. I also had visions of dumping the dummy and having to jump with the pilot. With control regained, we climbed to six thousand feet and found the hole in the cloud. The green light flashed. I swung my legs over the side, grabbed the wing strut and started to pull myself out, my other hand firmly grasping the ripcord handle. As I emerged, I found that halfway out of the plane the seat pack was jammed in the tubular mountings of the front seat that had been removed. I managed to pull myself back in, readjust the harness and then dive out.

After the necessary delay I pulled the rip cord, and the forward lift webs that ran down my back to the seat pack snapped over my head as the pilot 'chute ran out. Not only did the lift webs nearly knock my head off, due to the arms of the dummy obstructing their free run, but the dummy itself was freed. Fortunately, through instinct I made a successful grab at the dummy as we became parted. Had I missed, we would have landed separately and ruined the shot. As I passed the camera plane it followed me down in order to complete the shot right up to the landing, before returning to Elstree Aerodrome.

The Argos remained circling above the spot where I had landed so that a car could come and pick me up. The car had the other two 'chutes in it. By the time it arrived I was ready to jump again. I was certain that they would need further shots as back-up. The production assistant, who was in the car, told me that they had the shot they wanted and that we were to return to the studios. This was not what I wanted to hear. I needed the money for a somewhat delayed wedding and honeymoon. I had had a professional heavy-weight match the night before, in which my nose had been broken, so my nuptials were slightly delayed until the plaster could be removed. I married Marguerite Clemow, a biographer who worked for the J. Arthur Rank Publicity Organisation at South Street, London.

After *Stop Press Girl* there was another period of inactivity, so we decided to go to Juan les Pins on our belated honeymoon. We had been there for about ten days when Jock arrived. Having not met for a long time, he and I had a lot to talk about. His boat, the *Whispering Wind*, had been caught and impounded by the Spanish Navy while smuggling cigarettes from Tangier to Spain and its crew arrested. I therefore found myself on my honeymoon in France having to keep Jock, who had no money to return to the UK. When I think about it, as a man who could escape from a prisoner-of-war camp, get from Naples to Switzerland, then once again escape to France to join up with the French Maquis and eventually return to England, Jock really didn't need my assistance.

As it turned out, I greatly appreciated his presence when the car broke down at Lyons and we couldn't find a garage open. Eventually we were introduced to a garage owner who informed us that he couldn't do anything for a week. Jock had a furious row with him. How different things were now that the war was over and France no longer needed our help, he raged. He then produced his *laissez-passer*, the permit issued to him when he had been fighting alongside the Maquis. The garage owner's attitude changed immediately, and he couldn't do enough for us. He assembled a couple of mechanics to work on the car while his friends entertained us. In a couple of hours the car was ready. We were asked to stay for a few days, which would have been nice, but we had to push on, although the lavish hospitality had taken effect and really we were not in a fit state to travel.

On our return to England, we continued to run the stunt team from the pub, until we were reported to the London County Council for operating as agents without a licence. This was news to us, as we weren't making much from our efforts and a licence would cost us money that we could ill afford. We now had to find an office, as it was illegal to run an agency from the pub, and in any case, it would have been frowned on by the brewers had they found out.

Jock was very good at meeting people, and one day, while in a pub, he found himself talking to a builder who owned an office in Silver Place, off Beak Street, in central London. Behind this office the builder had a spare room into which he threw all his empty paint cans and various building equipment. He agreed to rent it to us for a very nominal sum. It was filthy dirty, with peeling paint and wallpaper hanging off the walls, but we decided to take it. With the help of some of the boys, we cleared out all the rubbish, stripped the walls and re-painted the whole room. We bought a second-hand desk and a few chairs, and obtained an agent's licence.

We were now the Jock Easton Stunt Team, running under the name of the Jock Easton Casting Agency Limited. Though this sounded fine, we had a few drawbacks. In the first place we had little money and couldn't get a telephone installed. The builder came to our rescue by letting us have an extension of his phone in our office. This meant that when somebody phoned, the call was answered by a secretary who, after enquiring who was calling, put the call through our office. This proved to be of considerable help in securing our first major contract.

13

Winners and Losers

One day Gerry Walker of Associated British Corporation phoned on behalf of Warner Bros to ask us to provide an audition for twenty-five stuntmen for the movie *Captain Horatio Hornblower* (1951), starring Gregory Peck. Warners had already held one audition for men to act as crew, and although forty had been picked, the director, Raoul Walsh, was not very impressed. It had been decided to see what we could come up with. Those chosen were to be the ships' crews, providing the action in the battles between Hornblower's ship and the French and Spanish navies. There was just one problem, we only had thirty men on our books, way below the amount a Casting Director would expect to choose from for the twenty-five required.

On the morning of the audition, the office of Gerry Mitchell, production manager for the film, rang to say that when their casting man arrived he was to phone him at once. Jock and I looked at each other as the same thought struck us both: no salary for the men had been agreed. As soon as the casting man arrived, we quickly installed one of the boys, Paddy Ryan, in the front office under the builder's secretary's desk with her telephone. Paddy's instructions were to listen in on the conversation taking place on our extension with his hand over the mouthpiece.

When the casting man arrived he was told to ring Mitchell. I left him and Jock in our office on the pretext of checking that all the men had arrived, but went straight to the front office so that Paddy could brief me on the conversation. It was as we had thought; the casting man had not been briefed on the question of salary. Paddy told me that Mitchell had told his representative to offer fifteen pounds a week. Although some stunts might need to be individually assessed, under no circumstances was he to go over twenty pounds. When I returned to our office the representative said to Jock, 'Before we start the audition let's sort out the salary to be agreed.'

He added that as the contract would be a long one, the figure should be reflected in that price. Jock thought for a moment, and then asked me what I thought. I said the figure should be twenty-five pounds a week, with adjustments for individual stunts. 'That is totally unacceptable,' said the casting man and stood up as if to leave.

'Look,' I told him, 'for the first time you have an American film company over here to make an action film. Fill your ships' crews with a lot of useless extras and they'll never come again. On the other hand, give them really good action scenes and they will. Remember, the price we're asking is a mere fraction of what it would cost in America. We have to show that we can match what they have in the States. We will be judged by Hollywood standards. The future of American action films shot in this country could depend on the professionalism now required and which has been recognised by George Archibald, the managing director of Independent Producers. I tell you what I'll do. I'll go outside and have a word with the boys and see what they think.'

After a short pause outside the office I returned and said, 'They're not happy to work for less, but they would accept twenty pounds, plus adjustments. They added that they thought that you were "a particularly hard man to negotiate with".' A slight smile crossed his face. He made one more attempt to get me to drop the price, but finally accepted the twenty-pound contract, plus adjustments, and the audition got under way.

The audition was for twenty-five men. Some were selected, others rejected. Fortunately, only five men at a time could get into the office, which gave the ones turned down the opportunity to quickly change clothes outside with the successful ones and to reappear for a second chance to get picked. One of them, Larry Taylor, was asked, 'Haven't I already seen you?' to which Larry replied, 'No, that was my brother.' He was accepted. Under these circumstances we felt that we had done rather well in fulfilling the contracted number.

The following day we all appeared before Raoul Walsh after being fitted out in our sailors' costumes. After inspecting us, Raoul, who was a director of international status, asked Jock, 'Could we find another forty like these men?' No problem, Jock told him, although neither of us at that time knew where this new forty would be coming from. Raoul then turned to the first assistant, Cliff Owen, and told him, 'Cancel that first lot from the FCA.'

Incidentally, Cliff later on became a director himself and even directed in Hollywood.

Jock and I returned to our office cockahoop, as *Captain Horatio Hornblower* would undoubtedly establish our agency beyond all doubt in the British film industry. We now started recruiting for the second contract solely from within the Equity membership. This was our opportunity to draw a line between the FCA and ourselves. In a very short time we found forty suitable men, some with ex-service experience and others with a stage or radio background. Subsequently a second audition was arranged at the studio. To our delight, Raoul picked them all.

It was also to be the start of the first of our many battles with the FCA. Imagine the chagrin of the British film producers when they found out what had happened. We two ex-servicemen, whom they had greeted with indulgent smiles when we first arrived on the scene, had suddenly become in their eyes two of the biggest bastards left unhung, who had nicked from under their very noses a highly prestigious Warner Bros movie which was being shot in their own studios. They hadn't been pleased when we obtained the first contract and now we had obtained a second, a total of sixty-five men in all. We were about to feel the full wrath of the British producers.

Under the terms of studio hire all crowd artistes had to be recruited from the FCA. Although the artistes themselves did not pay commission for their engagement, the operating company paid the FCA seven and a half per cent on the total crowd wage bill. Obviously this represented a sizeable income to the FCA spread over an estimated shoot of six months. To us it was even better. As licensed theatrical agents we were working on ten per cent. Our claim was that the work we had undertaken was not crowd work, but stunt work, which came under Equity. To press home the point even further, all sixty-five men had to sign an indemnity form against any claim for injury or death during the production. Our case was solid; any court in the country would have upheld our claim.

The producers now brought out the big guns. They arrived at the studio threatening to halt the production. We phoned Equity, but they failed to show up, leaving us to sort out our own problems. Here the producers were plainly contravening standard studio agreements between the two unions, Equity and the crowd artistes' union, the FAA, but Equity were not prepared to stand up for their own members. This set back professional stunting for years, and very nearly put an end to everything for which we had worked. A meeting was hurriedly set up to which Jock was called. Here I made the big mistake of letting Jock handle things alone. Together we were an effective double act, but since Jock had been a captain and I only a sergeant, I deferred to rank and didn't press the point about accompanying him. So Jock was alone, with Warner Bros on one hand fearful that the row could escalate and hold up the whole production, and on the other the British Film Producers Association (BFPA) representatives who had the backing of some sixty British production companies, of which the J. Arthur Rank Organisation was just one. What chance did we have? There was no way in which we could have taken them to court.

The outcome of the meeting was that the second contract was transferred to the FCA. All forty Equity members had to join the FAA and register with the FCA. Jock did, however, reserve the right to re-open the case direct with the BFPA at a later date. As a result of Equity letting us down, we lost several contracts to the FCA, which remained a thorn in our side for a great number of years.

Captain Horatio Hornblower was really the first film to bring together stunt artistes and special effects experts who today work hand in glove with each other. Warners also brought in an expert to instruct us in the authentic naval gunnery drill of the period. While we were working on the film, the actor James Robertson Justice told me that he had in fact been a naval liaison officer to Lord Lovat when we were stationed at Troon.

Our efforts to ensure stunt work on *Captain Horatio Hornblower* was up to professional standard did not go unrewarded, as we were to receive several contracts from Warners over the years. Jock and I were invited to the première of the film at the Warner cinema in Leicester Square, after which Raoul entertained us at Jock's local pub. He told us that he was so pleased with our work that he would recommend us to a great friend of his, another director, who would be coming over to England to make a film at the MGM Studio. We also received assurances from UK managing director Gerry Blattner that we would be considered for all future Warner Bros movies in this country.

Although we continued to supply stuntmen and stunt doubles for the film industry, there was no doubt that to a large extent the BFPA had put the block on our agency with their associated companies. Work was getting very hard to come by, and Jock and I were to all intents and purposes broke.

Some time prior to all this, the SAS had been re-formed in the Territorial Army, and had been merged with the Artists Rifles with headquarters just off Euston Road. The regiment had a fine record and had produced some fine officers. It now became the 21st SAS Regiment. Jock had joined in his substantive rank of captain, and I joined as a private. This meant that at least we could get some free parachute jumps in at weekends, and also get some shooting in at Bisley.

Later on the government decided that, in addition to the territorial unit, they would rebuild the SAS into a unit of the regular British Army. It would be placed immediately on a war footing, and there was a call for volunteers to go to Korea. As it looked as though we were going to eventually be squeezed out of the film industry, Jock and I decided that we might as well volunteer. We were both accepted – Jock as a captain and me as a sergeant. As far as I remember, there were eighteen of us. We reported to Maida Barracks, Aldershot, where we were fitted out and immediately underwent re-training. As we were about to go on active service, we were given priority on the rifle range, which upset all the regular regiments who had to book months ahead for rifle practice. The sooner we left the better as far as they were concerned.

During this period we did a deal with our secretary, Mary Merryweather, to keep our office open. Mary had been employed by us on a small wage, but also used the office for her own purposes as an agent in another line. We mutually agreed that she could stay there as long as our funds could still supply her small salary. Should she make a success of her own business she could take over the office.

After a short time at Aldershot, it was rumoured that the operation we were about to undertake was to parachute into North Korea to take out the North Koreans' headquarters. This was never confirmed, although it seemed to emanate from a fairly reliable source. Time passed and we had been at the barracks for some six months. Jock had the authority to sign leave passes so, armed with one of these, I used to take one of the Land Rovers assigned to the unit and drive up to our office, where I changed out of uniform and chased up stunt work. I also used the vehicle to visit the studios. Finally, a signal was received from General MacArthur saying, 'Home for Christmas', and the North Korean operation was cancelled. It was probably a good job that it was, for a few weeks later; the Chinese army poured down across the 49th parallel and entered the war. I had a feeling that the eighteen of us might have been slightly outnumbered!

One day, a major general arrived at Aldershot, and we were paraded before him. He told us that as the situation in Korea had changed, the operation for which we had enlisted had been cancelled. As we had now been officially incorporated into the regular Army, it had been decided to send the unit to Malaya to become the 22nd SAS and chase bandits in the jungle. He added that as we had volunteered to fight in Korea, if anyone wished to return to Civvy Street, they would be entitled to do so. No one took up the offer. Later, an advance party was to be sent to Malaya to set up camp, with administration offices to handle more volunteers to form the regiment. Jock was one of those to be detailed.

Meanwhile, on one of my trips to London I heard that Warners were to make a movie, *The Crimson Pirate* (1952), on location in Italy, in which Burt Lancaster was to be the star. There was news, too, of a film entitled *Ivanhoe* which MGM were planning to produce at their studios in Borehamwood. Richard Thorpe was to be the director and Yakima Canutt was in charge of the stunts. Both were very big names in Hollywood. Raoul Walsh had kept his promise and had passed our names to them.

Jock said that he now had to go to Malaya and there was no way in which he could avoid it. In my case, however, there was maybe still time to pull out. Jock advised me to write to Major General Lathbury and ask for my release. Before flying out, Jock signed another leave pass for me. This time, though, I wasn't able to take the Land Rover. Just as I was about to go on leave, I was sent for by the commandant of Maida Barracks, who was furious that I had had so many leaves. 'Make no mistake, Sergeant Powell. When you return, I will personally see that you are put on the plane to Malaya.'

'Thank you very much, sir. I'm looking forward to it,' I replied. When I arrived home I immediately wrote to Major General Lathbury, saying that my situation had now changed, and that I would like to take up his offer to be released. I explained that Captain Easton, MC, had applied to the Officers' Association for a business grant, which had now been given. Now that Captain Easton was in Malaya, it was really up to me to try and make a go of our business in order to repay the association. I also stressed that it would also ensure that Captain Easton had a business to come back to after he returned from completing his service in Malaya. All this was quite true. Jock had indeed received a grant from the Officer's Association.

On my return from leave the camp commandant again sent for me. Red in the face and obviously very agitated, he sat at his desk glaring at me for some moments. It rather reminded me of a caricature I had seen of Colonel Blimp. Suddenly he burst out with, 'You didn't tell me that you had written to Major General Lathbury.' I said I was very sorry. 'It must have slipped my mind, sir.'

'Get this man out of here!' the commandant roared to the regimental sergeant major who had marched me in. 'Return all his kit to the stores. I want him out of the barracks in double quick time.' So ended my military career and I was left to return home without my sergeant's pay and no job in the offing. I had to find some work.

When I returned to our office I soon found out that Richard Thorpe and Yakima Canutt had arrived in England and were already established at MGM Studios, Borehamwood. This was most convenient, as by now I was living only two minutes away from the studios. I phoned Richard Thorpe and explained that I had been working with Raoul Walsh, who had suggested that I got in touch with him. True to his word, Raoul had already highly recommended Jock and me, so a meeting was arranged.

After the trouble we had had with the BFPA and the FCA over *Hornblower*, Jock and I had obviously had our cards marked and I had not been able to get past the security on the main gate of the studios. On this occasion, however, when I turned up and said that I had an appointment with Richard Thorpe, the suspicious security guard phoned through to Thorpe's office, and was told to send me straight up. While he was giving me directions to Thorpe's office, he had an expression of incredulity on his face as if to say, 'How did you wangle that?'

As well as being a top film director, Richard Thorpe was also one of the most wealthy, having acquired a lot of real estate in the early days of Hollywood when land was cheap. Yakima Canutt was also world famous. A champion roper, bronco rider and steer rider, he had topped rodeos all over the United States and Canada, before becoming a star in the cowboy films of the silent movies era. When talkies came in, Yak's voice didn't record very well, and his acting career came to an abrupt halt. He then turned to stunting, and soon became top in this profession. He went on to specialise in setting up action scenes in hundreds of cowboy productions, doubling for John Wayne and other stars. One of his most amazing stunts was on *Stagecoach* (1939), the classic Western directed by John Ford. In the film he chases a runaway stagecoach on horse-back and leaps on to the lead pair of a six in hand. He falls between the two lead horses and holds on to their traces while being dragged along the ground between them as they gallop furiously along. He lets go of the lead horses, then catches hold between the next two horses and again gets dragged between them before losing his grip and ending up with the last pair of horses. He lets go for the last time and allows the stagecoach to pass over him, but catches its rear axle and hauls himself back on the coach. Grabbing the reins, he brings the stagecoach to a halt. The whole sequence was carried out in one take at a flat-out gallop. The director had considered the whole stunt so dangerous that he refused to be there when it was performed. He sent Yak off alone with the film unit to shoot the sequence.

Perhaps one of the best action scenes ever shot was the one Yak set up in the chariot race with Charlton Heston in *Ben Hur* (1959). When I went to see the film I was so bored that I thought about walking out – that is, until the chariot race started. I spent the rest of the time from then on sitting on the edge of my seat – it was fantastic. Yak used his sons Tap and Joe in that movie. He went on to become a top director in all types of movies.

As you can imagine, I felt honoured to meet Yak and Thorpe, but they were unassuming men to whom I found it easy to talk. We were soon discussing the requirements for *Ivanhoe*, the star of which was to be Robert Taylor. I had been with them for about thirty minutes when John Street, who was responsible for the hiring of the crowd and the men needed for the action scenes, appeared. Whether he had been tipped off by the studio security or not, I never did find out, but in any case he came straight in through the door of the office which had unfortunately been left open. He said that all the stuntmen required for *Ivanhoe* had been contracted, and he saw no point in me being there. I immediately thought of how we had been awarded the second contract on *Hornblower* by letting the director see for himself the difference between the men the FCA could supply and those we had to offer. If we could only arrange an audition, there was no way the FCA could compete with us. In preparation for this type of movie, and in addition to our regular boys, I had lined up a troupe of Don Cossacks, who formed a trick riding group that had toured not only the UK, but all over Europe. We also had another group of trick riders known as the Buck Ryan Group of Trick Riders. Buck Ryan had competed against Yak in the States, but rode in the rodeos on an English-style saddle. Making up the numbers, we had some steeplechase riders. If I could arrange an audition, I knew we would win the contract hands down.

'I'll tell you what I'll do,' I told Yak and Thorpe. 'I'll bring the whole group to the studios and put on an audition for free. There won't even be a charge for transporting all the horses. If you like what you see, then you can consider us for the contract. If you don't, we'll pack up and leave the studio. It won't cost the company a penny.'

Yak said immediately, 'I'm a great believer in seeing something for nothing.' John Street was furious and again insisted that everything had been arranged and the men were under contract. This was blatantly untrue. I knew that there had been no auditions, and in any case, Yak would have wanted to have seen and approved the men he was to direct.

Then there was a further development. Dora Wright, MGM's casting director, appeared on the scene to join John Street and back him up. Both Thorpe and Yak were rather taken aback by this combined move. As it was their first experience of working in England, they were reluctant to get involved in the middle of a studio and union dispute. Until this intervention by Street and Dora Wright, the meeting had been going very well indeed. *Ivanhoe* would have been a very prestigious picture for our agency to have handled. Apart from needing a great number of men, Yak was to rehearse all the action over a three-month period prior to the production start date. There were a great many jousting scenes in this film, together with numerous individual fight scenes involving the principal actors.

Thorpe was silent for a while before saying, 'I'm afraid that at this stage of production I'm not in a position to go against what the casting director has set up. But on Raoul Walsh's recommendation, I would be pleased to discuss with you any future film I might direct in the UK which requires stuntmen.' We shook hands and I left the studio.

The battle between our agency and the BFPA, FCA and the crowd union continued over a number of years. But Yak and Thorpe kept to their word, and we were to work with them, especially Yak, on a number of movies, including *Knights of the Round Table* (1953), *Quentin Durward* (1955), *Helen of Troy* (1956), *Zarak Khan* (1956), *Gordon of Khartoum* (1966) and *Where Eagles Dare* (1968). Apart from the MGM studios in the UK, filming took place on locations in Africa, India, Italy, Austria and Egypt. We also worked in Morocco with Yak's sons on *Young Winston* (1972).

In 1966, Yak was awarded a Hollywood Oscar for his achievements as a stuntman and for developing safety devices to protect stuntmen everywhere; in the same year he was placed in the National Cowboy Hall of Fame. In 1971, he received a Western Heritage Award and in 1976, he was included in the National Rodeo Hall of Fame. Two years later the Academy of Motion Pictures, Arts and Sciences held a dinner in his honour to which nine hundred of Hollywood's elite turned out.

Professional stunting in the UK owes a great debt of gratitude to Yak, from whom we learned a great deal. Anybody wishing to know more about the American stunt world in Hollywood should read his book simply entitled *Stuntmen*, published in the UK by Robson Books Limited in 1980.

14

First Stuntmen on Foreign Location

I was in a depressed state of mind with the loss of stunt work on *Ivanhoe*, as it was the only all-action movie available at that time. I began to wish that I had forgotten all about the film world and had taken the opportunity to join Jock with the 22nd SAS in chasing bandits in Malaya. Some weeks later, however, when all seemed lost, I heard that Warners were going into production with a film called *The Crimson Pirate* (1952). When I phoned Gerry Blattner, Warner Bros UK managing director, for whom we had worked on *Captain Horatio Hornblower*, he told me that there would be work on the film once it returned from location in Italy, but that would not be for some months ahead. He advised me to get in touch with Terry Hunter, the production manager.

While Terry was pleased to see me, he confirmed what Blattner had said – that there would be nothing for us until the production returned from Italy. During our discussion on the studio's requirements, he mentioned that there were some underwater scenes to be shot. Three doubles were needed and these could possibly be Italian ex-naval personnel, as they were trained on oxygen. I pointed out the problem in the first place of finding the doubles, and then the possible loss of production time caused through language difficulties when they failed to understand the requirements of the underwater cameraman. I also urged Terry to think of more possible time losses if mistakes were made under water. Each time the divers would need to return to the surface to regroup, and have the whole action restated. This also meant more frequent exchanges of oxygen bottles, and more time lost.

Terry had further told me that the cameraman was Jimmy Hodges from Siebe Gorman, the diving firm. I suggested that if he chose three of our men now, they could do some of the preparatory work at Siebe Gorman, working with Hodges. Terry thought this a good idea. Warners would pay for the training with Hodges, after which the underwater doubles would be wanted in Italy for a three-week period. He then contacted Siebe Gorman at Tolworth in Surrey to make the necessary training arrangements. I was chosen to double Burt Lancaster, Frank Howard was to be Nick Cravat's double, and Peter Mitchell, who was not a stuntman but an actor, was to double James Hayter, who was playing the part of a professor.

To obtain qualification for diving on oxygen meant that I would have acquired another string to my bow, a skill which hopefully could be used on some future production. It also meant that as an agency we would have the underwater sequences on *The Crimson Pirate* to our credit. It was also a great opportunity to train under an expert like Jimmy Hodges, who had been the first man to discover HMS *Thetis,* the submarine which failed to re-surface after making a practice dive. Making a free dive, Hodges had found the submarine before the Royal Navy had even organised a search. On *The Crimson Pirate,* Jimmy was not only the cameraman, but he also supplied the technical advice and set up all the sequences. Tragically, later on Jimmy was to lose his life filming whales for Hans Hass during an underwater film series for TV.

After thinking further about the underwater sequences, Terry thought that it would be a good idea if we doubles were to be on total location as members of Burt Lancaster's crew. This would establish us for the studio shots on return to the UK. I then suggested that, by the same token, it would be better to double our numbers, as three men would be very thin on the ground. He then agreed to make the number up to six for the location and studio work. Though this was terrific news, it was small beer compared to the loss of *Ivanhoe.* In order to boost the number slightly more I asked why not make the number up to eight? I offered to take the eight out by road in return for six men's airfares. The vehicle could then be used as a camera car on location. This would allow him to recoup the cost of the airfares. Terry, who couldn't resist a bargain, agreed.

The special deal with Peter Mitchell was that, apart from being a double for James Hayter in the underwater scenes, he would also be available for any acting roles which might suddenly be written into the script. This deal guaranteed him three weeks' work, a first-class hotel, virtually a holiday at the expense of Warners in Ischia, plus the added possibility of getting a small part on the film.

Having secured the agreement, we went out and bought an ex-army staff car that had large sand tyres. We were now all set to take British stuntmen abroad, the first time it had ever been done. This was in my eyes a solid achievement. It was another first for us, as we had already led the field in arranging a stunt insurance policy. Today, of course, it is obligatory to carry insurance. We had now got a foot in the door of the British film industry for locations abroad.

Our journey across France was pretty uneventful, until on a Sunday the bolts on one of the rear wheels sheared. It could have been a real disaster. Here we were in France, with a long way to go and barely enough time to complete the journey down to Naples to catch a ferry over to Ischia. Had the same problem arisen in England on a Sunday morning, there's little doubt that we would have been stuck. It being France, a mechanic was found who came out to tow us in, and then got to work. Within two hours we were on our way once more. Had the damage occurred a little later on while we were descending the Simplon Pass into Italy, probably none of us would have survived. As we had limited cash, we didn't waste time en route, and arrived in Naples tired and bleary eyed. We booked into a hotel for the night, and caught the ferry first thing in the morning. Having had luck on our side, we arrived in Ischia on time as per our agreement.

The whole unit, which included the producer, the director, Burt Lancaster, Nick Cravat, and all the supporting cast and technicians, booked into the Regina Palace Hotel, the best hotel on the island. The following day we were fitted out with our pirate costumes. A couple of days later, while we were waiting for the two pirate ships, *La France* and the *Marionique*, to arrive, filming started with the shooting of all the shore scenes. When the ships did arrive, *La France* ran ashore on the rocks. A tug had to be sent from Naples to pull her off. It was obvious the ship hadn't sufficient engine power to enable her to cope even in fairly calm weather. This was not a good start, bearing in mind that when shooting at sea started there would be up to two hundred members of the film unit aboard, let alone the ship's crew.

When eventually both vessels docked at Ischia we had our first opportunity to climb the masts. They were the first square-rigged ships I had ever been aboard, and I recall with pleasure the time I spent aboard them. The main mast was about one hundred and twenty feet high, which was just over half that of ships such as the *Peking*, one of the last tall ships still under sail. The rigging didn't seem to me to be all that secure. The first time I went aloft I made the mistake of climbing on to the top, by going through the 'lubber hole' in the platform. This is an unforgivable sin as far as a true rigging man is concerned. Anyone who does so is regarded with contempt. We learned in time the correct way to get to the top mast. First you scale the shrouds until you reach what are known as the futtock shrouds. These are fixed to the mast and run out to the edge of the top platform, from where they continue up to support the top mast. On reaching the futtock shrouds, you then lean backward, still climbing, until you are able to pull yourself over and on to the top. I found it hard to visualise what this tricky manoeuvre would be like when the ship was ploughing through rough seas under full sail. The axiom for this drill is to climb the shrouds on the weather side and descend them on the lee. My first impression on reaching the royals, the highest part of the ship, was that from that height the hull didn't seem large enough to support all the masts and rigging, let alone the pressure of the wind against the sails.

I took every opportunity of climbing the masts when we were filming at sea. When not required in any of the shots, I assisted the Spanish crew in setting or furling sail. It is quite an experience when you first go out on the yardarm when the ship is under way. You stand with several other men on a foot-rope that moves as you haul in or set loose the sail. This movement is in addition to the pendulum effect high on the mast accentuated by the pitch and toss of the ship below. It certainly brings home to you the dangers experienced by the sailors who manned such clipper ships as the *Cutty Sark* and the *Peking*, with masts around two hundred feet high, when they rounded Cape Horn in bad weather. It is surprising, however, how soon you become accustomed to it all. It not only becomes enjoyable, but preferable to being on a deck crowded with two hundred people sweltering in the heat and getting in each other's way.

What I learned on this film in a few months was to stand me in good stead over the years and instil in me an interest in square-rigged ships for the rest of my life. *The Crimson Pirate* was also to introduce me to like-minded men from different walks of life with whom I struck up a lifetime friendship. We were joined by two

92

American stuntmen, one of whom was Charlie Hogarth. As stunting had been part and parcel of American movies over a great number of years, they had naturally acquired knowledge of an art in which we were mere beginners. As the first American stuntmen we had worked with, they were radically to change our thinking and approach to stunt work. We owe them a debt of gratitude.

While trying to establish ourselves as a professional body within the industry in the early days, we had considered it rather sissy and beneath our dignity to pad ourselves when taking falls. We therefore found it incredible to see these experienced Americans come aboard carrying stuntbags full of assorted padding. But after sustaining innumerable knocks and bruises, we finally got the message. We hadn't taken into account that after taking a fall, you could be required to repeat the same action a dozen times or more. Without any padding you could finish up severely bruised, if not incapacitated. You had to be ready over the next few days, weeks, perhaps months, to perform similar actions. If unable to continue, you would be replaced without any compensation for loss of work. This was the name of the game. You just could not afford to become injured. Of course it is not possible to eliminate all the risks, but the art is to avoid them as much as possible. Our American colleagues taught us a valuable lesson.

Working with the special-effects department also gave us a new understanding of the film industry's requirements and greatly improved the quality of our work. This learning curve continued with the help of Burt Lancaster and Nick Cravat, both of whom had been circus trapeze performers and acrobats. They had turned their past experience to good use within the film industry. Some of this circus expertise came into play in the film when they were flying around in the ship's rigging. It was a pleasure to watch them and learn skills that we could use or adapt and add to our repertoire for future work of our own. It was also instructive to see how they kept fit in their spare time in order to retain physical excellence during the whole of the shooting period.

The army command car in which we had travelled to Ischia was now the camera car, as planned. I was called upon to load up first thing in the morning and transport all the camera equipment to the ship. After this I returned to the hotel for breakfast, and then left with the rest of the boys for the day's shooting. This meant that I was working more hours than a lot of the stuntmen and some of the technicians. At the end of the day's shooting and when the ship had returned to harbour, I still had to reload the car with the equipment and offload it back at the hotel. This was, of course, very tiring, but after some time Peter, who was not required on board as a stuntman, took over the camera-car duties. The car then became used for additional errands, such as ferrying people about while we were filming at sea. The company was certainly getting its money's worth. We gained from this experience on our return to the UK, by setting up a separate company named Studio Services, to provide camera cars and sound trucks to the industry and in this way subsidise the agency.

Eventually the underwater sequences started. The plot of *The Crimson Pirate* was along the lines of a mutiny by the pirate ship's crew, who manacle their captain, played by Burt Lancaster, his deputy, Nick Cravat, and James Hayter as the professor and cast them adrift in an open boat to die. The professor has the brainwave of turning the boat upside down, sinking to the seabed and walking ashore in the airlock trapped in the hull. This might look possible at a first glance, but there are several snags. Upturning the boat was no problem, but the trapped air kept it buoyant. This was remedied by tying lead and sandbags to the gunwales and, of course, excluding all the air. Our next problem was that the boat was then so heavy that we doubles were struggling to walk with it on the seabed.

As mentioned previously, we had trained using oxygen. Our Salvus equipment was a self-contained unit where the exhausted air is cleared within the system, and not into the water, so as to prevent any air bubbles rising to the surface. Frogmen on active service have this system so that they can remain undetected. It was estimated that we had an hour's supply of oxygen. However, due to the physical exertions required to carry a very heavy boat and also push it through the water, the oxygen supply was lasting less than half an hour. This meant frequent stops and returns to the diving boat to change oxygen bottles and the protosorb (the material which absorbs the exhausted air). As a result we were taking much longer to shoot the sequences than had been planned.

We were regarded as a separate team, and operated on the other side of the island from the main unit. The day started with Jimmy Hodges explaining what he required us to do. We dived to the appointed spot on the seabed, had a rehearsal, resurfaced to discuss the action, and then were instructed by Jimmy on any modifications he decided would improve the shot. We then went back and shot the sequence. For quite simple shots, the actual rehearsal was often sufficient.

The procedure was that we would dive down to the boat, lift it over our heads and wait for Hodges to knock on the hull. On receiving this signal we slowly counted to ten, to give him time to swim back to camera position and start shooting, when we moved off with the boat in the direction he had specified. When he had shot sufficient footage, he swam to the boat and again knocked to tell us to halt. He then ducked down so that we could see him and indicated by sign language whether to return to the start point for a re-shoot or drop the boat and return to the diving boat to be briefed on the next sequence. The system worked well, but with our frequent returns to the surface and briefing between shots it was a slow process. There were times, too, when Jimmy needed to go off on his own to find new interesting underwater locations.

The main unit was also progressing very slowly, as the script was changed so that from a pure pirate story the film became a comedy. This necessitated a rethink on the special-effect requirements. The special-effects man was from Hollywood. Working with him certainly expanded our knowledge of the film industry even further. With the re-scheduling of the script, some of the actors were not required for a number of weeks. One of them was Noel Purcell, the Irish actor, who used to come out with us on the diving boat as a way of getting away from the hotel and pleasantly filling his day. We greatly appreciated his company, for he had us in fits of laughter with tales of his experiences at Dublin's Abbey Theatre and in the film industry. What with his stories, the very enjoyable diving, the sun, the beautiful surroundings and the vino, our days passed very quickly and very pleasantly.

One evening as we finished the day's work on this particular location, Jimmy suddenly decided that there was one additional shot that he wanted. It was, he said, a very quick shot that would take only a very few minutes and which he could just get while we still had the light, which was fading fast. Known as 'one on the hurry up', this type of shot frequently occurs on films and has been the bane of my life. Inevitably such shots lead to problems. Professional American stuntmen refuse to do them, but we, being new to the game and all out to please, frequently agreed to cooperate.

I looked at my atmosphere gauge, which was showing very low. It was not an accurate reading as we were using oxygen above the estimated rate. I pointed this out to Jimmy, who said that if he didn't get the shot now he would have to leave it. He promised me the shot would be very quick. No doubt he was right – that is, if the shot went as planned. He stressed that we already knew exactly what he wanted, the boat was in position, there was no need to rehearse and we could do the shot straight away. Reluctantly I agreed.

As arranged, we dived straight down on to the boat, picked it up and put it over our heads. Frank and Peter started to move forward, so I presumed that Jimmy had given the signal although I hadn't heard him knock. We walked on and on. By now I was getting very nervous, as this was turning out to be anything but a short shot, and I had been very low on oxygen before we started. The other two seemed unconcerned, as they just kept walking. Presently I knew that something was wrong and pulled back, which made the other two turn around to see what I was doing. I gestured to them to stop and motioned to Peter to duck out and see what was happening. After a few seconds he returned and signalled that something was wrong, so Frank and I dropped the boat.

Oxygen can have a strange effect on different people. Whether it was due to our exertions with a heavy load and the abnormal amount of oxygen we were using I don't know. With me I tended to become rather morose and short-tempered. It had the opposite effect on Frank, who became light headed and childish, which I found very annoying. Frank suddenly disappeared, looking for Jimmy, although in training Jimmy had instructed us always to remain together at all times. I looked at my gauge, which was now showing empty, and on looking up discovered that we had walked into about fifty feet of water. While on oxygen we should never have exceeded thirty feet. I immediately signalled to Peter that I was out of oxygen and was going to surface, and pushed off from the bottom. With the Salvas equipment, the air is breathed from an air bag around your neck which, when full, can provide buoyancy. Halfway to the surface, when trying to breathe, I found that I was sucking for air which was no longer there. The result was that the two sides of the air bag were drawn together, and there was no air to draw upon. I made a fantastic physical effort to reach the surface, tearing off my face mask in readiness to gulp the air as I surfaced.

I was now in serious trouble. Not only was I without any buoyancy, but I also had the extra weights we had donned in order to walk along the seabed. These were distributed on belts around our waists and under our double's costume. I made a desperate attempt to tear off the costume to release the belt, but it was of a very tough calico material and I couldn't remove it. I started to sink. Peter had seen my plight and at once came to my rescue. Without his help I couldn't have kept my head above water and surely would have sunk to the bottom and drowned. Had Frank remained with us as he had been instructed to do, there would have been no problem.

While Peter was fighting to keep my head above water, he pulled off his facemask to shout for help to our dive boat. Though they heard Peter's shout, I saw to my horror that the boatman was pulling up his anchor hand over hand instead of cutting the anchor rope and heading straight for us. As far as the rescue boat was concerned, I had had it. I was now getting weaker and the strain was telling on Peter. No longer capable of holding my head above water, he could only lift me up to take a breath at a time. In tearing off his face mask to shout to the boat, he hadn't turned off his air supply, and he too was beginning to lose buoyancy. While this was going on I was still making frantic efforts to get out of the costume. By now I really had accepted the fact that I was going to drown. I still had a mental picture of the boatman slowly pulling up the anchor. If Peter released his hold on me I knew I was a gonner.

During the time that we had been shooting the underwater sequences, nobody had ever visited us. Now we had an amazing bit of luck. The fastest boat we had on location, which was with the first unit, had been sent round to us with a message. Luckily the two Italian boatmen saw our plight, opened their throttle and made straight for us. I was no longer aware of what was happening by this time, but I was told that one of the Italians tied a rope around himself and when near enough made a great leap and grabbed Peter and me. The impact apparently took all three of us under water, but the coxswain, who had shut off his motor, hauled on the rope and pulled us to the surface and eventually into the boat. Seconds later, Peter would have had to let me go to save himself.

Why we had gone off without instructions I do not know to this day. I can only conclude that the rush to get the shot and Frank's lightheadedness on oxygen may have been contributory causes. I learned a valuable lesson from this incident. The following day I went into the wardrobe department and cut off all the tapes which tied the costume over the weights belt, and equipment, replacing them with elastic. When the alterations were finished, I was satisfied that I could get out of the costume and dump the equipment and weight belt in seconds. It just shows that nothing should be overlooked and every detail checked, constantly thought through, and revised according to circumstances.

I must state for the record that Frank was a very good stuntman, with natural physical strength, and normally very reliable. During the war he had served in the Merchant Navy, and as far as I can remember afterwards became an adagio dancer. He often entertained the unit with his fine singing voice.

We came across a shoemaker on Ischia who made the best sandals I have ever seen. In his spare time he built and sold kayaks. I had a single kayak built, while Jack Cooper and Del Watson had a double made. On our day off on Sundays, I used to paddle over to a small island a mile or so from Ischia. At this time of year Ischia was full of holidaying Italians, in addition to the film unit and the local inhabitants. It was very pleasant to get away from all the noise and bustle. A couple of times we took the ferry to Capri, which also made a pleasant break. Capri was much more popular than Ischia, and as a result much more expensive. Ischia hadn't yet become the main tourist attraction it is today.

Following my trips to the neighbouring island, I became rather adept in handling my kayak. One Sunday I decided that I would paddle around the complete island of Ischia, which I was told was a distance of twenty-six miles. I mentioned the idea to Jack and Del, who decided that they would like to go along with me. We arranged for Peter to meet us halfway round with the camera car and some food and drink. On the appointed day we set off, despite the sea being a little choppy. Built of unseasoned wood and lacking buoyancy tanks, these kayaks were not intended for serious journeys. As a result, we had to make several landings to empty them, though because the island was rather rocky, there were few suitable places for us to land on en route. Half the time we were paddling waterlogged kayaks. Beaches on which we could empty out the craft became less frequent. By the time we had reached the halfway mark, Del and Jack decided that after a rest and refreshments brought by Peter, they were going to turn back.

I was determined to complete what we had started to do. I asked them if they'd seen a map of the coastline, to which they said no. I told them I had. 'We've already completed the hard part. I'm going to go on and not make life more difficult by turning back. You can go back if you like. But I'll be waiting for you, because I shall certainly be back before you.' Of course I hadn't seen a map either.

Reluctantly and misguidedly they agreed to carry on. The next part of the journey saw us finding even fewer landing places, with the coastline becoming even rockier than ever. Our progress was becoming even slower, and the physical effort greater. As time went on the light began to fail. Then we came across the best beach we had found so far, and paddled furiously to land there. We threw ourselves down to take a well-earned rest. In a matter of seconds we were being attacked by thousands of horseflies. The onslaught was so furious that we retreated back to sea without even emptying the boats. The physical effort under these conditions was taking its toll. As we got further around the island and darkness descended, we could see the lights going on in the villages. Music from the cafés drifted out to sea, as the nightlife was beginning to stir. It had been a very long day but at last we saw in the distance the lights of Port Ischia.

Eventually we arrived. Jack and Del were slightly ahead of me and beached their kayak first. They both got wearily out and Del started staggering up the beach. Jack shouted, 'Del, give me a hand with the boat!' Del didn't even turn around, and kept walking, but shouted back with considerable feeling, 'Fuck the boat!' As far as I can remember, Del didn't ever get back into that kayak again during the rest of time we were on location.

Charles Farrell, an actor who was an Equity representative, together with another member of the cast, entered into negotiations with Warner Bros regarding a location allowance for the actors. The technicians' unions had received this allowance for some time. The company agreed, which set a precedent and became part and parcel for all future locations. The amount was ten pounds, which was gratefully received. Future location allowances were based upon those of the technicians' unions.

On our next free Sunday, Peter and I decided to walk up Mount Epomeo, the summit of which is the highest point on the island. It was very hot on the way up, and I was amazed to find Italians suddenly appearing from holes in the ground offering us iced Coca Colas and cold beers. For those not wishing to walk up, donkeys were available to the summit, which rises to a peak and has a church, with adjoining rooms carved out of solid rock. Monks were serving both alcoholic and soft drinks in these rooms. In the very pinnacle itself, a table and bench seats had also been carved out of solid rock, where we were able to sit and order drinks to be brought up to us. From this vantage point, we found we could view the whole island. This was especially wonderful when night fell and the island was dotted with lights from the villages. The lights of cruise liners sailing to and from Naples, which itself could be seen twinkling in the distance, added magic to the scene. As the ships approached, we were able to hear the strains of the music being played aboard them, wafted up to us as we sat in the cool air knocking back a couple of bottles of vino. Afterwards, when we made our way down from the summit, we realised how the hazards of the descent in the dim light were in proportion to how much alcohol one had consumed.

Having now received the location allowance, we could afford some of the evening pursuits, such as the conviviality of the Michaeliss beach café, which consisted of a thatched roof supported by poles stuck in the sand under which lanterns were suspended. Here, after midnight swims, we enjoyed late barbecue meals and bottles of wine, while a small group of musicians and an Italian singer entertained us.

Some evenings after work, having cleaned up and eaten at our hotel, we sat in the cafés on the main street watching the young girls of the town parading up and down. This seemed to be their way of passing the evening. They were known as the 'click-clack girls' because of the leather sandals they wore, which had no strap around the heels, and made this sound as they walked along the road. They were featured on local postcards, so we sent an assortment to Jock in Malaya, where they were dropped by air into the jungle where the SAS were operating. Some of the cards carried the message, 'Wish you were here – from the boys.'

Jock wrote to me describing his life in the jungle. He revealed that the main problem – worse than the bandits – was caused by the leeches. After brief spells of sleep, he and his comrades woke to find the leeches had taken hold on the most delicate parts of their bodies. The only way to make them release their hold was to touch them with the glowing end of a cigarette. This was the first chore to be carried out each morning. At one stage they were joined by Indian troops who had been sent to acquire the latest jungle warfare techniques for fighting terrorists. They were non-smokers on religious grounds. Horrified at finding themselves covered with leeches when they awoke on the first morning, they quickly cast aside their religious scruples and became avid smokers.

Back in Ischia, once the main shots on land had been completed, we now spent every day at sea. I enjoyed climbing the masts and assisting with the setting and stowing of the sails. The skipper drilled into us the safety maxim: one hand for the ship, and one hand for yourself. This wasn't possible when pulling in sail, however. When out on the yardarm standing on a footrope, you lie across the yardarm on your stomach and use both hands to furl the sail. It's surprising how quickly you become accustomed to the ship's motion and the movement of the footrope caused by the other crew members standing on it. You don't even think about whether you are on the lower or upper yards. Of course Burt Lancaster and Nick Cravat were completely at home in the rigging, and moved about with the agility of monkeys. They taught us several of their circus tricks, which were to be of great value to me on future movies.

Quite suddenly, seemingly overnight, the holiday season on Ischia came to an end. The previous night had been full of holiday-makers, bright lights and music and gaiety. The next day, nearly all the cafés were closed, and apart from the local inhabitants, the place took on the appearance of a ghost town. This left us with very little to do in the evenings. As a means of passing the time we went to see showings of the film rushes, which had been processed in London and flown back for the production unit to evaluate. The production company was named Norma Productions, after Burt's wife. At one showing, I was sitting behind Burt and his wife. Featured in the sequence being screened was a character named Slimy Sam. The actor who played him always had the unit in stitches; he was undoubtedly the funniest character on the production. This film, remember, was now a comedy being played for laughs. His appearance always evoked laughter from us, which was quite a feat seeing that we were becoming a very tired and hard-bitten cynical unit. Norma had only just joined Burt, having flown in from the States, and these were the first rushes she had seen. She was also laughing along with all of us. 'Burt, who's that?' she asked. Burt replied, 'Oh, he's our funny guy.' I thought at the time that he had made the remark in a very peculiar tone of voice. When the movie was released, some of the sequences were missing. Without the punch lines, the scenes fell flat. After seeing the film myself, I wondered whether the actor concerned had been considered a little bit too funny and was stealing the scenes from the principal characters. I thought at the time that *The Crimson Pirate* would have established him within the film industry, but strangely I never heard of him again.

Generally speaking, *The Crimson Pirate* film unit was a happy one. This was only marred on one occasion by a dispute between Paddy Hayes and Jack Cooper. Paddy had been a professional middleweight champion in Ireland. Jack was a keep fit enthusiast and professional high diver; he was also a very strong swimmer and an amateur wrestler. Following some trivial row, Paddy threatened to give Jack a good hiding after work. Now while I'm sure that Jack would have given a good account of himself, I thought that the chances of not receiving a good hiding were stacked against him. Jack obviously gave the matter serious thought, and while sitting in the bus that was to take them down to the ship, shouted to Paddy, who was just boarding, 'All right, I'll see you tonight, but we'll meet again when we swim under the ship. That's when I'll get you.' He was referring to a sequence to be shot in which the two ships drift together, and the crew of the larger ship wait until they are close enough to board. Burt Lancaster's crew, hiding on the far side of the smaller ship, dive off, and swim under their own vessel and the other ship. On surfacing, they climb aboard the larger ship to take the crew completely by surprise and overpower them. It was quite a way to swim underwater, quite apart from having to remain well down to clear both hulls. We had to be in water at least eighteen feet deep. Now, though Paddy might well be a good fighter, he was not a great swimmer, and certainly no match for Jack under water. This obviously gave Paddy food for thought, as the threatened punch-up never materialised.

Script changes continued to be made and shooting on location dragged on into the fourth month. Everyone was weary with the long hours. Despite Peter Mitchell helping me out with some of the camera-car duties, I was especially tired because the vehicle was

102

also being used as a general pick-up, which meant it was needed before the day's shooting started and quite often after it had ended. The car started to develop gearbox trouble and needed repair. I cornered Terry Hunter, the production manager, on the hotel staircase. Pointing out that the company had enjoyed considerable service from us over a long period, I said that it was only fair they should bear the cost of repair. We still had a long way to go on this location. It was the first time I had been able to reach Terry who, when he was not caught up in production meetings, was chasing all over the island sorting out innumerable problems, which seemed to increase daily. The original time scheduled for the location had been two months. I admit that he must have been under tremendous pressure, but then so was I.

'You did a deal with me in return for the airfares, so it's down to you. You'll have to pay,' he snapped. I suddenly saw red and called him all the names under the sun. I told him he had reneged on what had been agreed. In any case, the verbal agreement we had made was for a camera car only. I had no wish to continue working with such a cheapjack, and I was going to leave, taking with me any of the stuntmen who wanted to come, leaving the company responsible for any who remained.

Our confrontation took place outside the main dining hall. I was told later that the whole unit, including Burt Lancaster and the stuntmen, stopped eating and talking in order to listen to the argument. The stuntmen especially had no wish to lose out on the remainder of the movie production, which of course also included work in the studio back in the UK. At this point Terry sat down on the stairs, with his head in his hands. I'm sure that he thought I was about to whack him. Still in a raging temper I marched into the American producer, Norman Deeming, to tell him that I wanted out. He had evidently heard the fracas. 'Look, Joe, I'll release you, but stay on for a few days in case you might be needed for some retakes or continuity shots. You needn't come out on the ship, and I'll pick up the cost of the car repairs,' he said. His calm manner took quite a bit of wind out of my sails, and I agreed.

For the next five days, when the shooting unit had left Port Ischia, I went down to the beach, jumped into my kayak and paddled off for a few hours. On returning to the beach, I spent the rest of the time swimming or sunbathing, and having the odd bottle of wine at the Michaeliss cafe. After five days, Norman Deeming sent for me. 'Now that the dust has settled, there's a lot more work to be done. So why don't you come back on the film, Joe?' Having become slightly bored with my lazy days, I was very happy to accept. Back at work, no one mentioned the incident, and everybody behaved towards me as if nothing had happened. It was, of course, only a matter of time before I ran into Terry, who stopped me and said that I had caught him at a very bad time. But in any case, the deal that I had given him was so good that he was sure that he was being conned somewhere along the line, but he couldn't see where. We shook hands, and that was the problem resolved.

When the location work finally came to an end, additional men were needed for the studio work. I left the location and flew back to England to audition for new men. Although we had lost the *Ivanhoe* contract, this additional work was compensation to some degree. Again I couldn't help regretting that if Equity had backed us, we would have secured both contracts. I felt, however, that our agency had regained some ground, with the added prestige of having completed the first foreign location supplying stuntmen.

After the production returned to England, there was still quite a lot of studio work to keep us going, but there was no other employment in sight. There was no doubt that the Film Producers Association, and their Agency the FCA, had marked our cards, and obtained a block on our services throughout the whole of the British Film Industry. The studios politely received me when I approached them, but no offers were forthcoming. The FCA could see that we had opened a new and untapped market within the industry, and they were determined to oust us, and secure it for themselves.

15

Open Air Shows

In the lean times following *The Crimson Pirate* we started looking for any work opportunities. One of the boys, Gordon Baber, obtained a contract for a publicity stunt in Wales, which involved appearing with a python in the window of one of the main stores in Cardiff. Gordon had experience of working with animals over a long period, including some time he spent in South Africa. Gordon and the snake made several appearances which attracted large crowds. He explained to me that you had to keep the snake moving round you, taking care not to let it anchor its tail between your legs or under your arms as this would enable the python to begin constricting with its coils around your body.

The stunt inevitably drew reporters and photographers from the local press who joined the watching shoppers. One day the camera flash bulbs repeatedly going off seemed to wake the snake from its passive state of semi-hibernation. It swiftly obtained a grip with its tail and started constricting. Gordon managed to bow to the crowd before backing into the shop and shouting for help, as he was now in serious trouble. All the shop assistants, however, were terrified of touching the snake. Gordon by this time was on the floor, yelling even louder for someone to help him. Fortunately two policemen arrived on the scene to see what all the commotion was about. Gordon shouted instructions to them to release the tail, but by now the python was fully awake and they had great difficulty in doing so. Eventually Gordon and the policemen managed to partially release the snake's hold, then a further two policemen arrived to help and a tragedy was averted. Eventually they managed to get the snake back in its container, and the dramatic incident came to its close. During the whole episode the terrified shop assistants stood by petrified and unable to help.

Back in the office, Gordon demonstrated the predicament he'd been in, even down to how he writhed on the floor in the struggle. He

105

had the stunt boys in absolute hysterics. As he said, he was able to laugh about it afterwards, but at the time he had been very frightened.

Chasing film work was made even more difficult because petrol was rationed, and we couldn't afford to pay the exorbitant price being asked on the black market. We did have some luck, however. Some of the boys were engaged to appear in a stage show re-enacting scenes from the movies. The authorities used to give petrol coupons for artistes to transport their props to the next town or theatre. The Ford I had taken on my honeymoon was pressed into service. I cut the saloon body in half, and built a van body on to it. I then re-registered the car as a commercial vehicle and joined the Showman's Guild, because petrol coupons were only issued to people registered with the Guild. Paddy Hayes, one of the stuntmen, took the logbook on tour with him. He then showed it to the authorities with the name and address of the next theatre at which they were playing, and coupons were issued for that journey. Of course, the boys all travelled by public transport to the next job, and the coupons were posted back to me. This enabled me to drive around the studios chasing up information I'd received about possible films requiring stuntmen.

I decided that now was as good a time as any to settle the question of which union represented the stuntmen. I wrote to Sir Henry French, Chairman of the BFPA, requesting a meeting with him to settle the question, particularly after the diabolical tactics of the FCA over the *Hornblower* contract. With the date set for our meeting, I informed Equity and asked them to attend as it was vital that they did so.

Equity failed to turn up. Unbeknown to me, they had phoned Sir Henry to ask what the meeting was about and accepted his explanation that it was solely about agents' commissions. Had they attended the meeting, the position would have been resolved and professional stunting would have been established years earlier.

To present stunting in an entirely new light to the BFPA and drive a wedge between the crowd union and Equity, I took along with me a number of people I said constituted our agency's representatives. I introduced Jock to Sir Henry, along with Captain Seeley from Newman's Airways, who represented our stunt flying team, Captain John Gillanders, who was in charge of our riding section, Lieutenant Commander Barry du Boulay, our seaborne activities representative, and two others representing our fencing and car stunting sections.

Sir Henry, who had expected to meet just Jock and me, was nonplussed. Ordering coffee and biscuits, he commented that he hadn't realised it was going to be 'that sort of meeting'. Also present were Mr Francis, head of the BFPA's personnel management, and Gerry Dearham from Denham Studios, who now was in charge of the FCA. My team really had little idea of what it was all about and what was at stake, but their presence ensured our agency being seen as a professional organisation with an entirely new approach to action scenes in the British film industry, far removed from merely supplying crowd artistes.

I opened the meeting by pointing out that as a crowd casting agency, the FCA had no right to become involved with the casting of stunt artistes. I stated that the second *Hornblower* contract had been fulfilled by our agency, and all of the men we provided were Equity members over whom the FCA had no jurisdiction.

I demanded that the FCA should not get involved in stuntmen's recruitment in the future and never use the name of the BFPA to obtain contracts fraudulently, and gain commissions on those contracts to which they legally had no claim. The discussion became very heated. Dearham was speechless – he could see that the argument was going against him, Francis came to his aid, and refuted all the charges laid against him. For the rest of the meeting Dearham remained silent.

Bringing the meeting to a close, Sir Henry commented that it had been very constructive. Without doubt the two separate organisations would keep to their separate fields in future. He glossed over Dearham's skulduggery, and said that there was no justification for the BFPA to consider the question of compensation. The whole episode had been one of misunderstanding, he concluded. Although we left empty handed, I had a feeling that for what it was worth, we had made our mark. While we had lost the battle, we had not lost the war. Although there was no way that we could have taken legal proceedings against a powerful organisation like the BFPA, I realise with hindsight there was some action we could have taken. As it was soon after the Second World War had ended, national newspapers might well have been interested in the shabby way two ex-servicemen had been treated, particularly as Jock had served in the SAS and I had been in the

Commandos, prestigious units that received a great deal of wartime news coverage.

I was furious with Equity, who had now thrown away two chances to establish stunting on a professional basis. It was obvious that having got away with the *Hornblower* contract, the FCA had no intention of vacating the market we had opened. Unfortunately, due to the registration of the men of the second *Hornblower* contract, the FCA now had nearly as many men registered as stuntmen as we had. The Crowd Union, of course, welcomed the outcome, as the increased membership swelled their coffers. From this point on, we had not only the BFPA to contend with but also the FCA and the FAA. This was a long and hard one to crack, more especially as we didn't have the backing of our own union.

It was at this time that I teamed up with Bill Munt, the owner of a riding stable in Borehamwood, who was already established in the film industry, providing riding horses, coaches and fours in hand. We discussed how we could cooperate to our mutual benefit by laying on auditions for both horses and riders which had not been previously available to casting departments. We also made arrangements for riders registered with our agency to visit these stables to exercise the horses. Soon it became known within the film industry that a group of professional riders was in regular training for movie work. It wasn't long before we had an influx of national hunt riders, which added prestige to our team. As I've mentioned previously, we also had on our books a troupe of Russian Don Cossack trick riders, as well as another trick riding team who toured open air shows under the name of Buck Ryan.

The FCA couldn't compete with us, and no other agent had entered this field or considered entering into this potentially large studio requirement, although the need for it had been exposed by the film *Ivanhoe*. As time went on, film companies were coming to us for straight riders, riding doubles and stunt riders. As the demand developed, it was this side of the business that kept us alive, along with what we earned from Studio Services. As riding was mostly associated with period films, we also registered Equity artistes with fencing experience. Among them was Pat Crean, fencing coach to the Rank Charm School. In addition, we had an Olympic fencing coach.

Period films requiring fencers and riders kept our heads above water when stuntmen were not required. We had by now cornered the market in both these fields. However, the scene can quickly change when a spate of modern gangster or romantic screenplays emerge, so it pays the individual to acquire as many skills as possible.

In the States, films and TV series featuring cowboys have always been in continuous production. This means that for example, a young man can enter the film industry as a rider, and make a good living throughout his lifetime doing nothing else. But he will do even better if he can earn enough to buy his own mount or mounts, and spend time when not employed training his own falling horses and perfecting his own particular range of stunts. He can also enter rodeos to supplement his income. He can rely on the fact that over the years cowboy films will continue to be produced. Unfortunately when things slacken off over here in the UK, there are no similar opportunities for employment.

In a bid to overcome dead times in the industry, I began concentrating on the possibilities offered by fetes and other open-air events, including outdoor ones put on by large companies especially for their employees. We had a great line-up of performers to offer. The Don Cossacks and the Buck Ryan shows proved to be very popular, as did the motorcycle and car stunts we could provide. Also on our books was a circus artiste named Saballa, a former lion tamer, who was also a sway pole artiste. He also performed what is known in the entertainment world as a dental act, where he was suspended spinning at a great height holding on only by gripping with his teeth.

One day I was contacted by a member of a local Round Table who were thinking of putting on an open-air act at Bury St. Edmunds. I was invited to meet them at a dinner they were giving in aid of one of their charities. They wanted ideas for an act that was completely different from anything previously performed at any show.

Some time prior to the meeting, I had paid seventy-five pounds for a 1925 Hispano Suiza, which must have weighed nearly three tons. It was reputed to have been owned by King Zog of Albania, and given by him to his paramour, Madame Lupresco. Of impressive appearance, it was a sedanca de ville, which meant that the roof over the driver's compartment could be folded back, leaving the driver in the open, while the passengers remained under cover. Alternatively, the whole roof could be folded away so that it became a topless vehicle. Had we known the eventual value of the vehicle forty years afterwards, we would have maintained it in its original condition. This is, of course, being wise after the event, and what I actually did was replace the eight-litre engine with a Perkins P6 diesel engine. With its high back axle ratio, huge wheels and twenty-five gallon tank, the car could be driven from my home in Borehamwood to the Spanish border without refuelling.

The main attraction for us was that it was a great calling card when parked outside any studio. No matter how many dozens of Rolls, Mercedes or other high-class limousines there were lined up in a car park, our vehicle was instantly recognisable. People would know that either Jock or I, or perhaps both of us, were there. The car was known throughout the whole film industry. It also took stuntmen to Italy, France and Spain on various locations. It was this car that I drove to Bury St. Edmunds to meet the Round Table organisers with my wife.

As we arrived at the hotel where the dinner was being given, Round Table members turned out en masse to view our monster of a car. When they saw it was me, I'm sure they thought that as the owner of such a vehicle I must be quite eccentric, and therefore the ideal person to come up with an original act for their show.

After the meal we got down to discussing possible acts, but none of my ideas found favour, including a suggestion for a jousting tournament, which I had made as jousting was one of the acts perfected at MGM by Yakima Canutt for *Ivanhoe*. No, it had to be completely new and spectacular. Given this brief, I drove home wondering what I could possibly dream up that would prove to be acceptable.

Sitting in the office one morning, trying to come up with something for the Round Table open air show, I was more than just a little worried. Time was getting short. A few days earlier, there had been an article in the *Daily Telegraph* featuring a crazy couple about to be married. After their reception at the Ritz in Piccadilly they were planning to climb into a balloon basket suspended beneath a cluster of balloons. When the balloons were released, the couple hoped to drift down to Wales. Their honeymoon would start from wherever the balloons landed them. The Regional Air Authorities had vetoed the plan for the obvious reason that if they drifted in the proposed direction, this would have brought them directly into the path of planes landing and taking off from Heathrow. I thought nothing more about it until Saballa, the circus artiste, walked into the office. Suddenly an idea came to me.

'Could you do your dental act beneath a cluster of balloons that are tethered, but at a reasonable height?' I asked him. When he replied immediately that he could, I told him to give me a few days and I'd come back to him with a possible offer. First of all I had to find out who the owner of the balloons was, so I phoned the *Telegraph* and spoke to the writer of the article, who gave me a name, but this was insufficient to enable me to trace anyone, so I tried the Ritz. A member of staff told me that it was a relative of the couple who had made the bookings. He seemed to remember he was a curator of the Tate Gallery. I phoned the Tate, made contact with him and eventually tracked the balloon owner down. I explained that the Round Table were planning a fund-raising show for charity and asked if he would cooperate. He agreed, but with the proviso that his balloon pilot should supervise the whole operation. Although the balloon pilot was living in France, eventually everything came together and a fee was agreed with Saballa.

I now had to put the proposal to the secretary of the Round Table. I wasn't exactly brimming with confidence at it being accepted, as everything else I had suggested had been turned down. To my surprise his committee jumped at the idea. Time was now pressing, as I had accepted a contract to work in France, so I tied up all the ends and introduced everyone concerned to each other, leaving the final details to be completed by the Round Table and the Saballa contract to be arranged through the office. I insisted on the one condition, agreed with Saballa, that the balloon had to be tethered, with a proviso that Saballa should determine the height. I must say that I was very surprised to find that Saballa seemed completely unconcerned and supremely confident that there was nothing to the act. While in France, I couldn't help wondering how he was to become suspended below the basket and by what means he would be liaising with the balloon pilot. One thing was for sure – with a dental act, there was no way in which he could open his mouth and shout out the order to be lowered!

On my return from France, I phoned the Round Table secretary to enquire how the act had gone. I was told that Saballa had done everything that he had promised to do. At the time the wind was quite strong, and they told Saballa that in these conditions they wouldn't ask him to perform. Saballa insisted, however, and was allowed to go ahead. The watching spectators were scared out of their lives, while all the Round Table members were petrified. Saballa brought his act to a finish by swinging himself onto the tethering cable and sliding to the ground. Although he had been contracted to do two further performances, the Round Table had had enough thrills for one day and refused to let him repeat the act.

We became involved in these open-air shows for a couple of years, but the problem was always that their success depended upon the weather. In the UK this is of course notoriously unpredictable, and most of these shows had to be one-day stands. I had tried to get the BBC and ITV interested, but at that time the range of their recording facilities was strictly limited by distance.

Around this time we were experiencing another slack period, so I applied to Tottenham Council to put on an open-air aqua show. Four of the stunt boys had been involved in such action before – Jack Cooper, George Leech, Peter Perkins and Mike Eversfield, who acted as compère; in addition there was Betty Slade and, last but by no means least, Roy Franson who used to dive sixty feet from a tower into a five-foot round tub. The council drew up a contract and decided that featuring the show in the publicity handouts as an event presented by the British Film Stunt Team would ensure the show's success. We had tried to negotiate a contract under which we received a smaller appearance fee but also had a percentage of the gate takings. Fortunately for us this was refused, for after the opening two days and nights, which were highly successful, the weather deteriorated, and the show lost money.

16

The Rodeo at Harringay

We were still fighting for survival in the film industry and battling with the FAA, the FCA and the BFPA. Some time had elapsed since we had finished the studio work on *The Crimson Pirate* back in England, after being on location in Italy. We resigned ourselves to being in for a quiet spell until we heard that Yakima Canutt and Richard Thorpe had returned to the UK and were once again at MGM Studios, to film *Quentin Durward* (1955). They kept their promise, made after our failure to get the *Ivanhoe* contract, to consider us for any of their future UK productions by agreeing to audition our riders and stuntmen. Yak was able to see for himself that all I had previously told him about the standard of the people we represented was no exaggeration. As a result of the audition, we provided all the riders and stuntmen for the film.

Quentin Durward was a milestone. It established that henceforth only Equity riders were to be used in British Films. It was also the first of many films on which I was to work for Yak over a great number of years. Shortly afterwards, opportunity was again to come our way with another period movie, *The Master of Ballantrae*. Things were starting to hot up.

I wrote to Jock in Malaya, enclosing two letters in the envelope. One said: 'I have not been able to generate enough work for the office to warrant me keeping it open. Only you can do that, as I have a family to look after. I'll keep the office open for one month more. If you can't return to take over, I shall regrettably have to close it down.' The second letter, for his eyes only, read: 'Jock you must somehow get back. The office is buzzing and I can't cope alone with all the work.'

He showed the first letter to his commanding officer, who gave him compassionate leave on the strength of it. Jock was returned to the SAS Holding Battalion in Wales, which happened to be run by an ex-wartime SAS friend who fixed things for him. So while Jock was officially still a captain in the SAS on the active list, he was taking stuntmen out to Sicily on location for *The Master of Ballantrae*. I reckon this audacious action should qualify for some sort of mention in the *Guinness Book of Records*!

In the meantime, the impresario Tom Arnold was planning a Texas Rodeo at Harringay Arena. The high quality and standards demonstrated by our boys on *Quentin Durward* enabled me to clinch a contract to supply all the riders for this rodeo, riding in which I consider to have been another highlight of my career as a stuntman. It was fortunate that I had that working arrangement with Bill Munt, owner of the stables at Borehamwood, near Elstree. With my riders and his horses and equipment, between us we were able to provide riders, horses and coaches to film companies requiring them, and could lay on an audition for them at very short notice.

Clem Butson, director of the Harringay Rodeo, was most impressed by the abilities of the men and girl trick riders included in the audition I organised for his benefit. This show established the principle, too, that all riders should be Equity members. Rodeo riders had been brought over from America for the show. The glittering line-up included Tex Ritter, the singing cowboy, who was famous all over the US, and Buff Brady, the world champion trick rider and roper, together with the Asah Indians; from the UK the Don Cossacks, Buck Ryan, and, of course, our riders who provided the broncobusters and rode in the colourful Texas Carousel event.

One of the acts to be included was a horse jumping over a Jaguar sports car. Several riders from the show world turned up with their show jumpers. Horses and riders were very smartly turned out and groomed to perfection, with all their tack gleaming. The only problem was that, during rehearsals, try as they might, none of the horses would jump over the car. Looking on was Johnny Roc, a stable owner from Ruislip, who claimed that he had a horse which would perform the feat.

The horse, named Mandy, arrived next day for the attempt. Looking rather like a shire, the horse had huge hooves and long shaggy hair. Quite a lot of mud was hanging from her coat as she lived in a field, and the tack left a lot to be desired. When she appeared, everybody just fell about laughing. So this was the horse which was to perform a feat that some of the best show jumpers had jibbed at? In fact Mandy cleared the Jag with ease, much to the astonishment of everyone. I could never understand why Clem Butson didn't include her in the show. If you first brought on the show horses which all refused the jump, then introduced Mandy to demonstrate how it should be done, it would have been a show stopper.

Johnny Roc had an open bet on Mandy against all comers. It involved a race drawing a cart carrying a ton, a gallop over a quarter of a mile, plus a jumping contest. Johnny had evidently won thousands of pounds in bets on Mandy all over the country. Sadly, one day Mandy jumped out of her field into a cornfield. She had an enormous feed of grain which swelled in her gut and killed her.

At the end of the Harringay Arena, four chutes were built for the bucking broncos. A chute is a wooden structure into which the horse is shut so that the rider can mount. Once the rider is on, one side of the chute opens out to release the horse into the arena. A further strap was tightened well back under each horse's belly. Not being used to this, the horses reacted violently and as soon as the gate was opened, they rushed out, bucking like mad all over the arena. The rider was supposed to stay on the bronco for several seconds without being thrown, but few managed it. If a rider did manage to stay the course, another rider would be on hand to take him off the horse's back out of harm's way. With shows every day of the week, plus matinees, there were plenty of spills and thrills involving some heavy bruising being sustained by the riders. After a couple of weeks, I was asked to renegotiate the contract, which I succeeded in doing. The management was not happy with this new arrangement, however, and said that if I continued to work on behalf of the performers and not in the interests of the company, I would have to leave the show. I had no option but to go, but we parted on very amicable terms.

I told the boys that as I had had so many laughs watching their tumbles, on my last night I would ride any horse they cared to select, so that they could then have a laugh at my expense. One of our riders was Jimmy Tonge, an Australian, who had been a boundary rider and horse breaker in his native land. He was probably the rider best suited to performing the bronco act. While riding one of the wildest horses in the show, he had had a very heavy fall. This was the bronco they selected for me.

As I was now part of the show, I had to be suitably dressed for the role, so I was rigged out in a cowboy outfit, complete with leather chaps. Well, I mounted the horse, the strap was pulled tight and the gate opened. I managed to stay on until we reached the centre of the arena in what seemed but a fraction of a second. As I was thrown, one of my chaps caught on the saddle pommel. From then on it was not just a case of staying on – I couldn't get off. Here I was, upside down, with the horse bucking all over the show. Suddenly the chap ripped loose and I was thrown under the hooves of the bucking horse. Why I didn't get my head smashed to pieces I will never know. To those watching it must have appeared horrific. The boys all rushed over to see how I was. I stood up, and said, 'I have to leave the show for re-negotiating your contract. If I'd known what fun it was, I would have volunteered for each performance.' The boys turned their backs on me and walked away.

I left the arena to find a quiet spot out of view of everyone. I was in agony. When I got home, I found I was heavily bruised from my knee up to my crotch, and when I say bruised, it was black. It was days before I could walk properly. Years later, Tap, Yak's son, told me that some time after he had retired from rodeo riding, he felt something was wrong. He suddenly realised what it was. For the first time in years he didn't have a pain in his body.

These shows were helping to establish us and, more importantly, providing a small income to pay for the office expenditure. The news of our activities came to the notice of circus performers, as well as stage balancing and acrobatic acts. We also registered a professional test parachutist who had perfected a method of ultra-high drops on oxygen for the SAS. A number of professional wrestlers were also registered. We had to use a number of men registered with us who still held two tickets, but wherever possible I gave preference to Equity card holders. My argument was that stuntmen working as extras cheapened and reduced their professional status. The latest additions to our books could only be recruited for films through us and not through the FCA. We had an advantage over the FCA in that we knew the capabilities of the men we supplied and worked as a team. After reading the script and talking to the director and the artistes, between us we worked out the action, then we rehearsed the stunts while the director was engaged in planning other sequences. This saved a considerable amount of production time, which offset the additional cost of the higher wages of the men we provided.

Aboard the *Mayflower II* in 1957.

Port Watch on the *Mayflower II*.

On the wheel of *Mayflower II*.

Two of my scenes from *Billy Budd*. [*Billy Budd* (1962) © Anglo-Allied Pictures Limited. Licensed by Warner Bros. Entertainment Inc. All rights reserved.]

With the Hispano while filming *Billy Budd*.

Learning basic flying technique. [*Those Magnificent Men In Their Flying Machines* © 1965 Twentieth Century Fox. All rights reserved.]

Putting my flying into practice for *The Man Who Would Be King*. [*The Man Who Would Be King* (1975) © 1975 Devon Company. Licensed by Warner Bros. Entertainment Inc. All rights reserved. © 1975, renewed 2003 Columbia Pictures Industries, Inc. All rights reserved. Courtesy of Columbia Pictures.]

Under fire from a machine gun in *Golden Rendezvous* with Richard Harris.

Playing chess with Anthony Quinn during a break from filming *The Passage* in 1979.

One of the first companies to recognise the value of this, apart from Warners, was the Hammer Production Company. Although all Hammer films at this time were produced on a small budget, the company realised that though we were more expensive, in the long run they were getting first-class action in their films as well as saving on production costs. We worked on many Hammer productions, and to a large extent they were responsible for our survival. The FCA, on the other hand, provided none of these services nor had the knowledge we had acquired by performing stunts ourselves.

The fight with the BFPA had not yet been lost. I read in the Equity rule book that a motion could be placed before the Equity Council at the annual general meeting, provided thirty or more paid-up members put their names to it. I thought that if we were going to gain recognition in the industry, we needed Equity firmly behind us. I called a meeting of the stuntmen at our office, and pointed out that unless we could get our own stunt sub-committee in Equity, then nobody was going to accept us as a separate professional body within the film industry. I got a motion to that effect typed out and obtained the necessary thirty signatures to put it forward at the forthcoming annual general meeting. I submitted it to Eddie Lattimer, who was in charge of the film section of Equity.

The meeting was held on a Sunday at the St Martin's Theatre in St Martin's Lane. When I arrived at the theatre, I looked around for some of the men who had signed the motion, but not a soul was in sight.

The meeting opened and there were a number of speeches made from the stage where, behind a long table, sat the Equity chairman and the committee members. Seated in the stalls, I found myself among film stars, Shakespearean actors then appearing on the London stage and other well-known stage and screen performers. I felt very honoured to be with such distinguished people. As I sat there listening to the speeches and proposals, Eddie Lattimer called me over to him. 'You'll be on after the next two speakers,' he said. I was flabbergasted, but he explained that as I had tabled the motion, it was up to me to put it before the members who would then vote for or against. I was totally unprepared for this, and with no speech prepared, my mind went completely blank. Shaken rigid, I sat almost paralysed until I heard my name called. In a complete daze I made my way forward towards the stage. Fortunately, as I was doing so, the chairman read out my proposal. I breathed a sigh of relief, as I hadn't worked out how I was even going to start to move the motion. Now at least I had something to work on. When I stood on stage in front of the microphone, it was more than a little daunting to see the famous faces in the audience looking up at me in the crowded auditorium.

This was my first experience of addressing a public meeting, but I surprised myself once I got into my stride and started thinking on my feet. First I stated that as none of us stuntmen had acting experience, people might well question what we had to offer Equity, the actors' union. Then I pointed out how unsatisfactory the present situation was, where casting departments just picked untrained people from the crowd to take part in action scenes. Most of the people I represented were ex-Army, some of whom were from Special Service units, who took a pride in their physical fitness and had acquired a range of skills useful to the film industry. They also had a professional approach to everything they were required by a director to undertake. Though cinemagoers accepted the fact that stars had doubles when it came to dangerous stunts, this did not affect their enjoyment if the action was believable. A good stuntman was an asset to the actor he doubled for and the better the performance, the longer the film would be remembered.

I added that with an established stunt team available, there was no reason why an actor should be called upon to risk life and limb doing a dangerous stunt. It was further evident that a great number of films in the future would be about wars, and who better to depict the action than the people who had actually fought in them? If we were to attract American film companies to this country, I argued, their producers ought to be safe in the knowledge that the British film industry could provide professional stunt action as good as any they would expect to find in the States. We had already acquitted ourselves well with the American director Raoul Walsh – so much so that he had recommended our team to other American directors planning to produce films in the UK. One of these had been Yakima Canutt, Hollywood's top action director.

I mentioned, too, the fact that we had recently returned from filming *The Crimson Pirate* on Ischia, which made us the first British stuntmen contracted to work abroad. I then finished my speech by referring to the use of horses in films, stressing that it was criminal to bring on to the set animals that only the previous

118

day had been used for hacking by a riding stables. To ask actors to ride such horses in scenes where large crowds were screaming and waving swords about was just asking for trouble. With this in mind, we stuntmen had already started to train horses for exclusive use within the film industry.

As I walked off the stage, I was aware that the committee had allowed me to run over my allotted time. There was mumbling among the audience, and I returned to my seat feeling that I had muffed a great opportunity. The chairman asked for a show of hands from those in favour of incorporating a stunt sub-section into Equity. To my utter amazement, every hand in the theatre shot up. No one voted against.

The tide was beginning to turn against the FCA and FAA, but while there was still a lot to do, the FCA had seen the writing on the wall and signed an agreement with Micky Woods, an agent who ran a gymnasium and had on his books a number of wrestlers who called themselves Tough Guys Limited. Woods was invited to submit names from this group to be registered as stuntmen and women. Through this move we lost a lot of what I regarded as bread-and-butter jobs. We still had the problem of the forty Equity members we had signed up for *Captain Horatio Hornblower*, who remained registered with the FCA and accepted work through their office.

However, by this time our riding section was firmly established and we had built up a very good fencing section. Neither Micky Woods' wrestlers nor the FCA could compete with us in these fields. But riding jobs were few and far between, and our agency was not going to get very fat on these commissions. If we were to survive, we had to find some supplementary form of income.

17

Studio Services Branches Out

I suggested to Jock that, having provided the camera car for *The Crimson Pirate*, we should set up a company to provide similar vehicles for the film industry as a whole. This would open up for us more contacts with the production managers with whom we had to negotiate stunt contracts, and we would also be able to keep in close contact with current movies. And while the stunt boys were not actually working on set, they could earn a few quid driving the vehicles. Jock agreed, so we put the proposition to the film studio company transport managers. To our surprise the idea was well received, but we were advised that we would need to apply to the Ministry of Transport for 'B' licences, which were difficult to obtain. We applied to the court for four licences, our reasoning being that if we were lucky we might receive two. I couldn't believe it when British Rail opposed our application. I was told later that British Rail automatically objected to every application for carriers' licences, no matter for what purpose. Jock insisted that as it had been my original idea, I should be the one to state our reasons for wanting the licences when we attended the hearing before a judge.

I started by giving a brief outline of our stunt agency, and explained that the vehicles we wanted licences for were used to film action scenes such as car chases at high speed. On the front of the vehicle would be a platform, on which would be a cameraman, a focus puller and possibly the film director. In the rear of the vehicle would be two sound technicians and, if filming involved night scenes, electricians. An assistant director would also be aboard. When two camera crews were operating, there would be platforms both front and rear. Such vehicles could only be driven by highly skilled, responsible drivers whose competence was well above the standard of HGV licence drivers. Our own stunt drivers had the necessary skills. Everything was fully insured.

The British Rail solicitor cut in here to inform the judge that his client could provide such a service. I said, 'If that's so, how many films has your client completed, and how many vehicles have British Rail available right now which are already equipped with front and rear platforms?' The solicitor cleverly avoided answering the question, and the judge came to his rescue by stating that as British Rail already had the licences, they were in a position to provide this service.

I then entered into a long explanation on the technicalities involved, and gave an example of how a car chase was built up in the film *The Small Voice*, with part of the action shot on location and part in the studio. American producers were now coming to Britain, and if this service was not available to them, they would insist on bringing over American stunt drivers, which meant the British would lose out on employment opportunities. I added that there was therefore an urgent need for at least four more of these adapted vehicles to be available to the industry.

The judge leaned back in his chair, and his eyes started to have a glazed look. I turned to the British Rail solicitor and asked him if he really thought that his client could supply this specialised service and be prepared to take responsibility for possible accidents caused by the limited experience of their drivers. A major accident, I said, could result in the cancellation of a film which had perhaps already been months if not years in preparation, at a possible cost of several million dollars. This could lead to a claim of negligence for damages against his employer, British Rail. The solicitor remained silent, and looked completely nonplussed. The judge broke the silence by snapping, 'Well, what's your answer?' The solicitor, after a moment's silence, asked if he could consult his client. As he turned to do so, he hunched his shoulders and spread his hands out in a manner that suggested he had run out of argument. After a brief pause, he turned and told the judge, 'Our objection is withdrawn.' The judge announced abruptly that our application for four 'B' licences had been granted. All through the proceedings I hadn't dared to look at Jock at the rear of the court; I knew that if I had caught his eye, both of us would have burst out laughing.

With the four licences, we obtained four Volkswagen microbuses and started a separate company called Studio Services. The earnings of these vehicles subsidised the agency and kept us in business. We were fortunate that we didn't have to employ regular drivers; instead, when any of the vehicles were hired, we always could call upon one of the stuntmen for the job. This suited the stuntmen, because they picked up some money when there was nothing else on offer, and they also became better known to the camera crews and production managers. We ran these vehicles for eight and a half years. We hired out to the BBC, who became regular customers, and on one occasion, were sent with them to cover a strike at Longbridge. This was our undoing. The strikers' union made much capital out of the BBC using German vehicles, and it was widely reported in the national press. As a result, the BBC told us that unless we turned to British vehicles, they would be unable to continue using us. We replaced the Volkswagens with BMC microbuses, but unfortunately these proved to be unpopular, and so we lost the work in any case. Overall, though, the Studio Services period proved to be advantageous. We had maintained contact with the production companies, even when stuntmen had not been required, and the stuntmen themselves had become known in the industry. We also kept the open-air shows going, but they only occurred in the summer months, and the councils and companies which used this service were notoriously slow in settling up.

We now had a full-time secretary, and our telephone bill and running costs had escalated at an alarming rate. This was quite apart from the cost of all our trips to the studios and the obligatory drinks at the bar. But I'm the first to admit that Jock's bar-room sessions did often result in work coming our way.

One day when things were slack, not only for the stunting, but also for the vehicle service, I had another idea. I went to the studios to see a production manager with whom we had done a lot of work. I was well received, but he opened the conversation with, 'I'm sorry, Joe, but there's no call for stuntmen, camera cars or sound trucks on this production.' I said that I had come to see him on an entirely different matter. He sat back and said, 'Go on.' I told him that I'd come to sell him tuppenny insurance. He looked at me for a while as if I'd gone stark raving mad. After all, he was a man dealing with hundreds of thousands of pounds' insurance. After while, he said, 'What the hell are you talking about?' I replied that all film companies employed buyers to buy or hire anything required for a production, from studio props to aircraft and ships. This also included horses, veteran cars, in fact hundreds of things. The production manager had to rely on his buyer to obtain the best deal he could for the company.

'Let's suppose,' I continued, 'that a company known as Studio Services had also been contacted to quote for whatever was required. Knowing this, the buyer would have to be much more on his toes in fixing prices. If Studio Services quoted a price for the same article that was well below that of the buyer, then the production company would save money, perhaps a great deal of money. If, on the other hand, a buyer quotes a price well under that of Studio Services, then a production manager knows that his buyer is doing his job. Either way all it will have cost the production manager is a tuppenny phone call.'

But where, he asked, was the profit for Studio Services? I said that as it was part of our agency, we would be charging fifteen per cent of the hiring cost. He suddenly beamed. 'That's a fabulous idea. It's really worth consideration.' Over the months to come we put this proposition to a number of production managers. The idea caught on, and soon we were being asked to quote for all manner of things for various productions. One day we were asked for a quotation from Moby Dick Productions for a tug to tow the *Pequod*, the ship featured in the movie. The *Pequod* was also to be re-vamped as a second ship, so the tug would be needed over several months. It turned out that our quote was five hundred pounds a week cheaper than the one that was accepted. I just couldn't believe it, for we had also inflated the price we quoted to cover our fees. When I asked why our quote was not accepted, I was told that they couldn't believe we were providing a reputable registered tug for the price. Had they bothered to check, they would have found that the tug in question was from the Tyne Tees Towing Company, which was registered at Lloyds and was well known throughout the shipping world. It's little wonder that film companies are often regarded as a soft touch.

On another occasion, when we visited Twickenham Studios where a film unit had recently returned from Italy, we found that there was no shooting in progress. In fact the only activity was the crew playing football. The reason for this halt in production we found out from Phil Shipway, the first assistant. It turned out the unit had arrived back in the UK to find that they needed extra shots involving the latest car Lancia had produced. But they were unable to track one down. When I explained to him what Studio Services had to offer. Shipway burst out laughing and shouted to the crew, 'Let me introduce you to Studio Services, who will undertake to find anything.' This was greeted with even more laughter. It was only when we got back to our office and spent all day on the phone that we began to get some idea of the problem. Not one of the latest Lancia models they had been shooting abroad had been sold outside Italy. Then I had a thought: had anyone approached the Italian Embassy?

On phoning the embassy, I was put through to the head of transport. He laughed heartily when I explained our requirement. There was only one of the new Lancias in Britain, he said, and it was owned by the Italian ambassador himself. But the car was the ambassador's new baby and he would never allow anybody to touch it. He again lapsed into laughter at the very thought of a film company wishing to use it. When his mirth had subsided, I asked him if I could speak to the ambassador direct, and I would pass on the message to the company concerned. He gave me a number on which to reach the ambassador.

After many phone calls I eventually got hold of the ambassador and explained the situation. The ambassador, too, laughed. There was no chance of him lending his car to anyone, he said, particularly as he'd only had it for a couple of weeks. I pointed out that as the film when completed was due for international release and to be shown all over the world, this was a tremendous promotion opportunity for the Lancia Company. At no cost to themselves, the publicity gained could result in a boost to their sales worldwide.

The ambassador stopped laughing and was silent for a moment. He said it was still not possible to lend us the car, because he was waiting for an audience with the Queen at Buckingham Palace. I replied that the film company only needed the vehicle for two days, but should he be required to attend Buckingham Palace during the time his car was at the studio, we would provide him with a Rolls Royce. Another pause, and then he agreed.

The following day, Peter Mitchell picked up the car and drove it to the studios. The main gate and the studio doors were open, as there was obviously no shooting. It was a hot summer's day and the crew were lazing about. He didn't stop for a security check, but drove straight onto the set giving blasts on the horn. 'Is this what you're looking for?' he shouted. The whole unit gathered around in absolute amazement.

I forget what exactly we charged for this service, but whatever it was we could have charged much more. During the shooting we received an urgent message telling us that the audience at the Palace had been confirmed and we had to lay on the Rolls. Delighted at our success in obtaining the Lancia after the studios had derided us and failed, we allowed our elation to overrule commercial good sense. We finished up losing money on the deal, as the audience at the Palace went on for some considerable time and resulted in the hire of the Rolls being more expensive than anticipated.

18

Transport Troubles

The professional standard of our stunt work on *The Crimson Pirate* resulted in us being highly recommended. We secured a contract for a second foreign location, in Spain. Jock drove the boys out there in the Hispano Suiza, behind which he towed our caravan, which was to be the stunt office. The film was an American production entitled *Alexander the Great.*

This second job helped to further establish our position when it came to contracting stuntmen for working on locations abroad. When it had been successfully completed, a third contract soon followed. We were asked to provide twelve men to work in Sicily to work on the Warner Bros film, *The Master of Ballantrae* (1953). Transporting them by road to the location proved to be a bit of a problem, as by now the poor old caravan had been written off, we had only one vehicle free, and there was very little money in the kitty.

Jock found a cheap ex-Canadian Army-type shooting brake. Whether or not the vehicle had taken part in the Second Front in France we didn't know, but it certainly looked as if it had. The body was in a very dilapidated state to put it mildly. Time was running out, but a friend of Jock's who owned a garage in Borehamwood said he would check over the mechanics for us. Jock and I set about rebuilding the wooden frame on the back of the vehicle, which included constructing a new tailgate. The work had to be done over a weekend and by Sunday night the car was fit to make the journey to Sicily.

Two cars set off, with Jock driving one and Jackie Cooper the other. The journey turned out to be a nightmare. Our first vehicle, not the one we had repaired, kept breaking down, and valuable time was lost with it receiving attention in a number of garages en route. Each time when leaving a garage, the car would perform perfectly, but after a few miles the trouble would start again and slow down progress. To make up for lost time, Jock pushed on through the night. Travelling under these conditions without stopping for a night's rest in a hotel had a disastrous effect on morale.

The car, however, seemed to perform perfectly at night, which should have given some clue to the problem. First it was thought that it was dirt in the fuel system, so the whole fuel system was cleaned out, including the petrol tank. Then an ignition problem was suspected. Each new theory meant the car going into yet another garage, and yet another bill. Jock began to worry whether he would have enough money to complete the journey. Due to the non-stop motoring, Jock was not paying hotel bills, which was just as well, because he didn't have enough money to pay both garage and hotel bills, but the twelve men still had to be fed. Time was crucial, as the contract would only be valid if the team turned up on time.

By now Jock had spent nearly all the money for both the outward and return journeys. There was still a long way to go, as they had only reached the South of France. With the situation becoming more desperate with each passing hour, Jock came up with a startling idea. He decided to take all that remained of the travelling expenses, and gamble in the local casino. The boys were horrified, but agreed that in such a serious situation there was no other option. As Jock's fortunes waxed and waned, the stunt boys could scarcely bear to watch. In fact half of them left the table and sat outside convinced that all was now lost. After some considerable time, those who had been brave enough to stay to the end emerged with Jock laughing hysterically. Jock had won sufficient money to continue the journey. They jumped into the vehicles, and sped off into the darkness towards Italy.

Everybody was getting exceedingly tired with the travelling, which often meant towing one car to the next garage. The heaviest burden however was on Jock and Jackie. Garage after garage tried to find the fault. At the last garage the distributor was taken off and bench tested. It performed perfectly, but a close examination revealed a hairline fracture in the Bakelite distributor cap, which opened once the engine became overheated.

Once the fault had been rectified, Jock and Jackie drove like demented men and pushed the cars to the limit to make up time. The passengers were just about flaked out and having a very rough ride when some miles past Naples, the radiator of the first car blew up. The radiator was taken off and taken in the ex-Canadian Army car back into Naples to yet another garage. Once the radiator was repaired, Jock drove like mad to get back and reassemble it. As he rounded a comer at breakneck speed, the body of the car twisted, and the tailgate dropped open. Dickie Newman, who was sitting in the back faithfully clutching the radiator, fell out. Still holding on to the radiator and protecting it, he turned over and over, bouncing in the roadway. As Jock pulled the car over to park, a number of the boys who had gone along for the ride jumped out before it stopped and ran back to Dickie.

They gathered round him as he lay in the roadway hugging the radiator and shouted anxiously, 'Dickie, are you all right?' Jock, now at his wits' end, pushed them aside. 'Fuck, Dickie!' he yelled, 'Is the radiator all right?' Dickie didn't speak to Jock for at least a month, unless he had to during the filming. It was to the credit of both Jock and Jackie that the team had arrived on time. The return trip presented no problems.

When they got back to the UK the agency was awarded another contract for all the studio work on the film. Having now completed three successful locations, we felt that at last we had made a permanent mark on the industry. We were now definitely hated by the FCA and FAA, and our progress hadn't endeared us to the BFPA either. Although the FCA accepted they would not get the location contract, it irked them that they had missed out on all the studio work.

During the making of *The Master of Ballantrae*, Jock became friends with Errol Flynn, who was talking about making his own movie later on in Italy. The future seemed bright for us. Warners, who had been pleased with our work, were also planning to make another film, *Helen of Troy*, at Cinecitta Studios, Rome.

19

Some Sword Play

Errol Flynn's picture *Crossed Swords* eventually went into production, and Jock and Dave Crowley were placed under contract. Flynn put up half the money for the movie, while an Italian company guaranteed the balance. Flynn's money was to be used first. According to Jock, after this money ran out, the promised Italian contribution failed to materialise. Some weeks passed without any filming being done, while negotiations with possible new partners were started. These, too, failed.

Although Jock's hotel bill was paid, he received no wages. While the negotiations were going on, a restaurateur arranged for Flynn to open his new restaurant as a publicity stunt. Jock was invited along, which meant that at least he would receive some free booze and a slap-up meal. Jock meanwhile had heard that Flynn had acquired some new finance. At what seemed an appropriate moment, Jock asked Flynn if there was any chance of a small advance on his wages. By this stage in the proceedings, Flynn, who was renowned for frequently engaging in drunken brawls, had had a few drinks. He took great offence at being asked for some money and started calling Jock all the names under the sun. Jock, he added, was a fake SAS officer. Jock told him to withdraw the remark or he would put one on him.

'You'll do what? I'd like to see you try!' retorted Flynn. So Jock did just that and put Flynn on his arse. Flynn's handlers grabbed Jock and started to throw him out of the restaurant. Flynn got to his feet and shouted, 'No, leave him alone, he's my friend!' He then went up to Jock and said, 'Let's forget it.' At the same time he put his hands on Jock's shoulders and tried to knee him in the groin. Jack at once started punching again, whereupon the handlers this time did throw him out into the street. He was put on the first plane out in the morning.

After considerable time had elapsed we heard that Flynn was to do two films for Herbert Wilcox in the UK. When these were completed, apparently Wilcox was to put up the balance of the funding for Flynn to finish *Crossed Swords*. We also heard that Flynn was going to bring over his yacht, the *Shallimar* to live on while filming was taking place. Jock began telling everyone that he would have a writ nailed to the mast and have Flynn's boat impounded subject to receiving the balance of his contract. I told him to keep quiet about it, as it was sure to get back to Flynn. Jock wouldn't listen and the inevitable happened.

Jock received a message from Flynn saying that he would arrange for Jock to be contracted on the picture for the full period as his double as a means of repaying the debt. Jock wouldn't hear of it. 'Jock, take the offer,' I urged him. 'If at the end you still want to nail him, do so. You will then have received in addition possibly three months' wages.'

Jock still refused, but we managed to get another double for Flynn on the picture. Flynn sent for him and asked whether he had come from Jock's agency. The obvious reply we'd told him to give if asked was a definite 'No'. Flynn told him: 'If ever you see any of Jock's boys, let me know.' Eventually we had quite a big crowd of our boys on the picture, all denying that they were in any way connected with Jock.

Flynn was a fine fencer, and towards the end of one particular sequence, had a fight in which he disarmed his opponent. With his sword at the throat of his adversary, he demanded, 'Who sent you?' The actor concerned, who had been set up by the boys, replied, 'Captain Jock Easton.' As you can imagine, this brought forth gales of laughter. Flynn threw down his sword and walked off the set. I never did see the film, so I do not know how this particular scene ended. Had all this happened years later, it would just have been handed over to Equity's legal department and no doubt Jock would have been paid. As it transpired, Jock had turned down the contract and Flynn never paid him, so he lost all round.

A couple of years before *Quentin Durward*, we had provided all the riders and stuntmen for *Knights of the Round Table*, which was also shot at MGM Studios. We had at last got our feet under the table at these studios that had formerly been closed to us. It therefore gave me great satisfaction working there. At one stage of the filming, Cecil Ford, the then production manager, told me that the crowd union had called a strike, which was upsetting his shooting schedule. The crowd extras were needed in a court scene as knights. I asked him why he didn't put stuntmen in. 'You know I can't put Equity members in crowd scenes,' he said. He could, I pointed out, if he gave them named parts and they were on the call sheet as such. This is what he did. Overnight, the stuntmen were given titles which would not have disgraced the House of Lords.

The following day, we arrived to find the crowd union picketing the studios. We walked through them, greeting them with 'Good morning, boys,' only to be met with a stony silence. The scenes were completed within a couple of days and the strike was called off. It gave me no end of satisfaction to put one over on the FCA and the union in the very studio where John Street and his boss on *Ivanhoe* had thwarted me. It also helped to level the field a little for the double dealing and loss of contract on *Captain Horatio Hornblower*. I was to work for Cecil Ford on many future movies.

20

Fair Helen in Rome

It was very difficult to find out what was happening in Rome. Italian Warners had been set up to produce the movie *Helen of Troy* (1956), so we were not able to get any information through our usual contact in London. Jock decided to fly out to Rome to see what he could find out. We thought we might be in with a chance because at this time there were no organised stuntmen in Italy.

Jock received a lot of help in Rome from Dave Crowley, the ex-British lightweight champion, whose Dave Crowley Bar had become the meeting place for a number of film types and American ex-pats. Jock hoped that his stay in Rome would not be long, because he had little money. Unfortunately, the man he needed to see – Gerry Blattner, Warner's Europe representative with whom we had dealt in the UK – was still in Hollywood, finalising the cast and production costs.

A top US government official who was in Rome to award aircraft manufacturing licences to Italian companies frequented Dave's bar at the time. He had a flat in one of the smartest areas of Rome overlooking the racetrack, but was often away from Rome and was worried about the security of his flat during those times. He confided in Dave about the problem. Dave told the American about Jock and his wartime training and experience, and suggested that if Jock lodged in the flat he could look after it when the owner was absent. Not only that, Jock could act as a minder when necessary. The idea of having an ex-SAS officer around found immediate favour with the American, who offered Jock free accommodation. In return, Jock not only looked after the flat in his absence, but also acted as a minder when King Farouk was one of the guests at the parties the American organised for businessmen. This was perfect for Jock, who was financially on his beam-ends, although you would never know it from his appearance: tall and slim, Jock

135

was always elegantly dressed. This enormous stroke of luck for him didn't end there – amazingly, the American let Jock use his Cadillac to visit Cinecitta Studios whenever it was whispered that Blattner was due there. When Jock drove into the studios with the CD plates the Italians were greatly impressed, as were the local industrialists, who concluded that Jock must be a close confidant of the American. The staff at the studios were further impressed by the fact that Jock was waiting to see none other than Gerry Blattner, whom they regarded as the top man heading Warner Bros European arm.

At long last Blattner did eventually arrive, and Jock secured from him the contract for stunt work on *Helen of Troy*. Initially this was for eight men, to be transported out by road, to be followed at a later date by another seven, who would be flown out. This time we decided that I would take the first batch. The cost of the trip was partly funded by us accepting the airfare for half their number. We would, however, recoup the remaining cost if filming overran, in commissions from the second contract. This proved to be the last time we did this, as on all future contracts, the stuntmen were flown out either in the company's charter planes carrying the main unit, or on individual flight tickets travelling first class.

We travelled to Rome in an old American ambulance. While driving down the main street we heard a bellow of welcome from none other than Yakima Canutt, who was to direct all the action. Assisting him to set up the action sequences was Alan Pomeroy, an American stunt arranger, who had already signed up some sixty Italians. He had recruited them from circuses and gymnasiums. Some boasted that they already had chariot experience, and in the training period that followed, they proved to be extremely athletic. A number of them were fantastic acrobats – I swear they could climb a rope hung from the studio roof faster than monkeys. We began to worry that we were about to be severely outclassed.

While Alan Pomeroy was to take charge of all the rehearsals, we were to assist in training the Italians for the film work. We learned a lot from Alan, but, at one stage in the rehearsals he told us not to take part in the falls; he said it was the Italians who needed the practice. At the time we thought nothing of it, but one night one of our team went to a club where Alan was drinking with other Americans working on the unit. He overheard him say, 'You didn't see any of those British boys rehearsing the falls, did you?' The

136

obvious inference was that we were dragging our feet, and that as long as he could train the Italians, we were not needed.

This argument was shot to pieces in the first fortnight of shooting. All the scenes were scrapped and had to be re-shot, with all our boys in the foreground. This was due to the performance of the Italians as athletes rather than stuntmen. If they were required to fall, then they selected their spot, so the fall would be similar to that of a tumbler, unlike that of a man who had just been run through by a sword. As far as acrobatics was concerned, they could run rings around us, but when it came to authentic-looking battle scenes, they were not in the same class. The loss of the first two weeks' shooting must have cost Warners hundreds of thousands of dollars, and justified Blattner's decision to employ us on an Italian production. It also reinforced our position in the industry.

There is no doubt in my mind that Alan's ploy was to try and convince producers that they really didn't need either British or American stuntmen, as he could train locals in any country and save on production costs. I have always held the view, which I've put into practice, that the greater the number of your own team on location, the better the results appearing on screen. The saving in time of one day's shooting can result in the saving of the entire cost of the stuntmen's salary on a major production. This is quite apart from the quality of the action, which is what puts bums on seats. Then there is the principal artistes' safety to be considered, which professional stuntmen always do their best to ensure. An injured star can hold up film production for weeks, if not months, or even cause the film to be scrapped. I often wonder why insurance companies, in their own interests, don't write into their policies clauses to the effect that only professional stuntmen are to be employed for all action scenes.

After learning of Pomeroy's comments, we insisted that we took part in all rehearsal falls. There was one occasion during rehearsals when one of the Italian stuntmen objected to being asked to do a back fall of just fifteen feet. It was, he said, beneath his dignity to be asked to rehearse such a stupid small fall. He was, after all, an Olympic high diver. We insisted, however, that he went ahead with the fall. Taking his time, he climbed up on to the rostrum with a silly smirk on his face, grinning at the other fifty nine Italians and gesturing with his hands as if to say it was child's play, spun on one foot and fell backwards. All at once his diving experience and conditioned reactions came into play. Just as he has about to hit the pad, he looked backwards to see where he was going, landed on his neck instead of his back, and immediately began screaming. To our amazement at least half a dozen of his compatriots ran forward and grabbed him, and, despite his anguished screams, half of them started to pull him one way while the others began tugging him in the opposite direction. All the while they were arguing and shouting at each other, while the injured man kept screaming. We made a vow then and there between ourselves that if any of us did get injured, the others would make sure that none of the Italians touched us.

At a later stage in the rehearsals, however, George Leech did a jump from about the same height. He landed with one foot between two mattresses, and hit the ground with one almighty yell. What we saw appeared unbelievable: his foot was no longer at the end of his leg, but to the side of his shinbone. An Italian first aid man nearby shouted at us to hold George down. There was such authority in his voice that we jumped to carry out his instructions. Our resolve not to allow any Italian to become involved in any accident to one of our men was forgotten. We jumped on George and pinned him down. The Italian, using great strength, grabbed George's foot, and heaved it back in place. After he had tightly bound up the foot, George was sent to hospital. It speaks volumes for the skill of the first aid man that although George's foot remained bandaged for the rest of the time on location, he managed to carry on working.

Chariot training was next on the list, using horses that had never drawn one before. There was a pair of horses to each chariot. The sound of the chariot wheels thundering along frightened some of them and they bolted. This happened on several occasions. Yak called us all together. 'If this happens again, and you can't pull them up, drop one of the reins, and pull like hell on the other, because those bastards can't run cross legged,' he said. Yak knew what he was talking about because apart from his rodeo experience, he and his two sons, together with other American stuntmen, had produced those unforgettable chariot scenes in the *Ben Hur* chariot races.

The rehearsals came to the point where the second group of stuntmen joined us. I had included Paddy Hayes, to whom a number of the men had objected. He had been branded a troublemaker, who was often getting into fights. Personally, I had never heard of Paddy being involved in a fight with any of the other stuntmen, or anyone on a production unit. Anyway, it was unlikely that any of them would pick a fight with Paddy, a former professional middleweight. I wanted Paddy along for several reasons. It was my way of rewarding him for his loyalty to me by not working in the crowd, at the time when a number of those who were now objecting to him being included had been among the men with the two union tickets, which had caused me problems. He had also been my sparring partner while I was training as an amateur boxer and obtained permission for us to use the police gym in Chelsea. He also had a lot of guts, and was well able to cope with the work involved. There was also one other reason. Mary, his wife, was a devout Catholic, and Paddy had promised her that if he got the job in Rome, he would bring her out so that she could hear first hand the Pope's address in St Peter's Square.

Knowing that there might be difficulties between him and the other boys, I phoned him before he left the UK to warn him that if he did get drunk and became involved in fights, I could not stand by him. He would be sent home, which would bar him from ever working on a location again. I also reminded him of what it would mean to Mary if the only opportunity she would have in her life to stand in St Peter's Square listening to the Pope speak was thrown away.

For the first couple of weeks everything went well, with Paddy performing as well as the rest of the boys. One evening I took Paddy under my wing and we went to a restaurant near the Spanish Steps. Just as we were about to leave, in came several of the stuntmen. They were rather noisy and a little the worse for wear, having been celebrating. They drew up chairs and sat at our table. When you are cold sober, it isn't always possible to be in tune with those who aren't. After staying a while, I said to Paddy, 'Come on, let's go.' Paddy, who like me was quite sober, was talking very reasonably with the noisy newcomers and trying to quieten them down. 'I'll stay for just a short while,' he said. I noticed that one of the boys had put some rum in Paddy's glass. As I left, I told him not to drink it. 'No, I shan't,' he promised.

The following morning, Alan Pomeroy approached me and said Paddy had become drunk and had beaten up Frank Howard. He had seen the two of them staggering down the main street, the Via

Parioli, with blood streaming down Frank's face. Paddy had been with me for the best part of the evening, I said. I'd investigate and find out what had actually happened. Alan said that he was not interested. Paddy had to be fired. I found Paddy and asked him what had gone on. He admitted that foolishly he'd drunk from his glass, forgetting that I'd told him that his drink had been spiked, but everything seemed fine. Everyone was seemingly enjoying themselves. He was the last to leave the restaurant, and as he went through the door someone punched him in the face. He immediately struck out at the first person near to him, who happened to be Frank Howard. The others by that time had disappeared, and Frank had sworn that he hadn't hit him. To my mind, the fact that the two of them were seen by Pomeroy walking together down the main street with their arms around each other gave Paddy the benefit of the doubt. As far as I was concerned his version of the incident was truthful and correct.

I went back to Pomeroy and told him what I had learned, including my own account of the evening up until the time I left the restaurant. Paddy's story seemed to tally, I stated. His reply was, 'Paddy's fired – and that's the end of it.' Although I'd previously told Paddy that I wouldn't stand by him if he got into trouble, it looked to me as though Paddy had been the victim of an arranged set-up. Why had they all disappeared after the two blows had been struck? Alan refused to change his mind, so I said that under the circumstances I had no alternative but to put the case before Tinny Wright, the producer.

Alan was furious. As I didn't have the opportunity to do this immediately due to rehearsals, this gave him an opportunity to talk to some of the boys and, of course, Tinny Wright. Later that afternoon Tinny Wright sent for me and I had the opportunity to put the case before him. What surprised me was that during the short time leading up to this meeting, Pomeroy had actually enlisted the aid of some of the boys prepared to give evidence against Paddy. They included at least two who hadn't even been at the restaurant. In this affray, only two punches had been thrown, and here we were in a major confrontation with the production company. We had played straight into the hands of Pomeroy, who obviously didn't want any of us out there in the first place. The outcome was that four of us got the sack. The only consolation I had was that Gerry Blattner, who had also been at the meeting, had weighed up the situation for himself. He stood up, extended his hand to me and commented, 'Well, Joe, Alan is in charge of this job, and he doesn't want you, so you must go. But equally if the situation was reversed and you were in charge and didn't want Alan on the job, then undoubtedly Alan would go.' I shall never forget the perplexed look on Alan's face. Over the years that followed I was to work on several Warner movies. The hurtful thing about the whole situation was that my wife, Marguerite, had planned to join me in Rome.

We were due to leave by road the next night, but Paddy Brannigan, one of the sacked men who was a Catholic, wanted first to attend the Pope's address in the morning. We greeted with amazement his announcement that he was 'putting an Irish curse' on the movie. By hearing the Pope speak he would be able to strengthen his curse, he claimed. Was it just wishful thinking from a superstitious Irishman? All I can say is that afterwards we heard that the action scenes in the film rushes were so bad that a new director was being flown out from Hollywood to re-shoot them all. Evidently the falls and other stunts appeared highly comical on film. So much for Alan's boast that he could train anyone around the world to do stunts.

As we were packing our bags into the car, the minibus arrived to take the remaining stuntmen to Cinecitta Studios for the day's work. Only one of them, John Sullivan, held the bus up just as it was about to leave so that he could wish us luck and shake our hands. The rest of them in the bus all looked the other way.

After all the effort I, and particularly Jock, had put into gaining the *Helen of Troy* contract, we were astounded by their sheer treachery. They were stupidly cooperating with a man who was trying to get rid of all of us. Had he had his way, no one would have worked on the movie. We were dumbfounded to think that people who had secured a well-paid job in Italy as a result of our efforts could turn against us like this. However, in principle we had shown the advantage of taking British stuntmen abroad on locations as an integral part of a film unit. This set the stage for productions in the future.

The final twist to this saga occurred about a month after we had returned to the UK. The complete set of Troy was burned to the ground. Whether it was due to Brannigan's Irish curse or not, we shall never know.

The director who took over the movie was none other than

Raoul Walsh, the director of *Captain Horatio Hornblower*. I was told that while looking over the ramparts of the mock castle he spotted the stuntmen and shouted out, 'Where's Joe Powell?' He was met with stony silence.

In a funny way, I was grateful to Pomeroy, as he had proved to me that the way in which he taught us to fall was completely wrong. It was from this experience that I devised my own method of falling. I reasoned that a person who is stabbed or punched and slips or falls from, say a roof top, is not going to do a swallow dive. I still see this type of fall performed, even on American movies, particularly on cowboy films. I have never been a high diver, and so my falls always look untidy, with my arms and legs thrashing about. I trained myself to forget the height and just concentrate on the crucial last twenty feet. Fortunately, I was lucky enough to be born with tremendously fast physical reflexes, as these are something that cannot be acquired by instruction. If you're falling onto boxes, then it's essential to land on your back. Hitting the boxes face down from a really high fall could break your back. If you're falling into water, you have either to enter feet or head first, but even then from a really high fall there's a good chance of you being heavily bruised. But to my mind if the fall ends as a perfect dive into water, then the shot is ruined.

21

A Whale of a Time

As soon as I arrived back in the UK, I phoned Jock, who told me that Jack Martin, the first assistant, had asked for me to work on a movie named *Moby Dick* (1956), based on the whaling classic by Herman Melville. The film was to be directed by John Huston, a legendary name within the industry. I didn't realise it then, but this film was to have a great influence in my life on and off for the next forty years.

I was instructed to go to Hull, and join the crew of a ship sailing to Youghall in Ireland. The vessel, which featured prominently in the film, had been specially converted to give her the appearance of a square-rigged old-time whaling ship. Originally named the *Rylands*, she had plied between Ireland and Liverpool. The second mate and I were the last to join the ship. The camera and production crews had already taken all the available accommodation; we couldn't even find space in which to sling a hammock. The second mate, however, hit upon a brilliant idea. As part of her conversion the superstructure had been changed and she had been fitted with a false bow and an extra deck above the original one. The space between the two decks, according to him, was an ideal place in which we could sling our hammocks.

The ship was to be towed from Hull to Ireland. Every time the ship dipped her bow into the waves, the sea rushed like a torrent through the hawse pipes and along the original deck. When we were lying in our hammocks, the water was only a few inches below us, and to reach our hammocks without getting our feet wet, we had to judge the right moment to scramble into them. The rest of the company and crew delighted in watching our antics when we got into our hammocks or vacated them. Our dodging of the cascading torrents was one of the main sources of amusement and diversion aboard ship during the crossing to Ireland.

The ship's false bow began to leak, however, and as a result the space between the original bow and the false one began to fill up. It was estimated that eventually some ten tons of water filled this void. This caused the bow to dip even lower, as she met the waves, and an even greater torrent flooded the deck. But the last laugh was ours. The extra deck above our hammocks had been newly caulked, so that when it rained the second mate and I remained dry. But the original deck had not been re-caulked, and it was only a matter of time before leaks opened up letting water in on the crew settled in below. Everything they had became wet and damp, and plastic sheeting had to be spread over all the bunks and equipment. We pulled into Plymouth for repairs, but as filming was scheduled to start within a week or so, it was decided that a proper job would take too long, so the repairs were bodged. First the water was pumped out, and the void filled with cork. This at least allowed us to continue the tow to Youghall. Had we met any really heavy seas the flooding of the false bow could have had disastrous results.

When we arrived and had tied up, the star of the film, Gregory Peck, and the rest of the cast who formed the crew came aboard and we were introduced to John Huston. I was to work on subsequent films with both Peck and Huston. Although the possibility of the false bows flooding hadn't been taken into consideration, everything else had been thought out and meticulously researched. The whaling boats had been built as exact replicas of those used in the whaling period. They were completely practical and seaworthy.

The houses around the harbour at Youghall had been painted by the film company to represent a whaling village of the time in America – that is, all except one. The owner of this house had held out for higher compensation. He reasoned that if his property remained unpainted, it would stick out like a sore thumb, and the company would have no option but to accept his terms. All the dockside scenes were completed at Youghall, but by slightly altering the camera shots the unpainted house was completely excluded. The owner therefore never did receive payment, and neither did his house get painted, so he lost out all round.

While in Ireland, we had many very early calls, so the film company found it more convenient to organise early morning breakfasts for the whole unit. An old warehouse was used as a dining room, with breakfast served by location caterers. At that time in the morning, nearly everyone turned up, bleary eyed and for the most part pretty quiet.

144

One day at breakfast while talking to Del Watson, I told him about the Japanese propaganda film describing how prisoners of war could be fastened to telegraph poles by their legs. John 'King' Kelly, who had overheard the conversation, shouted in his very loud and raucous voice, 'I've never heard such a load of bullshit in my life!' The commotion made everyone suddenly become wide awake, and all heads were turned in our direction. I tried to explain what I'd been telling Del, but more loud shouts of 'Bullshit!' reverberated around the warehouse. Indicating the steel posts supporting the floor above, I asked Kelly, 'Do you want a demonstration?' 'Yes,' he said, smiling at the assembled company, who were all now eagerly watching.

Having instructed Del on what he was to do, I got Kelly to face one of the posts, and supported him from behind. Del pulled each of Kelly's legs either side of the post and placed Kelly's right foot behind his left leg, which was then pulled behind the post. I then allowed Kelly to sink down in a squatting position, and Del and I returned to the breakfast table. At first Kelly appeared confident that he could release himself. Gradually this confidence was replaced by despair, and then followed by sheer panic. The thing with this position is that the harder you struggle, the more your legs tighten around the post.

Kelly shouted to me to get him off, to which I replied, 'Kelly, I told you that I knew how to put you on. I didn't say that I knew how to get you off.' Kelly really started to panic, screaming for me to release him, accompanied with a stream of obscenities. I thought that if I didn't do something, he would have a heart attack. I lifted Kelly up from behind, while Del unfolded his legs. The post was of a much smaller diameter than a telegraph pole, so any prisoner who received this treatment must have suffered excruciating pain. There was no way they could have escaped, and if abandoned, would undoubtedly have died. It was interesting to note that for the rest of the day, Kelly remained silent. Several of the technicians asked him how the trick was done, but no answer was forthcoming. He really had had a scare.

With the shooting completed at Youghall, the ship was towed to Fishguard, Wales, this time in a comparatively dry state. We were to stay here for several months while the main shooting was carried out. The company took over the Fishguard Hotel, which had originally been built for the railway, but had fallen into disuse. The company renovated it and practically the whole unit was accommodated there. An aptly named Moby Dick Bar was established, with a licence to sell intoxicating liquor at cost price. As we used to finish late most evenings, it was very convenient to be able to go there straight from the ship, without first having to wash and change after being cooped up all day in a ship with two hundred people on board, counting all the artistes and production unit, plus the professional crew. Additionally, there were the cameras, props, electrical gear, and all the other equipment required for filming at sea. When shooting was in progress, everyone not required for that particular shot would have to disappear below decks, sometimes for the whole day, in artificial light and practically no ventilation.

It was for this reason that I looked forward to the sailing sequences, where I assisted with the sail setting and appeared in general sailing shots. There were also the scenes where we were featured rowing the boats in pursuit of the whales. To simulate being pulled along by whales we had harpooned, we were sometimes towed by RAF rescue boats. There was one occasion when John Huston wanted a completely deserted ship apart from one or two principal artistes. He decided to send off the five whaling boats with their crews, which would leave more room for those who had to go below decks to remain out of sight. We were literally set adrift. When we were needed again, the unit was to send our supply tenders to find us and get us back to the ship. This was, in fact, an incredibly foolhardy thing to do. On a number of occasions after a few hours we completely lost sight of the ship and land. None of the boats had a compass, and had mist or fog descended we would have been in trouble. We had no flares, water or food, as well as being dressed only in our *Moby Dick* costumes.

It was purely a question of whether the small tenders could find us before darkness descended. These boats were currently engaged in transporting production personnel and food supplies, and generally standing by for the needs of the production unit. As a result, they had no idea of our position at sea. It would have made much more sense to have left us in the harbour, to be ferried out as required.

On one occasion we had been drifting for some hours, the quiet being continuously broken by Kelly, who was one of our crew members. He kept up an incessant chatter about nothing in particular, all the while moving around and upsetting the trim of the boat. He was a great source of annoyance, and I believe delighted in making himself so. He was getting on everyone's nerves, but there was no escape. Also in our boat was the actor Bernard Miles, who had opened the Mermaid Theatre in London, and Count Frederick Ledebur, an Austrian nobleman who owned a castle in his homeland and was a big game hunter and a friend of John Huston. Frederick was playing the part of Queequeg, the Indian harpooner. This particular day, after we had already spent some hours adrift, Kelly had been told to keep quiet on several occasions but to no avail. Turning to Frederick, he said, 'Why don't you entertain us by making some animal noises like those you've heard as a hunter in Africa?' Frederick shot his eyes heavenward, and a look of complete exasperation crossed his face. After a few seconds, he commented, 'Look, Kelly, I will make a noise like a lion for one minute, if you make the noise of an animal I name for the rest of the day.' The thought that he would be in a position to annoy us for the remainder of the day obviously appealed to Kelly, who readily agreed. 'Go on, Frederick,' he urged. 'Let's hear your lion noise.' Frederick took out his watch, and started roaring like a lion with exasperation on his face the whole time at the sheer stupidity of it all. The effect, in fact, was hilarious. After a minute he stopped. Kelly was now eager to find out which animal he had to imitate. 'Come on, Frederick,' said Kelly, 'what animal am I to do?' Frederick had sat silent for a while as if exhausted by his effort and the futility of it all, and then turned to face Kelly. 'I want you to make a sound like a fish.' He then pursed his lips, opening and closing them like a goldfish in a bowl. It was brilliant. Every time for the rest of the day Kelly started to say something, we all pursed our lips like a fish to remind him of his agreement.

There was, however, a little more drama to follow. Kelly couldn't sit still, and decided to rearrange one of the oars. In so doing, he overbalanced, and the oar fell and Bernard Miles received a glancing blow to his head. Although not badly hurt, he was furious. He sat, head in hands, shaking with anger, and obviously trying to control himself. There's no doubt in my mind that he could have killed Kelly at that point. The incident did, however, have the effect of breaking the tension, and I couldn't refrain from laughing. Still holding his head, but without turning, Bernard called out to me. 'Joe', he said. 'Yes, Bernard?' With great

147

feeling and in a very pained voice, he said, 'Joe, not now.' My laughter had brought him very close to breaking point.

We suffered a few more days of being cast adrift. One day we were all lying half asleep in the boat enjoying the sun and after some hours had passed the *Pequod* was nowhere in sight, nor was the land for that matter. Frederick woke up as a result of Kelly's fidgeting and presently nudged me. 'Joe, look, we're taking on water.' In fact a considerable amount had come on board unnoticed. I reached down in the water to discover that the boat's bung had come out. Fortunately a short length of cord was attached to the bung, so it was not difficult to locate. We realised at once that while moving about the boat, Kelly had caught his foot in the cord and pulled the bung out. Everyone now turned on Kelly and berated him. Fortunately we had a bailer on board and after considerable effort and time bailed her out. The contrite Kelly kept very quiet for the rest of the day, and peace descended.

On the numerous occasions we were told to remain below decks, I opted to assist the crew aloft. For the purpose of the film, the sails were continuously required to be reset, furled or stowed. I found this far preferable to being cooped up below. Not only was I in the fresh air, but from the high vantage point I could watch all the bustle during the shooting on deck. Our captain was Alan Villiers, the famous authority on square-rigged sailing ships, as well as author and TV personality. Evidently my efforts aloft had not gone unnoticed by him. This was to stand me in good stead, because he forwarded my name to several film companies for whom he had worked. Later on he also accepted me as a member of his crew to sail the replica of the *Mayflower* from Plymouth to Massachusetts in 1957, to commemorate the original voyage of the Pilgrim Fathers.

At times, of course, work in the rigging was not required, and we were banished below decks. Here again I was fortunate, as Bernard Miles taught me to play chess. This enabled us to pass the time oblivious to our surroundings and the cramped conditions. We held chess tournaments and the British actor Leo Genn, who was in the role of Starbuck, would take on several of us in a consultation game. He used to set up a chessboard in one cabin, while we were grouped around our own chessboard and pieces in another. He shouted his moves to us, and we in turn relayed back to him each answering move after some deliberation among ourselves.

148

Although we had some good players among us, he always won. Leo was a quietly spoken man, but a tremendously interesting and entertaining person to talk to once you knew him. Following the end of the Second World War, he had appeared as a counsel at the Nuremberg war crimes trials.

The weather at Fishguard worsened, and for several weeks we remained moored, spending the time with some playing chess or poker, while others kicked a ball around on the dockside. Huston seemed completely unconcerned about the delay and escalating costs. He used to come on board in the morning and disappear below decks to play poker with Gregory Peck, Richard Basehart, and other principal artistes. Thousands of pounds used to change hands, and the proceedings were always viewed by a small group of those lucky enough to squeeze around the cabin door to watch.

To break the monotony and gain publicity for the film, our publicity department laid on a rowing race between our boat crews, in which the local sea cadets were invited to compete. Being one of the strongest rowers, I was chosen to crew Gregory Peck's boat. The odds were stacked in favour of Peck winning the race. The publicity boys reckoned a win by Peck would be good publicity for the film and it was thought that we would walk away with it. The race was from one side of the harbour to the other. The men in our crew were three times the size of the sea cadets, whom we thought offered little competition; the other boats also had strong crews, including some professional seamen.

The race was started, and immediately we started to pull away from the rest of the field. After a while, however, I noticed that our lead over the sea cadets didn't appear to be increasing. At about the halfway mark, they started to gain on us, slowly, but perceptibly, then gradually they drew level. Peck became rather agitated and increased the stroke, but we still couldn't shake the youngsters off. Their challenge made Peck even more agitated, and he again increased the stroke. With each shout, he leaned forward as if to add weight to the stroke, whereas the cadets' coxswain hardly moved and seemed confidently in charge. He was not a big man; in fact, he was short, rather rotund, and wore a blue peaked cap and pebble glasses. We heard him quietly encouraging his crew by calling to them, 'Long and strong, long and strong, long and strong ...' We, on the other hand, were trying to keep pace with Peck's frantic yells, but merely stirring the water, only gaining a quarter of the effort we were putting in. The cadets just pulled away from us and easily won the race, to the utter disgust of Peck and the publicity department. There was no point in trying to explain what had happened. Later that evening, in a local shop, the owner told us how pleased all the townspeople were that we had allowed the cadets to win. It was much appreciated, he said. I replied by saying that he shouldn't say that, as the cadets really had won, but I secretly hoped that the tone of my voice confirmed the conclusion everyone had come to. As they say, pride comes before a fall!

In London, Jock had been asked to find a double for Count Frederick Ledebur in his role as the Indian harpooner Queequeg. Frederick was about six foot five, and built like a beanpole. There were no stuntmen around with a physique even remotely similar. But all credit to Jock, he found a man by the name of George Pearson, who duly arrived at Fishguard. It was a two-hour job making up Frederick as the heavily tattooed harpooner, so by using Pearson in a number of shots, it allowed Frederick time off without make-up until the times that he was required in close up.

After some weeks at Fishguard, even Huston became bored with the continual poker games, and started organising other diversions. Although Pearson was apparently well educated, he was young and impressionable. As the days dragged on, we sometimes put to sea in the forlorn hope that the weather would improve sufficiently for us to sneak a few shots or at least to gain some ship-handling experience. Pearson enthusiastically joined in the hauling on the ship's halyards and lines. Although well educated, he was young and impressionable, and Huston, a great practical joker, told Pearson how amazed he was that a person so slim could generate such strength. I treated it as a mild leg pull, but hadn't appreciated that Pearson was really being set up for one of Huston's more elaborate jokes. Pearson was very flattered, and agreed to Huston arranging a wrestling match ashore between him and Tom Clegg, who played a harpooner in a rival whaling boat. Tom, a South African, was a former professional fighter and wrestler, and built like an ox. Without doubt he could have disposed of Pearson in seconds. But he was under instruction from Huston to take falls in a convincing manner, which he did to loud cheers and hand claps from the crew, who were all enjoying the spectacle. Encouraged by shouts from Huston, Pearson was the only person unaware of the set-up and became convinced that he possessed greater strength

150

than he'd realised. I looked upon it as harmless fun, which helped to keep up the morale of the film crew.

Apparently at the outset Huston had wanted to make the film in Las Palmas, where the sun was more or less guaranteed. He wanted to complete most of the sea shots there. His plan was ruled out because the *Pequod*, for insurance purposes, was limited to sailing shots no more than ten miles off the coast, and always with a tug in attendance. It was a wise precaution I thought, considering the state of the ship. Huston often exceeded this limitation by a large margin, however, to take advantage of light winds and good lighting conditions. Had he not done so, even less filming would have been completed.

One day we received a message to say that the film's backers were coming to see for themselves the reason for our lack of progress. As it happened, they appeared on a particularly bad day weather-wise. This suited Huston, as it justified his original request to shoot in Las Palmas. The sky was grey and overcast, and there was a fairly heavy sea running, which made the ship pitch and roll under tow. Had the backers not turned up, it's probable we would have stayed in port. However, we steamed up and down rehearsing scenes that we hadn't the slightest hope of shooting. At least we showed that we were trying. Later in the day the weather worsened. After experiencing these conditions, the backers, who by now appeared rather green, decided that they wanted to be put ashore. Huston was in his element and, as usual, puffing away on his cheroot.

To bring out the tenders, it was arranged to give a series of blasts on the ship's siren. One blast was for number one boat, two for number two and so on for the five tenders. Although these blasts were repeatedly signalled, none of the tenders came out to us. It appeared their skippers had decided that if we were mad enough to put to sea in such conditions, we could count them out. Delays like this reinforced Huston's lack of progress. Huston said jokingly to the backers, 'If the worse comes to the worse, I'll send you ashore on the back of the whale.' Despite feeling rough, one of the backers retorted, 'Well, that's a great idea, John, because that whale has been on *our* back long enough.' I had to admire him for it. That night they returned to London.

One of the crew on board ship was an old sailor named Ted Hughes, who had finished up as a docker humping pig iron around in the Barry Docks. In his younger days he had sailed on many square-rigged ships, and had several times circumnavigated the world. When told that a film company was looking for seamen with square-sail experience, his mates suggested that he should apply. 'No, I'm far too old. They'd never consider me,' he said. His mates, however, submitted an application in his name, and he was interviewed and taken on as a crew member. I well remember the times when we were not shooting, with John Huston, Gregory Peck, Richard Basehart and Noel Purcell the Irish actor, sitting around Ted in a small circle hearing stories of his exploits under sail. They were as spellbound as small children listening to fairy tales.

Ted lived on board, and one night became so drunk while ashore that his shipmates had to take him back to the ship, undress him and put him in his bunk. As they took off his socks, they were surprised to see that all his toes were misshapen; they had obviously all been broken at one time. The following morning when asked about this, Ted explained that it was due to the ringbolts used for securing things on deck. Frequently during bad weather when all hands were called on deck in emergencies they didn't have time to pull on their boots. In the dark, with the ship pitching and tossing and the seas crashing over the decks, they occasionally smashed their toes against the iron ringbolts. There were no doctors on board in those days, and by the time the ship reached port after a voyage of many months, the broken bones had set, and remained like that for the rest of the sailor's life. Ted was a tremendous character, and after *Moby Dick* finished filming the ship was sold to a TV company, with Ted taken on as first mate.

Some considerable time later Ted became ill and was taken to a London hospital. I went with Bernard Miles and two other stuntmen who had worked on the film with Ted to visit him. He told us that working on films had been one of the most memorable periods in his life. Being elevated to first mate had meant a lot to him. Some weeks later his condition worsened, and he was sent back to Wales where he wanted to end his life. All four of us went to the station to see him off. He was obviously in great pain, but as the train pulled out he got up from his seat with a tremendous effort and did a sailor's hornpipe by way of farewell.

152

22

Jokers Wild

I had thoroughly enjoyed working on *Moby Dick*. Looking back, I think it was another one of the most enjoyable periods of my professional life and had a significant effect on my future. There was only one discordant note to spoil the harmony of that time, and that was the attempt by Huston to complete his setting up of George Pearson.

It occurred one evening after we had returned to harbour. I had to call in at the production office, where I found Kelly waiting for me. He said Pearson had been sent for by Huston and asked whether he had the guts to be tattooed all over his head, chest and back. If Pearson was to do this, stressed Huston, it would save hours in make-up time when he was doubling for Frederick Ledebur. He added that if Pearson was prepared to go through with it, not only could he name his own price, but at the end of the filming, the company would pay to have all tattoos removed. He assured Pearson that the remuneration would be enough to set him up for life.

Huston was indulging himself as a great practical joker and, having found that Pearson was a very gullible chap, was just playing games with him. By this stage I was getting very angry at this court-jester situation. I felt that by the way Huston was treating Pearson, all of us stuntmen were becoming something of a joke. I asked Kelly where Pearson was. Kelly told me that he had advised him to lock himself in the lavatory, where nobody from the production department could get him to sign any agreement that did not reflect the true value of what was being asked of him. Kelly had told him to leave it to me as an agent to negotiate a sum commensurate to the value it would be to the company. I was stunned that Kelly, too, had swallowed Huston's gag and was furious that the two of them had been so taken in. No doubt by then the story had been circulated around the film crew, and everyone would be laughing at our expense and regarding us stuntmen as idiots.

I got Pearson and Kelly together, and let them know in no uncertain manner how stupid they both had been. I was now determined to see whether Huston could take a joke himself, and I spent considerable thought hatching up a plot which depended on the cooperation of the chief make-up artist and the company's doctor.

A few days later, Huston, Peck, Basehart and other principals were playing poker in the cabin as usual. There was the usual group of onlookers watching the huge sums of money changing hands. While they were occupied, I took the opportunity to persuade our chief make-up artist to decorate Pearson's shoulder with a tattoo pattern like Frederick's film make-up. Pearson was stretched out for this purpose on the medical bunk, stripped to the waist and lying face down. The make-up artist did a fine job and it looked like a real tattoo. When the work was completed, we covered Pearson up to his neck with a sheet. The doctor stood nearby with all his medical paraphernalia laid out and his stethoscope around his neck, while I committed to memory the medical term for an extremely rare blood disorder he told me about. The scene was set. I went to the cabin where Huston was playing poker, roughly pulled aside the onlookers, and said to him: 'I want to see you outside – immediately!' Within seconds all the onlookers disappeared, not wishing to be in any way involved as the tone of my voice clearly indicated that there was a row in the offing. Peck was so embarrassed that he dropped his cards and disappeared under the table to retrieve them; the other players shared his embarrassment and didn't know quite where to look. Huston, a man who never refused a challenge, looked up. 'You want to see me, Joe?'

'Yes, and it's bloody urgent,' I replied. He stepped outside and walked a little way down the passageway. I said in a fairly loud voice, so that the poker players could hear. 'You've been making a fool out of Pearson for some time now, but your last jape has really misfired. Do you know what this stupid idiot has done? He took a copy of the make-up to a tattoo artist in Fishguard to have it tattooed on one shoulder. He wanted to find out what it would be like to be completely tattooed all over as you suggested. He's now seriously ill with blood poisoning.' And here I quoted the name of the rare blood disorder which the doctor had given me. 'Unless an antidote is found, within a few hours he will be dead.' I also said that the doctor had told me that the antidote could only be obtained in London. 'We need it immediately if it is to be of any use. The situation is serious.'

Huston just looked at me, stunned. As I returned his gaze, I was thinking to myself, 'Gotcher! You're hoist with your own petard!' He enquired abruptly, 'Where is he now?' 'In the medical bunk, being looked after by the doctor,' I said. Huston immediately turned on his heel and made his way there to find the doctor bending over Pearson. 'Is this true, Doctor?' he demanded.

At this point the doctor, who was rather in awe of Huston, looked a little frightened. He was no doubt wondering why he had agreed to get involved in my little charade and fearful of the possible repercussion. Luckily his nervous manner added a touch of realism to the scene. When I asked the doctor where we could get the antidote for Pearson's malady, he replied that it was only to be found in London. 'We need it immediately if it's to be of any use. The situation is extremely serious.'

A few moments passed, and then Huston asked to see Pearson's shoulder. The doctor pulled the sheet aside, and Huston bent down to get a closer look. He leaned forward to touch the skin around the tattoo. Pearson didn't react in any way to his touch. At that moment it suddenly struck me – I hadn't stage managed the drama expertly enough. Pearson should have been writhing in agony, and then, in all probability, Huston wouldn't have asked to see the fake tattoo.

I had planned to follow up with, 'It's bad luck, but don't worry about it. I'll phone Jock tonight and get a replacement. After all, he's not even a stuntman.' But Huston had accepted that he'd been set up and the joke was on him. He swung on his heel, avoided my eyes, and walked back to the poker cabin. He calmly picked up his cards, and said to Peck, 'Your twenty, and up fifty …' and the game was resumed. The incident was never mentioned again, but I felt Huston had shown that he could take a ribbing as well as dishing it out. No more japes were played on Pearson.

There was a further twist. I heard later that Jack Martin, the ever efficient first assistant, had also been taken in by my ruse. While standing on deck he overheard everything and rushed to get in touch with the production office ashore, telling them to find out urgently how quickly a helicopter could be sent from London, once an antidote had been located.

Kelly had been playing poker with the technicians, and from all accounts had not been faring very well. Several times he was heard to say that he'd like to play in 'the big league', meaning the Huston–Peck card school. This was greeted with derision by most of the unit, but Huston was evidently amused when Kelly's wish reached his ears. One night, while a large number of unit members were in the Moby Dick Bar, Huston's personal assistant appeared. He said, loudly, 'Mr Kelly, Mr Huston and Gregory Peck would like you to join them in a game of poker.' This was greeted with loud cheers and much laughter around the bar by everyone, who thought this was truly a case of the lamb being led to the slaughter. Apparently the idea was to teach Kelly a lesson by taking all his money, then return it and figuratively slap his arse and send him on his way with instructions to gain more experience before getting into a really big poker school.

The following morning when we joined the ship, we found that the poker school had been playing all night. When Kelly joined us, he had several hundred pounds tucked into his belt. Suddenly Kelly appeared in a new light to everyone. The games resumed each night after shooting, or during the day when bad weather put a halt to any production activity. As each day passed, Kelly became increasingly rich.

One morning, when I returned to the ship after having been delayed by a visit to the production office, I was told that the first assistant wanted to see me straight away. I assumed that it would be to discuss my scheduled fall from the mast into the sea. Instead, Jack Martin informed me that Kelly had been selected to do the fall instead of me. I pointed out immediately that Kelly was not capable of doing the fall. 'As you well know, Kelly hasn't even climbed the mast, because he doesn't like heights,' I said. It transpired that one of the actors had told Huston that Kelly had been cheating, which Huston had believed. Making Kelly do the fall was Huston's way of saying, 'Don't mess with me, boy, or you'll have to answer for it.' I found this hard to believe. Huston had played over the years in very big and tough card schools, and I am sure was capable of being aware of any cheating. What made cheating further unlikely was that, as I understood it, the cards were shuffled by a player other than the dealer. There was certainly no one in that school who would have cooperated with Kelly to cheat. But it seemed everything was now set for Huston to get even over alleged cheating.

156

I again stressed that Kelly had no idea of how to do the fall, and if he attempted the stunt, there was every possibility it could end in tragedy. He was just asking for trouble. Jack Martin told me to talk Kelly out of it. We were now leaving harbour as I went down below decks to speak to Kelly, who was getting dressed ready for the fall. He was pale and shaking. 'What the hell do you think you're doing?' I demanded.

'Huston believes I've been cheating, but I haven't. He thinks that if I turn the job down in front of the whole unit, it'll make me look a coward, and that's his way of getting even. He just wants to show me up in front of the whole unit. I'm going to do it, and show him up instead. I'm not going to back down; I'll accept his challenge,' he said.

There was nothing more I could do to dissuade him. The yard from which he was to fall was more than sixty feet high. The fall was made even trickier because he would be standing only on a foot rope, with the ship pitching and rolling in heavy seas beneath him. I knew that the current off Stumble Head, where the fall was to take place, was quite treacherous and the sky was black and overcast. Here am I, I thought, in charge of the action, with the possibility of a bad accident or worse. Something had to be done, but the question was what? The trouble with a high fall into water is that, if all the wind is knocked out of you and you are unconscious at the same time, you lose buoyancy, and just continue to sink. In those black waters, with the ship under way, the chances of reaching Kelly and then diving to find him were slim; there would be little chance of recovery.

I suddenly had an idea. I broke open a life jacket, took out all the kapok pads and with a roll of camera tape, stuck them all to Kelly's body. Now even if he did get knocked out, he wouldn't sink too far and swallow a lot of water, and would very quickly return to the surface, where we would be able to get to him quickly; the pads would hopefully also absorb some of the impact on hitting the water.

We emerged on deck, with all the crew and performers standing quietly watching the drama unfold. Arthur Ibbertson, the cameraman, caught my eye, and then looked up to the sky, slowly shaking his head. There was very little light, and therefore no way in which this scene could have been caught on camera. Huston appeared on deck. 'Up you go, Kelly,' he said, lighting one of his favourite small cheroots. Kelly went to the shrouds and started to climb up the ratlines, obviously shaking as he ascended. Slowly he inched his way along the yardarm on the foot rope, until he reached the end. There was a look of satisfaction on Huston's face, as he watched Kelly's obvious distress and fear. After a short pause, Huston called 'Turnover!' to the cameraman. Kelly shouted down, 'Not yet, not yet. I'm not ready.' Huston shouted back, 'All right, Mr Kelly. You just let us know when you're ready', and took another long drag at his cheroot. After some moments had gone by, Kelly started inching his way back along the yard to the shrouds, and then descended. With obvious relief he reached the deck where he paused before walking up to Huston and saying, 'After all the money I've won from you, I don't need that fucking job.' It would appear that both sides had gained some satisfaction from the outcome. The ship was immediately ordered back to port.

Everyone expected Kelly to be sacked. To our amazement, nothing more was ever said, and things carried on as usual. Even more unbelievable, when that evening the poker school resumed, Kelly was included. The excuse Huston had made to Jack Martin for getting Kelly to do the fall instead of me was that the person doing the fall would be finished on the film. It was to indicate that he wanted me to continue on the film. This fracas had cost me the chance to earn some additional money. I then had to telephone Jock in the office, to contact John Sullivan to do the fall.

We finished shooting at Fishguard, leaving a second unit to complete a few additional shots of sailing scenes. We then started work at ABPC Studios in Borehamwood. The interior shots included ones below decks and all the storm sequences. It was not possible because of the total length of the ship to build a complete replica on one set, so half the ship was constructed on one stage and the other half on another. Both halves were built on hydraulic rams which, when activated, reproduced the rolling and pitching motion of the ship at sea, especially to enact the storm sequences. High up in both sets were water tanks, each holding a ton of water. Under each tank was a chute with a bend at the end. When the water was released, it shot down the chutes, hit the end and literally flew at the ship. The water gained added force with the help of a series of aircraft engines ranged in the roof of the studio, sixty feet up. With the engines on full throttle, the draught from their propellers hit the water to simulate a wave hitting the ship. Detergent in the water gave the foaming effect of the sea when crashing on to the vessel. The detergent was so strong that we all had trouble with our ears. The incoming water had such impetus that if you didn't hold on, you risked being smashed from one side of the ship to the other. To heighten the storm effect, the electricians rigged up electrodes which gave off brilliant flashes to simulate lightning. The total effect was fantastic. The filming of the storm scenes went on for several weeks. One of the reasons why these took so long was that the tanks had to be refilled and the aircraft engines refuelled after each shot. There were also many hold ups for repairs to the hydraulics.

A second film unit had been left behind at Fishguard, as the continuing bad weather resulted in a number of scenes still needing to be completed. Eventually Huston got what he wanted all along and the first unit was flown out to the better conditions offered by Las Palmas. We were there for several weeks, including the Christmas period. I was fortunate enough to have my wife and two children join me there. They came out on a banana ship, the *Monte Urgiola*, which plied between London, Las Palmas and Tenerife. Apart from the cargo, the ship carried seventy passengers who travelled first class, and had use of a swimming pool. I felt the trip would help to make up for the loss of the family holiday I had promised them in Rome when working on *Helen of Troy*.

Huston had planned to have thousands of seagulls featured on his film credit titles. To entice the numbers he needed to get on film, he spent hundreds of pounds on buying meat, which local workers were hired to cut up and throw into the sea to attract the birds. I couldn't begin to describe the expression on the faces of these people, who were too poor to afford such meat in the first place or had never handled it in such quantities. That they were being paid to throw it to the seagulls was beyond their comprehension. I felt really embarrassed watching these poor people, some of whom, believe it or not, lived in caves on Las Palmas. The only way to look at it was that had the film company not been there, they probably wouldn't have had any employment at all.

The only redeeming feature was a boxing exhibition that we staged locally, which raised a large sum of money for the poor. Jimmy Spearman and I fought two rounds each with Tommy Clegg, with John Huston acting as the referee and Richard Basehart and Leo Genn as the seconds. This achieved wide publicity for the film, as well as being a boost for Clegg's character as one of the ship's harpooners.

One of the last scenes in *Moby Dick* is when Peck, as Captain Ahab, harpoons the Great White Whale and in doing so is caught up in the harpoon line and dragged out of the boat. In its death throes the whale rolls over and over, dragging Ahab with it. Each time the whale rolls, so Ahab disappears under the water, then reappears as the creature continues its roll. To simulate this action, a section of the whale had been built on a pontoon, on a mechanical arm. Peck was tied on to this and dunked beneath the surface. With the camera running, the arm was rotated and Peck reappeared from under the surface; filming continued until Peck reached the top of the roll. That was the planned shot. There were said to be sharks in the area off Las Palmas, where this scene was being filmed, however. To prevent Peck being offered as shark bait, the production company had contracted a reputed 'shark hunter', who was flown out from Spain. He was to stand by in case any were sighted, and to dive in to fend them off if Peck was in any danger.

The shark hunter arrived, festooned with all manner of harpoons, knives and an assortment of other paraphernalia. He also had a large water glass, which enabled him to search the surrounding area prior to Peck being submerged. It was he who gave the go ahead to the lowering of Peck beneath the water. After the shot had been completed, I asked him, 'In fighting a shark, where do you start?' He waited until there were few people around us, and gave me a conspiratorial look as if to let me in on the secret. Then, turning his eyes to heaven, he spread out the palms of his hands, hunched his shoulders, and puffed out his cheeks, as if I he considered me potty to ask such a stupid question. It seemed that his sole function, as far as he was concerned, was to shout a warning for Peck to be quickly pulled to the surface should he spot a shark through his water glass. It became evident to me that had a shark appeared on the scene, there was no way in which he would have gone to Peck's aid. The presence of this so-called shark fighter, however, was sufficient guarantee to Peck that his safety was assured. To me it was a glaring example of how producers are prepared to get stars to participate in dangerous scenes in order to get realistic close-up shots of the artiste. Remember that this was the last shot of the film. Had Peck been attacked by a shark, I suppose it would have been tremendous publicity for the film.

Kelly remained employed by the company and continued to play poker while in Las Palmas. When the picture was completed, Huston owed Kelly quite a considerable amount of money, which it seems Kelly was reluctant to demand. When Huston went to the airport, Kelly went, too. After the usual goodbyes, Huston suddenly disappeared into the plane leaving Kelly disappointed and crestfallen without his cheque. But just as suddenly Huston reappeared, and called to his PA, 'Don't forget to give Kelly his cheque.' As usual, he played out the drama to its conclusion, complete with that poker face of his. I've no doubt at all that Huston derived great pleasure in keeping Kelly on tenterhooks right until the end.

23

An Eccentric Encounter

In the early days our agency office received a number of bogus telephone calls. Friendly production managers and assistant directors often played pranks on us, so we always had to be on our guard when answering the phone. On one occasion, however, I was completely caught out.

It was sometime in the mid-fifties when I received a call from a person with a German-sounding name. He told me that he was setting up an unusual concert at the Royal Festival Hall with Sir Adrian Boult as the orchestra conductor, but he also reeled off a host of other high-profile names in the musical world, such as Sir Malcolm Sargent and John Barbirolli. I had heard of them all, of course, but the caller's name was completely unknown to me, and I began to be suspicious. Listening carefully to his voice, I tried to place the would-be joker.

It sounded to me like a real send-up. He told me that the theme of the concert was to be hilarity, based upon the music of the classics. Some leading instrumentalists would participate, including the London Philharmonic Orchestra. There would be other musicians creating a whole range of musical sounds with jaw's harps and mouth organs, strumming washboards with thimbles on their fingers, blowing rubber hoses, and playing saws with violin bows. He mentioned a whole number of unlikely musical instruments, which sounded quite idiotic for a place such as the Royal Festival Hall. All through this conversation, I was trying to figure out who could have thought up such an elaborate hoax.

The caller then asked me whether I could contribute some wild ideas, which he could include. At this point, I thought that I'd enter into the fun, and match his outrageous ideas with some of my own. 'How about fixing a Kirby flying wire to Adrian Boult? While he's conducting, we whip him fifty feet up in the air, but he will take no notice and carry on conducting as if nothing had happened,' I suggested.

'Ho, ho, ho! Capital! Capital!' he said. 'But I don't think that he'd stand for that.'

'Well,' I said, 'at the end of one of the pieces of music, why don't we get one of our stuntmen, posing as an enthusiastic member of the audience, to stand up in one of the theatre boxes, overbalance and fall into the orchestra pit?'

'Ho, ho! Capital! Capital!' he enthused.

I went further. 'How about the Don Cossacks galloping across the stage, followed by Buck Ryan's Cowboys during the playing of the Post Horn Gallop? Then again we could have Babu, a highwire artiste, sliding only on his feet, down a wire stretched from high up in the hall over the heads of the orchestra to the back of the stage. We could have Saballa swing across the stage, holding on by his teeth, dressed as a fairy.' My wild proposals were punctuated with frequent 'ho, hos' and 'capitals' from my listener.

'Oh, Mr Powell, we must meet to discuss these wonderful suggestions further. But wouldn't these acts cost an awful lot of money?'

'No,' I said. 'You told me that the concert was for charity, and I'm sure that the boys would be only too happy to make a contribution.' All the time I was wondering who could have thought up such an elaborate joke. The caller then asked if it was convenient for me to see him that day. Anxious to find out who was perpetrating the joke, I said yes. He said that he knew where my office was, and that he would be in Lexington Street at eleven o'clock. If I walked down the street, he would be waiting for me in his car. 'Right,' I agreed, still trying to fathom out who the joker was.

At the appointed time I strolled down Lexington Street, glancing at the parked cars. I was about to pass a small Ford Ten when I heard my name called. The driver introduced himself as Gerard Hoffnung, but I didn't recognise him as anyone I knew. After we had shaken hands, he asked me to jump in. 'Where are we going?' I asked. 'Why, to the Festival Hall, of course,' he replied.

I was flabbergasted. I thought, my God, I've really put my foot in it now. This man is for real. As we drove along he explained the proposed concert in detail, but I was hardly listening. My brain was racing as I wondered how I was possibly going to get out of the mess in which I had landed myself.

On arriving at the Festival Hall, we went straight to the stage,

164

where men were busily arranging things for the concert. I was introduced to a number of the staff, including the theatre manager. They greeted me with smiling faces, obviously interested to hear what my contribution was going to be. I had no other option but to give an outline of what I had said to Hoffnung. As I continued talking I could see the smiles begin to fade from the faces before me, especially that of the manager. Brows began to furrow, then consternation was in turn replaced by looks of actual horror.

After a while, the manager said, 'These wire attachments and the horses' hooves, won't they damage the stage floor?' Inwardly I breathed a sigh of relief. Here, I felt sure, was my way out.

'Oh, I don't think so,' I said. 'It's true that we'll have to bolt a very heavy shackle to the stage, and beneath it. It will have to be substantial, as the wire holding Babu for his slide is quite heavy due to its length. We can't have Babu falling on the audience's head, can we? As for the horses' hooves, I'm sure that the marks could be sanded out. The holes drilled for the shackles could be plugged afterwards and also sanded over. I don't think that they would show very much.'

The manager's face was a picture of despair. 'We'll have to discuss the arrangements,' he murmured and shook my hand and thanked me for coming. Hoffnung, on the other hand, was delighted, and as he drove me back to the office was very enthusiastic about what he saw as the successful outcome of my meeting with the manager. I was hoping to myself that he'd got it entirely wrong. Much to my relief Hoffnung phoned me a couple of days later to say that the management wouldn't go along with the necessary stage arrangements. He thanked me very warmly for all my trouble and subsequently sent me a couple of tickets for the concert. Unfortunately I couldn't go, but gave the tickets to a neighbour, who said afterwards that he and his wife had had a most enjoyable night, one that they would always remember.

Gerard Hoffnung, I learned later, had come to England as a very young boy refugee. He died at the young age of 34. During his short life, however, he became famous for his Hoffnung concerts, which were staged in Norway, Japan, Israel, the United States and Australia. He was also renowned as a cartoonist, musician, broadcaster and raconteur. He lectured at both Oxford and Cambridge, and yet, up until the concert, I must confess I had never heard of him.

24

Mature Moments

After *Moby Dick* it was another down period for the agency. One day a production manager, Doug Twiddy, phoned me. Doug was an ex-Commando who had lost an eye at the battle of Salerno in Italy. He was working on a film at MGM Studios and wanted me to go there immediately to get kitted up to double as Victor Mature in a fall down a hole. It was a bread-and-butter job worth only a few pounds, but nevertheless it was money that I could have done with. The only problem was that Doug couldn't give me an actual date when the stunt was due to be shot. I told him that I was very sorry, but I could not guarantee to be available for the job, as I was chasing up a very big production which would employ a large number of stuntmen. Casting was due at any moment, and I just couldn't afford to miss the opportunity, but I promised to find him someone to help out.

Doug was annoyed at being turned down, and started putting a lot of pressure on me to accept the job. I was still on the phone to him when Harold Sanderson, one of the stuntmen, came in. He was a far better double for Mature than me. 'Doug,' I said, 'a perfect double has just walked into the office and I'll send him up straight away.' But Doug still insisted he wanted me to do the job. He knew my capabilities, whereas Harold was unknown to him. I was torn between upsetting a valuable contact, and possibly not being around when this other big production started casting. I wasn't acting just in my own interests; there were a number of stuntmen who looked to the agency to find them work, and the film I was after meant a lengthy location in Morocco for many of them. 'If I come out with Harold, and you find him suitable, will you take him instead of me?' I asked Doug. He agreed, but told me to make sure that I did accompany Harold.

At the studios, both the cameraman and Doug wanted me to double for Victor Mature, but eventually I persuaded them to accept Harold. I rushed back to the office to continue chasing the major production I was interested in. Harold carried out the fall down the hole so successfully that two weeks later, he was contracted to be flown out to Kenya to continue doubling for Victor Mature. After three months, he was retained for a second film called *Safari*. Work on this movie lasted a further three months, and then the film company wanted him to go on a third film in Africa. Harold complained that he hadn't seen his family for six months. They flew him home for two weeks, and then he was flown back out to Morocco to double for Mature yet again in the movie *Zarak Khan* (1956), which happened to be the production I was chasing and which was the reason I had turned down the job of falling down a hole. Incidentally, Harold went on to double for the star on several other movies, one of which was in Italy, and another in the West Indies. Altogether he worked as a double for Mature and Robert Mitchum for about seven years.

After filming on *Zarak Khan* had been going on some four weeks, eight more of us stuntmen were contracted to work on the film. During the shooting in Morocco, tragedy struck when one of the stuntmen was killed while doing a horse fall. He was Jack Keeley, an ex-cavalryman and one of the most popular of the men.

After his death, the contractual fee was increased to £60 per week all in. The indemnity against any claim for death or injury still applied. The trouble with an all-in deal, in which no top-up fees were received for any extra individual stunts, was that such stunts were performed by only a small percentage of those under contract. It encouraged those who became known as 'the stand back brigade'. These were men who, while quite happy to receive the contracted weekly fee, shied off performing individual stunts. Happily that is now a thing of the past.

All the stunt work on *Zarak Khan* was being directed by Yakima Cannut. Under Yak we learned a lot about horse falls and stunting in general. I was fortunate enough to work with him after this picture on numerous productions in many different countries.

At one stage during filming, the heavens opened up. Not only roads, but also the sides of mountains were washed away, making it impossible to reach the locations, or even to do any camera work. The setting was supposed to represent India, though it looked more like Wales in flood. Eventually the whole unit was sent home, and didn't return for several weeks until the floods had

168

subsided. On our return, we were based in the Dersa Hotel, Tetuan. Work was very slow, as a number of the roads were still impassable, and some days were spent drinking in the hotel, in local cafés, or in the Kasbah.

One night, I was joined in the bar by Tony Bevan, author of the book on which the film was based. He was very upset by the way that his story was being interpreted on screen. *Zarak Khan* was about the Pathans, whom Tony had a tremendous admiration for as a race. He told me in great detail why he held them in such respect. His tales of northern India, where he had served as a cavalry officer, were far more colourful than the story now being depicted on the screen. I started commiserating with him, and when we got into some pretty heavy drinking on Spanish brandy, I began to see why he was so upset.

After talking and drinking for some time, we both were certainly the worse for wear when in walked Victor Mature. Tony broke off in the middle of one of his stories, stood back from the bar and, glaring at Mature, said loudly, 'When I look at him playing Zarak, I want to puke.' Mature turned on his heel and walked out. Tony carried on telling me stories about the Raj and his adventures in India on the North West Frontier. Some weeks later, he told me that had it not been for me talking with him that night, he might well have seriously considered suicide. Later he sent me a signed copy of his book, *Zarak Khan*, in which he wrote, 'To our night out on Fundadore' (the Spanish brandy we had been drinking).

On our return from Morocco, there was another quiet spell until out of the blue came a contract for sixty stuntmen for a Hammer production, *The Steel Bayonet* (1957), a war film. Around this time we hadn't got that many on our books, but I was determined not to employ any crowd artistes. To fulfil the contract, we took on a number of Equity artistes who had all served in the Forces, and who could re-enact their experiences in the battle sequences. The main location was Aldershot, with all the interiors being shot at Bray Studios. It was here that we renewed our acquaintance with Stanley Baker, whom we met when he played a minor role in *Captain Horatio Hornblower*. Later on he and I worked together on several films. I was Sergeant Windridge in Stanley's own production, *Zulu*. I also worked on *The Last Grenade*, another film he produced in Spain, and on *The Guns of Navarone*.

We took our caravan while on location at Aldershot for *The*

169

Steel Bayonet. Not only did it cut out the travelling, but it was used as a stunt office. Eddie, my brother, who was one of the team, decided to bed down in the caravan with Jock and me during the time we were there. One night after the unit had packed up and left, we three went into Aldershot for a drink. We finished up making a heavy session of it, and returned very late. In the morning, we discovered Eddie was not with us in the caravan. We found him in his car in which he'd spent most of the night. Evidently, Jock and I had snored so heavily, that Eddie, in his desperation to get some sleep, wandered off in the pitch darkness to try and find his car. Not having a torch to see where he was going, he had fallen and become completely entangled in some barbed wire that was part of the film set. Although he was not far from the caravan, Jock and I did not hear his cries for help. Eventually he managed to extricate himself, and after some considerable time located the car in which he spent an uncomfortable night. After that, although we were in Aldershot for several weeks, Eddie preferred to travel all the way back to Twyford each night rather than repeat the experience.

Eddie, who had been serving in the 1st Battalion Grenadier Guards as a dispatch rider in Germany, was demobbed in 1948 and on his return to the UK, he'd decided to join me in the film industry and become part of our stunt team. Like me, he did six months' work as a crowd artiste in order to learn something about the film industry, find out where the various studios were located and acquire some knowledge of the general running of the business.

One of his first jobs with me was on a film called *The Death of Uncle George*, in which we both had to fall into a lake from a rowing boat. It was midwinter and there was snow on the ground, while three-quarters of the lake was covered in ice. We knew nothing about wetsuits in those days and we were frozen. Fortunately we had to only do one take, which is quite unusual; otherwise we might both have suffered from hypothermia.

We worked together on dozens of films, but where Eddie came into his own was in doubling for Christopher Lee in the horror movies Hammer Film Productions specialised in. In all, he doubled for Dracula six times. Among the many major productions he appeared in were *Chamber of Horrors*, *Howling II*, *Your Sister is a Werewolf*, *Dracula, Prince of Darkness*, *The Mummy* and *The Mummy's Shroud*.

170

He doubled for Clint Eastwood on *Where Eagles Dare*, sitting on top of a cable-car arm at Ebensee. At 2,000 feet up, this cable car run is one of the highest, if not the highest, in Austria, and Eddie hated heights! He appeared in *She, The Devil Rides Out, The Lost Continent, To the Devil a Daughter* and *The Alien*. Other contracts included *Flash Gordon, Hammer into Anvil, Batman, The Legend, The Keep, Daleks Invasion of Earth*, and *2150 AD*.

In *The Omen*, he doubled for Gregory Peck, and in *The Sea Wolves*, again as Gregory Peck, he did a back fall from over sixty feet into water and as a result ruptured his spleen. While on the plane returning from India, he passed out. Doctors on board thought he'd had a heart attack, and gave him injections that only made things worse. The pilot diverted the plane to Rome, where he was rushed to hospital and put on a heart machine. In the morning, a nurse who spoke English told him, 'We were very worried – for a little while we lost you.' When Gregory Peck heard the news, he phoned the hospital, and arranged for Eddie to be put in a private ward.

Eddie also worked on *Patriot Games, Boys from Brazil, The Chairman, Arabesque, High Wind in Jamaica, 633 Squadron* and *Nairobi Affair*.

171

25

The Gallant Mayflower

In 1957 building was completed on the replica of the *Mayflower*, the ship in which the Pilgrim Fathers sailed to America in 1620. The plan was to sail her to Plymouth, Massachusetts, following the route taken by her famous predecessor. It was the fulfilment of an ambition for a Fleet Street visionary named Warwick Charlton. The idea came to him while he was serving on Field Marshal Montgomery's staff in North Africa. He was inspired after reading the journal of William Bradford, the first leader of the Pilgrim Fathers, who had sailed on the original *Mayflower*. Commander Alan Villiers, whom Charlton had retained to captain the ship on her voyage to the States, invited me to become a member of the crew. It was an offer I couldn't refuse, so I gave up the opportunity to work in Norway on the movie *The Vikings*, which starred Kirk Douglas.

The *Mayflower II* was to be given to the people of the United States as a measure of gratitude from the people of Great Britain for America's aid during the Second World War. Warwick Charlton was helped in the fundraising by John Lowe, a co-founder of the project. I had gained my limited crewing experience while working on ships featured in movies. These included the *Angelina H.* and the *Marcel B.* in *Billy Budd* of which Captain Adrian Small was the skipper. He was to be second mate aboard the *Mayflower II*, while Godfrey Wicksteed was appointed first mate. Captain Jan Junker, a Danish ice pilot from Copenhagen, came as a third mate. Such was their enthusiasm for the voyage that these eminent seamen with worldwide experience in square-rigged sailing were prepared to sail in any capacity.

I felt highly honoured to be a crew member; it transpired that there were more than three thousand applications to join the crew from yachtsmen and seafarers with enormous sailing experience. The slight advantage I had, however, was that my experience had been on square-riggers. Also in my favour was the fact that I was known to both Allan Villiers and Adrian Small, who had seen me working. When not actually required during shooting, I had always taken the opportunity to assist in the crewing of the ships. This had given me practical knowledge of setting and furling sails, and more perhaps importantly, of the workings of the miles of rigging on a square rigger.

When I arrived at Brixham, Devon, to join the crew, I obtained my first view of the ship from high above the harbour. From that vantage point her smallness was accentuated, but she looked a very pretty vessel. Evidently when launched, she had all but keeled over due to lack of ballast, and then continued to list at an alarming angle. A sea captain who had sailed four-masters was quoted in national newspapers as saying that he wouldn't dream of sailing the *Mayflower II* outside the breakwater. Grave doubts were raised as to whether she would ever manage the voyage to America. It was reported that there would be only a fifty-fifty chance of survival. As a result, we were named the 'fifty-fifty crew'. Experts said that her sides were too high, but others said that if the sea forced *Mayflower II* on her side, her tender shape would encourage her to keep going.

The first couple of weeks were spent humping pig iron to provide the ballast – one hundred and sixty tons of it. Our next job was to load containers of goods for display in America, which were termed 'treasure chests'. Manufacturing companies paid five hundred pounds per treasure chest to have their goods transported and take advantage of the publicity generated by the voyage. This was the way in which some of the funding for the ship building and voyage was raised.

One of the containers contained a Coventry Climax engine. We picked it up from a point high above the harbour. The container was so heavy that it took a number of us to carry it down the many steps to the ship. Halfway down, a couple of the lads slipped, but we others managed to hold it long enough for them to regain their balance, and the chest was loaded aboard without further bother.

The following morning though, I was in great pain and had difficulty in getting out of bed. Another member of the crew living in the billet called for John Stevens, who was our ship's doctor. On examining me, he diagnosed a slipped disc. It was shattering news, because there was no way I could take part in the voyage. Fortunately our landlady, who had suffered for years from a slipped disc until receiving treatment, phoned her osteopath in Torquay and made an immediate appointment for me. While I was travelling to him by bus, I was in such pain that the sweat poured off me. I must have looked terrible, because several passengers asked me if they could help in any way. Luckily I didn't have far to walk after leaving the bus, although it was slightly uphill to the osteopath's practice and I began to think that I wouldn't make it. When the osteopath opened the door, he saw at once the bad state that I was in. He was built like an ox, and he practically carried me inside and somehow got me up a steep flight of stairs to his surgery. After an hour's manipulation, followed by a short rest, I walked unaided down the stairs, and went for a twenty-minute walk. The change was unbelievable.

When I arrived back at Brixham, I told the doctor that the trouble was only a pulled muscle. He refused to believe this, and sent me to hospital in Torquay for an X-ray, which revealed the real damage to my back. I was given a letter to take back him, but I opened it. The letter was quite detailed, but briefly the message was clear – I could not be considered as a member of the *Mayflower II* crew. When the ship's doctor questioned me, I told him that the hospital had confirmed that all I had was a pulled muscle. 'Didn't they give you a letter for me?' he asked. 'Letter? They more or less kicked me out of the hospital for wasting their time,' I told him, adding that he had made me look like some kind of wimp and severely embarrassed me by sending me to the hospital. Luckily he accepted my story.

When the voyage started, not all the work on the ship had been completed. There was a lot left to do, including quite a bit of painting. The caulking had to be smoothed out, which meant going down on your hands and knees and scraping. As I was still having trouble with my back, after a couple of hours the only way in which I could stand up was to crawl to the ship's side and heave myself upright. The good news was that after a few weeks of hauling on ropes, my back pain started to diminish and before we reached America it had all but disappeared.

The doctor and I were on the same watch. One night I said to him, 'Oh, by the way, Doc, do you recall that when I came back from the hospital you asked me whether they'd given me a letter for you? Well, I've just remembered that they did – and here it is.'

After he had read the letter, he turned to me and what he called me doesn't bear repeating. It was not the sort of language one expected from a doctor.

We were becalmed a couple of times, although on occasions there was some very bad weather. At one stage, Captain Villiers ordered lifelines to be rigged both port and starboard of the main deck, and all sails stowed and the wheel lashed. Things stayed like this until we had ridden out the storm. The high stern pointed the *Mayflower II* into the wind, but we still rolled and rolled. When we saw a tanker crashing through the waves, we realised that even modern vessels found it very heavy going. As the poop deck was about thirty feet high, you really had to hang on up there. To lose your hold would have meant being thrown high in the air and into the sea. With no engine and in those conditions, there would have been no chance of recovering a man overboard.

The skipper's cabin was on the poop, so that when the ship rolled, he was in the worst possible place for comfort. On one occasion when the going was rough, I was on the wheel, not more than ten feet away from Villiers's cabin. His curses were certainly in keeping with those of an old sea dog. He was not in the best of temper and being most uncomplimentary to the ship. After a while he appeared on deck and greeted me calmly with, 'Good morning, Joe.' He gave the impression of being completed unruffled. It was in complete contrast to the colourful language I had just heard. I couldn't help smiling to myself.

In an excerpt from how we sailed the *Mayflower II* to America, which appeared in the *National Geographic* in November 1957, he wrote:

> *It began to blow fresh and then hard on the third morning, and the shallow, choppy sea of the channel got up and started jumping, as is its well known habit. And the little ship began to jump with it. Not in wartime destroyers, or submarines, or LCAs, Assault Landing Craft for the invasion of Europe, or in big Cape Horners, or small yachts, had I experienced anything like this. She rolled and she lurched, she pitched and she stumbled, all with a wild and completely unpredictable abandon that was extremely trying to say the least. Even some of the old Cape Horners were violently seasick for days. She was like a wild little bronco constantly taking an uneven series of high fences and rolling and all but falling over as she came to each one.*

176

> *To climb aloft in the topmast rigging was to be flung round in circles, for all the motion was increased by a hundred fold up there, and the rigging alternately slacked and then whipped taut again as the little ship rolled, so that even the most skilful seaman had to hang on for dear life.*

Maitland Edey, a columnist aboard *Mayflower II* for *Time Life* magazine, wrote:

> *Steering the square-rigger was a difficult and strenuous task, and all too often, until they gained experience, the helmsmen found themselves with the sails taken 'aback'.*
>
> *The nights in the tropics were magic. I would spend my hours as lookout sitting on the foreyard, my back set comfortably in the rigging, the sail lifting softly against my feet hanging out over the yard. It was extremely beautiful.*

The reason for the lookout being stationed in the foretop was because the sprit-sail blocked the view of the helmsman. It was, however, a great place for observation, especially at night when other ships' lights could be reported long before they could be seen on deck. During the day porpoises would often gambol in our bow wave, sometimes as many as ten of them at a time. Their speed and agility were a real joy to watch.

Sailing through the Sargasso Sea was a weird experience. The weed was so thick that the sea itself could not be seen. You got the impression that if you jumped overboard you could walk for miles. Crew members hauled up on deck buckets of the seaweed, which was teeming with life, to examine the sea creatures living in it.

At one stage a British tanker, the *Border Sentinel*, steamed miles off course to see us. By the time she arrived, it had become quite dark. In order not to disappoint the other ship's captain, Villiers stationed all the crew in the rigging and on deck holding flares, which we lit at a given signal. It must have been a wonderful sight. The tanker sailed around us a couple of times, before resuming her original course. Her captain was obviously highly delighted and expressed his thanks over his Tannoy system.

En route we were visited by, among others, the aircraft carrier, HMS *Ark Royal*. We must have appeared like a rowing boat in comparison to this huge vessel. When she appeared, John Winslow, a serving pilot aboard her who had been released from duty to crew the *Mayflower II*, rushed below decks to don his naval jacket and cap, so that the crew of the aircraft carrier would recognise him. A helicopter from *Ark Royal* flew over and around us taking pictures – and also our wind. Villiers growled that the pilot obviously knew nothing about square-rigged sailing.

Later on, the American Coastguard training ship *Eagle* overtook us, and her captain and ours exchanged greetings as old friends. We were not far short of being in sight of America when a four-engine bomber was seen on the skyline heading directly towards us. The plane flew lower and lower until by the time it had reached us it was flying at mast height. As the aircraft flew past, we saw printed on the side *Mayflower III*. We had to laugh at their cheek. *Mayflower II* hadn't even sighted America at that point!

Out of courtesy, our first port of call was Provincetown, Cape Cod, where the original *Mayflower* had first dropped anchor on reaching America. Here we had a great reception from the people, with local dignitaries coming aboard. All our crew appreciated the hot showers and huge steak sandwiches we enjoyed on board a tug moored alongside us. The following morning we cast off for Plymouth, a mere twenty-six miles away. As we approached the port, hundreds of craft, including yachts, cabin cruisers and coast-guard boats came out to meet us. Yacht crews shouted greetings, and coastguards bellowed through megaphones ordering everyone to keep clear of us. Larger vessels steamed parallel with us, sounding their sirens, while planes and helicopters flew overhead. As we came closer to our landing spot, we could see thousands of people gathered on the shore. Some in specially erected stands were waiting to welcome us, including Vice President Richard Nixon and Senator John F. Kennedy. High in the stands were dozens of television crews. The noise of the welcome was deafening, especially after a voyage where the only sounds were from the sea as the bow cut through the waves, and the creaking of the masts.

After we had anchored, an American crew rowed to meet us and take us ashore. Their boat was a replica of the original shallop carried on the *Mayflower*, that was left with the first settlers when she returned to England so that they had a craft for fishing and reconnoitring the coast.

The voyage of *Mayflower II* had lasted fifty-four days and covered a distance of 5,500 miles.

I had to fly home from Plymouth to find some work. The ship, however, sailed on down to New York, where the crew was given a tickertape reception. On 21st July 2000, members of the crew still around were invited back to Plymouth to celebrate the 380th anniversary of the original landing. We were entertained royally in both Plymouth and Provincetown. American hospitality cannot be overstated. Friends I made on that voyage are still friends today. We also hear annually from the Plimouth Plantation, a reconstruction of the first settlement of the Pilgrim Fathers.

Mayflower II en route to Plymouth, Massachusetts.

Stanley Baker and me in *Zulu*.

Zulu hospital scene, also including Ulla Jacobsson. [© Paramount Pictures. All rights reserved. Courtesy of Paramount Pictures.]

Zulu group picture, 1964. [© Paramount Pictures. All rights reserved. Courtesy of Paramount Pictures.]

Stanley Baker, Ulla Jacobsson and me. [© Paramount Pictures. All rights reserved. Courtesy of Paramount Pictures.]

The Piz Gloria restaurant at the summit of the Schilthorn, featured in *On Her Majesty's Secret Service*.

Stunt supremo Vic Armstrong received a BAFTA from Sir Richard Attenborough in 2002.

26

A Chinese Puzzle Solved

The following year, 1958, I was offered a contract on another sea film shot in Spain, *John Paul Jones*. But I turned down the offer, because it was discovered that my wife had cancer. There didn't appear to be any other work about at this time, so I was very fearful of how we were going to survive. One day, however, Gus Agosti, a first assistant and one of the best in the business, phoned me. He was working on *The Inn of the Sixth Happiness*, a movie being made for Twentieth Century Fox at the nearby MGM Studios, Borehamwood.

Gus told me that the company was in great difficulties. They required two thousand Chinese extras for the movie and although someone had been working on setting up a crowd register, the situation was in utter chaos. They had thousands of names that didn't match the addresses, agents' telephone numbers or the thousands of photographs which had been taken. Shooting was due to start in a very short time. He offered me the job of co-coordinating the whole thing. Seeing that I had never before had any dealings with Chinese crowd extras, it was a rather daunting job to take over and a tremendous responsibility. But I was very grateful for the offer and felt honoured to have been singled out to solve the problem. I suppose that I had become known as a bit of a wheeler dealer in getting things done, so I accepted the challenge.

I was very impressed by the size of the office I was given at MGM studios. It amused me to think that I was in the very studios where previously I had had great difficulty in even getting past the front gate. For two days I sat there waiting for all the work which had so far been completed to arrive. Without it I couldn't start to solve the problem. It eventually arrived on my desk in a large pile of files containing long lists and hundreds of photographs. By this time I was getting really worried, as time was so short. It took me a further three to four days to realise that the only way to deal with the problem was to scrap everything and start afresh. Facing me was a nightmare.

I decided to see the casting director at Twentieth Century Fox's head office in London. I think that she was glad to see that someone else was now responsible for carrying the can if things were not sorted out in time for the film's start date. I told her that I had to start from scratch, as there was no way in which the files given me could be used. I said that I needed a secretary in the office, a photographer to accompany me on auditions, and the authority to hire audition rooms as and when needed. This was all agreed.

I dumped all the files and photographs I had been given, then contacted all the agents who had Chinese subjects on their books and set up auditions. I was fortunate enough to make contact with Mrs Farmer, who, as far as Chinese children were concerned, was more helpful to me than any of the agents. I signed her up as a chaperone for the children, which was a requirement under London County Council regulations.

The first auditions were held in London. After about the third one, I began to see part of the problem. Although I have a shocking memory for names, I nearly always remember faces. I soon realised that a number of the Chinese people were trying to get booked through several agents under different names. I soon put a stop to that little game. I told those who turned up a second time: 'You have already been booked, and if I see you again you will not work on the picture.' A further complication was remembering Chinese names. The solution to that was to have a master list of names, which gave each agent a block of numbers. In these blocks of numbers would be a certain percentage for males, females, children, old men and old women. In addition to this, I had a further list of Chinese people I had managed to contact direct by approaching Chinese restaurants and asking them to put the word around about my requirements and the conditions of pay. The office telephone was soon ringing non-stop.

The system was simplicity itself. With more than two thousand numbers on file, I could tell from each one if the person was a man, woman, child, old man, or old woman, and whether they came via an agent or from direct contact. These numbers were used for labelling wardrobe costumes, for payment, and for the call sheets. I would go on to the set and be given the numbers to be called the following day, or perhaps some time later. Looking at the numbers, I would say, 'Oh, yes, that's the little girl from such and such an agency.' Production staff used to look at me in absolute amazement, as if I had remembered each individual out of more than two thousand. I had the greatest difficulty not to burst out laughing; it was such a simple system that I could never understand why the production department couldn't follow it.

In the course of the filming, the director, Mark Robson, used to call me to the set to discuss some of the more distinguished-looking members of the crowd whom he required to be in close proximity to the principals in the shooting ahead. He was very meticulous about his crowds. In particular, he had very definite ideas about who he wanted to see as the village elders who would be shot in close up with Robert Donat, the male lead. Each time I went to the set, I carried with me sheets of hardboard onto which I had pinned photographs of new Chinese crowd actors. Robson would pick the ones he needed for the ongoing scenes.

This was fine until I failed to provide the exact type of elderly men he required. This situation carried on for some time, with him getting very irritated with me for not getting it right. I was at my wits' end until one day I came across some very old Japanese men who were interested in working on the film. Fortunately, the boards filled with photographs did not have names, only numbers, so taking a chance, I had the old men photographed. Putting the board bearing their photographs behind the others, I went to Robson on the set. He cast all the boards aside until he came to this particular one. To my utter surprise, he said, 'These are the ones I need.' Secretly I found this quite laughable, for he had let it be known that he was an authority on the subject. He then asked the opinion of his Chinese adviser, who confirmed his choice. So much for the experts! Had the names been included, I would have probably been fired on the spot.

Eventually, I met the whole of the Chinese crowd requirements, but when the big calls were put out, we had trouble getting all of them to the studios on time. They kept getting lost. We solved that problem by laying on a train from London to Borehamwood, then picking them up by coach and bringing them to the studio. It worked like clockwork. After being called from my master list by their numbers, the required crowd artistes on the call list were fitted out at the wardrobe with their individually numbered costumes.

Although they were paid their daily salary by their numbers, they signed for the money using their own name. When it was time for me to leave for Wales to arrange the Chinese crowds on the location, a first assistant was called in to take over the rest of the studio's calls. By this time things were running smoothly, with the secretary knowing the system backwards.

The place to find Chinese extras for the Wales location was Liverpool. I'd never been there before, and I didn't really know where to start. Then I remembered that among the Commandos there had been a Corporal Gubbins, a Liverpudlian who said that he would return to his career in the police. It didn't take me long to trace him, as fortunately he hadn't transferred to another part of the country and was still a policeman in Liverpool. Better still, his department dealt exclusively with the Chinese in the city. He was extremely helpful, and passed my name to the elders of the Chinese community. This enabled me to find without delay all the Chinese extras we needed for the location at Beddgelert. I had much more trouble complying with all the local council's rules and regulations relating to the employment of children. The accommodation had to be approved, the children could only be employed for a certain number of hours, and they had to receive a certain number of hours' schooling. A chaperone had to be allocated to groups of children, and Mrs Farmer here again proved to be a godsend.

One day, I had an advance warning that the Chinese Embassy was not happy with a film which showed how young girls' feet were bound to keep them small, a practice once carried out in China. The embassy wanted to promote China as a modern country and not as it used to be. They went so far as to circulate a false rumour to the effect that during filming the children were inadequately housed and fed, and were working long hours without breaks. Unfortunately the rumour was believed. Coaches were hired to bring all the parents to the location to pick up their children and take them back to Liverpool. The danger was that, once home, the parents would refuse to allow them to return. Had this happened, it would have been a disaster. Not only had the children been established as far as continuity was concerned, but it would have put paid to our chances of finding replacements from Liverpool. There were other considerations, too. The ramparts of a Chinese city had been built on the location. To rebuild such a set at another location would have cost considerable time and money – and where would we find the necessary numbers of Chinese extras as replacements?

On the day when the parents were expected to arrive, we sent all the children off in coaches. The shooting schedule was altered so that filming could continue on scenes where the children were not required. The irate parents arrived and demanded to know where the children were. We told them that we didn't know, because they had been given a day off as a 'thank you' for the work they had done, and the treat was a mystery trip. The parents then visited the children's billets, sampled the food they were being given, and were shown the conditions and regulations laid down by the council; the call sheets were produced as evidence of the times the children had worked on the set. To round off their visit, the parents saw some of the shooting in progress. They all left for home realising that what they had been told was a silly rumour and happy in the knowledge that their children were in safe hands.

There was one further setback. Some of the parents had children with different names due to the fact that while they had the same mothers, some of them had different fathers, and therefore some of the cheques couldn't be cashed. I left it to the accounts department to sort that one out.

Sadly, my wife died during the filming. To enable me to complete my contract on the film, my two children were looked after by my mother and sister. Later, I acquired the services of a housekeeper.

When *The Inn of the Sixth Happiness* finished, we were in for another quiet period. Fortunately an American company by the name of the Danziger came to Borehamwood and set up a studio. Their films were all made for television, and included some action. Although they never employed many stuntmen, when they did, even if it was only for a short duration, it helped the agency keep afloat financially.

Around this time, too, we managed to get a couple of men on the movie *Ferry Boat to Hong Kong*, then later on provided a number of men, who included horse riders, for a Hammer picture, *The Stranglers of Bombay* (1960). There was also the occasional income from the hiring out of our camera cars and sound trucks, which helped. From time to time we were also asked for a Chinese crowd, as it seemed I had established a reputation as the person who had particular experience of recruiting in this field.

One day we were phoned up by British Paramount, who needed

Chinese extras for their forthcoming *Suzie Wong* movie, starring Nancy Kwan in the title role with William Holden as Robert Lomax. Then I had a call from the King Bros asking me to take a small team of the boys to work in the Geisel Gustag Studios at Munich. My brother took over the *Suzie Wong* movie from me, and I left for Germany.

27

A Brush with a Lion

One day at the office I received a call from a lady lion tamer, who was working on a *Tarzan* film, with Gordon Scott playing Tarzan. She told me that previously while she had been on the set at MGM Studios, her representative had put her life in danger. It seems the director had asked if it was possible to snare the lion in a net and haul the animal up in the air, which the representative said was all right.

The net had evidently been disguised and was out of sight, but she had not been informed of what was about to take place. When the lion was caught in the net and hauled up in the air it had gone berserk. With the net lowered, she was faced with the unenviable task of releasing the lion while it was still raging and thrashing about. Despite being in mortal danger, the lion tamer managed to achieve this, and then sacked her representative on the spot.

She was now seeking a new agent, someone she could trust to look after her interests and find her work. Our agency had been recommended to her. I arranged to meet her at Elstree Studios.

On arrival there I spent some time trying to find her dressing room, until Gordon Scott himself came along. I asked him if he knew where I could find the lion tamer. 'In here,' he said, opening a nearby door and pushing me into a room, then quickly shutting the door behind me. It was an incredibly foolhardy thing to do on his part. The lady lion tamer was indeed inside – and so was a bloody great lion, which was jumping about the room. No doubt Scott thought it was a great joke, and expected me to panic and make a quick and frightened exit.

The lion tamer was standing in the middle of the room and I very smartly stepped behind her. She told me that the lion was having his exercise period. As the lion tore around the room, she turned with him, and so did I, always keeping behind her. All the time this was going on, we conversed and I took notes, keeping a wary eye on the animal. It was one of the most bizarre meetings I have ever experienced. Even more strange was that she had her small son sitting in one corner of the room. He was in a wire cage from which he could watch everything going on and he himself was completely visible to the lion. Probably he was being lined up as a future lion tamer.

After what seemed to me an awfully long time, the lion stopped gyrating and lay down on a settee in the room. Still keeping the lion tamer between me and the lion, I slowly reached the door and made my exit. I often wondered how she got the lion from the dressing room onto the set.

Afterwards, while on the set talking to someone I knew, I became conscious of Scott regarding me with a quizzical expression on his face. I was sure that he was dying to know what had transpired after he'd pushed me into the lion tamer's room, and wondered why I hadn't rushed out in sheer fright. The panic was there all right, but I wasn't going to let him know that. Eventually I looked across at him and said casually, 'Oh, thanks for your help,' and then went on talking as if nothing had happened. Right up until the time I left the studios he was still trying to weigh me up.

Unfortunately I never did manage to secure a contract for the lady.

A small film, *The Challenge*, came to my rescue during a quiet period in 1960. The stunt I was required to do was to turn over a police vehicle during a car chase in London. The turnover was to take place at night in a Bayswater square; a very large crowd had assembled to watch the filming. I had done several runs through for the camera, and each time I noticed the crowd had surged forward. I pointed out to a production assistant how dangerous this was, insisting that the people be moved well back.

I started being harangued by the production people to get back to my start point, as daylight was coming soon. I returned to the start point, but from there the camera crew and crowds were out of sight. The streets were watered down, followed by an assistant standing in front of the huge studio lamps and shouting through a megaphone to me to start up. The light was shining straight towards me and making it very difficult for me to see clearly. 'I wonder if they've moved the crowd,' I said to Jock.

I was just getting out of the car to query this when the assistant shouted, 'Everything's ready, start up!' This didn't really answer my question, but I got back into the car, started up, and on 'Action!' drove straight for the light, turning sharply to the right and straight on to the position where the car was supposed to turn over. At the very last moment, after I had cleared the light, I saw to my horror that the crowd were even further forward than they had been before. In the split second that remained to me I slammed on the brakes, swung the wheel over and, skidding sideways, managed to miss the crowd. But, unable to stop, I crashed into the camera platform. Fortunately this was protected by scaffolding and a wooden barrier, behind which were the camera crew on a platform with their equipment. The impact nearly resulted in them being thrown off.

Jock and I were furious, and berated the production assistant, who had obviously been under a lot of pressure from the producer and been panicked into giving the go ahead. Last-minute rush and panic can always have the potential for disaster. It was now too late to reset the shot and the unit packed up for the night. The shot was set up a few nights later at Twickenham, where the crowd was smaller and this time kept far away from the scene of the action. When the stunt was completed, I did a publicity shot with Jayne Mansfield against the upturned car.

28

The Guns of Navarone

This film which was made in 1961, was a long film, and the length of time it took to make can be gauged by the fact that I worked on it first in Athens, followed by some months in Rhodes, then there was a break while I flew from there direct to Israel to work on *Cast a Giant Shadow*, starring John Wayne and Kirk Douglas. When I returned to England three months later, *The Guns of Navarone* was still in production and I went back to work on it at Shepperton Studios.

Carl Foreman, who was the executive director, also wrote the screenplay. Even before the film had started he showed what he could achieve using the power of the film industry and his personal influence. Rhodes was only twelve miles from the Turkish coast and under a treaty signed by Italy, Greece and Turkey at the end of the Second World War, no military, naval or air forces were to be stationed on the island. Carl had secured the full cooperation of the Greek government though, so that during filming not only did one thousand troops land on the island, but tanks, armoured cars and military vehicles of all types were brought in as well. There were also some spotter aircraft and naval boats in the area.

The company took over an unfinished hotel named the Miramar, and as rooms became ready, so they were occupied. A huge production unit was assembled in London, and flown out to Athens for several weeks' shooting there. At the completion of the shoot in Athens, it was flown on to Rhodes, where the main shooting was scheduled. As with many movies, scenes were shot out of sequence. A start was made just outside Athens in rough mountainous country – the scene where the Allied Commando raiding party, having successfully landed on Navarone, have been detected and are being pursued by the German army. High up in the hills, Anthony Quinn is sniping at the Germans in a delaying action to allow the rest of the party to escape. In one particular scene, Quinn is seen taking aim and firing from a long distance at one of the German troops. Directing the scene was Sandy McKendrick. The German being shot was Jimmy Lodge, one of the stuntmen. To make the shot more dramatic, the director decided to attach a bungee rope to Jimmy, activated by special-effects men, so that when hit he would be thrown back at high speed among the rocks. Obviously this required absolutely precise timing.

After the scene had been shot about six times, the timing was still not right and Jimmy was getting heavily bruised. He shouted to the director, 'Why don't you let me take my own time without the bungee?' As nothing had worked up until now, they might as well try, was the reply. The scene was reset and shot. Jimmy, with perfect timing, got the shot in the can. As well as bruises, Jimmy had sustained a number of cuts and abrasions. Infuriated, he shouted, 'Sandy McKendrick, you're a ****!'

Some other scenes were shot in Greece before we moved to Rhodes. It was here that we were to film the raiding party landing before they climb the cliffs thought to be unassailable. They are disguised as fishermen in a traditional Greek fishing boat. When still some way from Navarone, they are spotted by a German patrol boat, which eventually draws alongside. As the German boarding party jumps aboard, the Commandos suddenly reveal their arms and open fire, catching the Germans completely unaware. A high explosive is then thrown down an open hatch on the German vessel to explode below decks and sink it. We stuntmen were both the boarding party and the German sailors shot on the open decks of the patrol boat.

Prior to this scene, when Quinn and I weren't needed, we played chess. We had been playing one game for quite some time when he commented, 'Joe; you've got two moves left.' I said there was only one. Quinn insisted that there were two. 'One,' I repeated, 'and it's checkmate.' He looked flabbergasted, as it was a very rare thing for me to win. 'OK,' he said, 'but let's go back to see what would have happened if I hadn't made that last move of mine.' I refused. 'If you want another game let's set it up,' I told him.

Quinn was now being called to work on the other boat. 'All right, Joe, you've won, but bring the board over on to the other boat with me and we'll see what would have happened if I hadn't made my last move,' he insisted. Again I said no. The calls for

Quinn were becoming louder and he had to leave. He was still calling for me to accompany him and I continued to refuse. That night I got a right telling off from the director, who said that because of me Quinn had been difficult all day.

Once the sequence of us aboard the German craft had been filmed, we were all transferred to the film boat for a long shot of the blowing up of the patrol boat. To simulate the explosion coming from inside the hull, a steel plate was hung over the side to protect the hull, and in front of this the explosive was suspended. On deck the special-effects team had rigged fires. What had been overlooked was that when the boat was under way, the steel plate was washed towards the stern, so when the explosion took place it actually blew a hole in the side of the boat. None of the crew left aboard to man the boat was aware of this until after the shot had been completed, and it was spotted when the camera boat came alongside her.

We shouted to Tony, the skipper, that there was a hole in the hull. During the rehearsals leading up to this scene, we had come to know him fairly well. He'd got used to our joking, so he ignored our shouts, thinking it was another of our pranks. But when we shouted again, this time he did look at the hull. Tony immediately shouted orders to his crew who, after taking a look for themselves, rushed below deck. We were impressed by what we thought was prompt emergency action on their part. In a remarkably short time, however, they all appeared above deck carrying their suitcases and possessions, which they threw down on to the camera boat deck. A case belonging to one of the boat's officers burst open to reveal cutlery, cups and saucers and various other items belonging to the location caterers, as well as bits of special-effects equipment.

Several of us jumped aboard Tony's boat to help move heavy equipment to the port side, in order to tilt the boat over and try to lift the hole above the water level. The boat then limped back to port. We heard later that Tony had been jailed for endangering the boat and held for some time until the cost of the damage was paid; an additional fee was included for the time the boat was out of commission.

Back on land, scenes were shot of German army movements, which involved dispatch riders, staff cars, tanks, and all the paraphernalia of an army on the move. We learned that one of the Greek dispatch riders had been badly injured. Later on we were told that as he could no longer work, his Greek army pay would be stopped. Whether this was true or not, we never did find out, but we decided anyway to have a whip round for him in the unit. When the money collected was given to him in hospital, he evidently burst into tears with gratitude, as the amount raised was apparently equivalent to several years' army pay.

On one of our free days, Cecil Ford, the production manager, sent for me to enquire who our Equity representative was. When I said that there wasn't one on the unit, he asked, 'Well, who knows most about the rules then?' I told him that would be Jimmy Lodge. 'Well send him to me, as there are one or two things on the film to sort out.' I sent Jimmy off to see him, and then thought no more about it.

As it was out of season on Rhodes at that time of year, there were only three things you could do if you had any free time: you could stay in the hotel, go to the Voice of America Club, to which we had an open invitation, or go to a club called Baby's. Someone once pointed out Baby to me. He turned out to be a small Greek man, who appeared to be about ninety years of age. While still undecided as to where to spend my leisure time on this particular day, I happened to pass the huge conference room of the hotel, which was glass-sided, enabling you to see at a glance what was going on inside. To my surprise I saw Jimmy Lodge at the head of the large conference table. Sitting around it listening to him were Gregory Peck, Anthony Quinn, David Niven, Anthony Quayle, Stanley Baker, Irene Papas, Gia Scala and James Daren. I found out later that the discussion was about seventh-day working and overtime pay. It seems that at one stage Cecil Ford opened the door and asked if he could join the discussion, but Peck told him, 'No, not yet. We're still talking to our Equity representative.' All Equity contracts abroad were based on six working days, which meant overtime rates of pay for all the principals would have been horrendous. The outcome of Jimmy's interpretation of the rules was immediately apparent to us stuntmen, who were also Equity members. Up until then we had always been the first people on call and almost the last to leave the location each day. From now on, we qualified for overtime pay if we worked longer than the agreed hours. The following morning, we received a later call and were allocated a faster car to take us to and from the location. Immediately we finished for the day, the car was there ready and waiting to return us to the hotel pronto. We were all very grateful to Jimmy.

The Guns of Navarone was a real action picture, and establishing the highly professional stunt team that played such a vital part in the success of the movie can be regarded as a feather in our cap. As well as the scenes shot as we climbed the cliffs, I was called on later to do a ninety-foot fall into the sea. It was the scene where Peck and Niven have arrived in the gun position, and I am the German abseiling down to enter the mouth of the cave and attack them. I think it is Peck who spots and shoots me. The fall went well, and I thought that I had made a clean entry to the sea. When I got back to the hotel that night, however, I found I was bruised black from hip to ankle.

There's another stage in the film where David Niven, the explosives expert, has successfully laid the charges to blow up the guns. He and Gregory Peck then both escape by diving from the mouth of the cave into the sea. The fall was about eighty feet and doubling for them were Jock Easton and Bob Simmons. I didn't see the actual falls, as I was doing something else at the time, but I did arrive back soon afterwards. Both had been picked up out of the sea, and were lying on the rocks in the sun. Jock, who was then about sixty, was not looking at all happy. He had received quite a knock on hitting the sea. When I looked into his eyes, I thought to myself, yes, Jock, that was your swan song; your stunting days are over. Though Jock continued doing action work for some time after, he never again got involved in a major stunt.

In another scene, Peck and his party are being sniped at by two Germans from their vantage point in the top of a minaret. The minaret was about seventy feet high and was climbed by means of an internal staircase. Once at the top, you went through an opening on to a circular concrete platform, about three feet wide; it was perfectly flat, but there was no handrail. Bob Simmons and I, as the snipers, were shot in fairly quick succession, and had to fall on a very narrow bed below. It was vital for Bob, as the first sniper to fall, to get away from the bed immediately after he had hit it. As the second sniper, I had no opportunity to see what was happening below and had to rely on him getting clear. Harold Buck was the production manager, and responsible for all stunt adjustments. He thought Bob and I were asking too high a figure for the stunt. After much haggling, Harold said, 'I'll come to the top with you both. If you move around, Joe, to the spot where the fall is to take place, I'll come round as well, as long as the Bob stands the other side of me. I'm not going to look down until we reach that spot, and then we'll agree a price.' So we climbed the stairs to the top of the minaret and stepped out on the platform. We told him when to look down. 'You're both mad – I agree to your price. Now get me back,' he said. In retrospect, I think that at that moment we could easily have asked him for twice as much.

By this time I had met my new wife and was able to bring my two children back home.

29

The Longest Day

In 1962 John Sullivan phoned to let me know he was stunt advisor on the movie *The Longest Day*, and that he'd arranged an audition and he wanted me to be on it. At that point I wasn't familiar with Cornelius Ryan's book on which the film was based. When I did come to read his account of D-Day, I was pleasantly surprised to find included in the book a war cameraman's picture of Peter Kelly and I carrying a stretcher. There was also mention of Lord Lovat and No. 4 Commando.

After being picked at the audition I spoke to Elmo Williams, the associate producer, who was American. I said that I was pleased to work on the film as I had been in No. 4 Commando. 'Everyone was in No. 4!' he snapped. I was very annoyed at the time, but on reflection, knowing the film industry as I did, I guessed that a number of actors had claimed they were in the Commandos, hoping that it would assist them in obtaining a part in the film.

The Longest Day was certainly a star-studded movie. Heading the list were John Wayne, Henry Fonda, Robert Ryan, Rod Steiger, Robert Wagner, Mel Ferrer, Eddie Albert, Red Buttons, Richard Burton, Peter Lawford and Christopher Lee, with a large supporting cast, which included the then relatively unknown Sean Connery playing the part of a British soldier.

The movie showed shots of the British, American and German armies. The French contribution was depicted as being a major part of No. 4 Commando. It was hardly an army, but it was highlighted in the production. On arrival at the location, we were given a generous location allowance and told to find our own accommodation. I had travelled down to Ouistreham by car with Ken Buckle, one of the stuntmen, and suggested to him that we should stay in the Hotel Normandy, as it was a Commando rendez-vous after we had landed at Ouistreham on D-Day.

We spent some time touring around trying to find the Normandy

197

hotel. We finally stopped and agreed that we would book into the first hotel we came to. But on looking up, Ken and I found that we had stopped right outside the very hotel we were searching for. We went in and ordered a couple of drinks, and I introduced myself as being a former member of No. 4. The landlady was a French heroine, a former member of the Maquis who had lost a leg during the war. She produced a folder with a great number of wartime photographs. Ken opened it up and, lo and behold, there on the top of the pile was a picture of me carrying a stretcher. He at once accused me of knowing where the hotel was in the first place, and that the photograph was all part of me setting him up. It was a great laugh, but in fact it was all purely accidental.

After we had visited the production office, received our location allowance and had our fittings at wardrobe, we took a look around Ouistreham. Naturally the whole place had changed over the years. It took me a while to find the wall I had sheltered behind when we were being mortared by the Germans; on the other side of the wall I found a memorial to No. 4 Commando. Eventually I recognised the long road up which we had had to travel en route to Pegasus Bridge, but I couldn't recognise anything else.

One day Lord Lovat himself arrived to be entertained by the film producer, Daryl F. Zanuck. I was very surprised and pleased when he recognised me immediately and called me over for a chat. In the film Peter Lawford portrayed Lovat. Later at lunch – a two-hour session in a huge marquee – I walked by Lovat and Zanuck, who were sitting together. 'There's Powell, one of my sergeants,' said Lovat as I passed. While his remark was not of great importance to anyone else, it was personally very gratifying to me to be thus pointed out.

In the scenes shot at Ouistreham there were times when we stuntmen were in British Army uniform and others where we were German troops. A number of French stuntmen had been contracted, although funnily enough they were nearly always cast as Germans. I was the only one on the unit who had served in No. 4 Commando and found myself reliving my wartime experiences. The attack on the six-inch gun battery we silenced was re-enacted, as was our crossing of the Pegasus Bridge, followed by No. 4 making their way inland to take up their position on the extreme left flank of the British army.

We moved location to Pont du Hoc, where the Americans had

landed during the war. Here the American Rangers joined us, bringing with them a large range of American army assault craft, which they made available to the film. This was of tremendous value to the company, as there was no way in which such equipment could have been duplicated authentically. Zanuck, reputed to be the biggest shareholder in Twentieth Century Fox, daily arrived by helicopter at each location.

On D-Day, No. 4 had landed on the beach, whereas the Americans had to scale cliffs before they could advance inland. At the tops of these cliffs were German pillboxes and heavily reinforced gun emplacements. Fortunately for the purposes of filming, these fortifications were still in existence. Looking at them I could well imagine the heavy casualties that were suffered in overcoming them.

When returning to our hotel after finishing rehearsal one day, I recognised Commandant Kieffer, who had headed the French contingent of No. 4. I went up to him and we had a chat. Kieffer, like Lovat, was also featured in the film. He hadn't met Zanuck, so I took him back to the location where the production was discussing the next day's shooting. I went up to Zanuck and asked him, 'Would you like to meet Commandant Kieffer in person?' Zanuck was highly delighted with the introduction and got the stills cameraman to take photographs with the two of them together; then he took Kieffer to other locations to ask his advice on the authenticity of what they proposed doing.

On several occasions before a day's shooting at Pont du Hoc, I heard the Rangers running along the beach chanting, but I couldn't make out the words. One morning I got close enough to the point where they passed so that I could hear them. I found it quite amusing. They were shouting, 'Make my muscles big and strong, big and strong' over and over again. Often at the end of the day after filming we met them for a drink. They were great fellows and we got on well with them.

The rehearsals for this part of the film were extensive and lasted for several days. These periods were lengthened even more by bad weather. At one stage while rehearsing their landing from the sea, the Rangers dragged up an American patterned anchor, obviously a relic of the original D-Day force. They proudly carried the anchor back to where their whole force was housed in tents and located it in a place of honour in the middle of the camp.

One afternoon it was very foggy and too bad even to rehearse. Everyone sat under cover waiting for the fog to lift. All the Americans were in their tents out of sight, so we decided to play a joke on them. Under cover of the fog we crept out and nicked their anchor, which we carried back to our own lines and hid under some props. We then hurried back to our tent and carried on talking as if nothing had happened. It was not long before the anchor was missed. Tom, a very large PT sergeant from the Rangers whom we knew well, stopped at our tent. Obviously we were the prime suspects. 'What do you think about the weather?' we asked him, 'Do you reckon that we'll eventually get some rehearsals in?' Tom said nothing, but scrutinised each and every one of us carefully before leaving. Later on the fog lifted and we were all called for rehearsals. Some Rangers were missing, however. We found out later that a number of them had been left behind as a fatigue party detailed to find the anchor. They practically tore the camp apart until they found it. No one said a word and it was as if the episode had never occurred.

After completing this section of the film we moved to a further location named Colombey-les-Deux-Églises, the town where Charles de Gaulle lived. It was here during an airborne assault on the town during the war that an American paratrooper's parachute caught on a church spire. Unable to release himself, he pretended to be dead and, while hanging there, had a bird's eye view of the battle for the town between the Allies and the Germans.

With the end of filming on location, the company gave a party for the film unit, the Rangers and the stuntmen. On arriving at the hotel which was the venue, we were ushered into a large room where we found some of the Rangers. Producing bottles of whisky, they said that they thought it would be a good idea if we had a drink together before the main party took place. Glasses were passed round and Tom, the sergeant, gave a toast to our cooperation and friendship. We knocked back the drink, only to find it was cold tea. Immediately afterwards a bugle sounded the charge and in rushed the remainder of the Rangers with one of then carrying the Stars and Stripes Flag. We were all figuratively made prisoners. They had waited a long time to exact their revenge for their anchor being nicked. It was a good laugh. 'Take the flag away and secure it before this lot nick that as well,' Tom said. They were a great bunch and we had a lot of fun working with them.

30

Arabs and Zulus

In 1962 I was very pleased to be able to work on the movie *Lawrence of Arabia*. Pleased is too mild a word really – I was highly delighted. T. E. Lawrence had been one of my schoolboy heroes. As well as reading *Seven Pillars of Wisdom* by Lawrence himself, I had read *Orientations* by Sir Ronald Storrs and the works of many other authors, including Lowell Thomas. While no one could find fault with Peter O'Toole's acclaimed film portrayal of Lawrence, as far as I was concerned he didn't physically fit the bill; he was far too tall for Lawrence.

The film, directed by the legendary David Lean, was undoubtedly a classic. It was shot in Saudi Arabia, Morocco, Spain and England and took some fifteen months to complete. I worked on the battle scenes shot in Morocco at Ouarzazate, and was only on the location for one month, but as far as I was concerned it was a most memorable time.

Ouarzazate, we were told, had once been a French Foreign Legion punishment station. Since that time a small hotel had been built there, but there was no room for the stuntmen, so we were accommodated in tents nearby. Most of the men had no experience of being under canvas, and as a result did not adjust the tents' guy ropes when necessary to meet the changing weather conditions. A couple of times they paid for this by having their tents and belongings blown away – never to be seen again – in the frequent sand and wind storms. Personally I much preferred living in a tent to the hotel.

Lawrence's Arab army was portrayed by a tribe known as the Blue Arabs. There were thousands of them mounted on camels or on horseback. On one occasion it had taken all day getting them into position. I seem to remember that this was the third day that had been spent lining up this particular shot. There they sat, under the blazing sun, waiting for the action to commence. The unit personnel were provided with ice-cold drinks and snacks throughout the day, but no provision had been made for the Arabs. This particular day, the Arab chief rose and without a word mounted his camel and rode off into the distance with his tribesmen following suit. They did not reappear for three days. Obviously negotiations had taken place, because when they did reappear several water bowsers were provided for them. Generally speaking, film companies take very good care of their employees, and in this case somebody had obviously slipped up, but on this scale it was inexcusable. The three days' filming lost must have cost a fortune – just for the sake of hiring a few water bowsers.

My daughter, who is now a film assistant accountant, was working in Ouarzazate comparatively recently. No doubt because of the number of films shot there it has become a tourist attraction and many hotels have been built since. In no way does it now resemble the place where we experienced a primitive way of life.

Back then it could be a violent and dangerous place. For example, one day an officer rushed out of the bar unbuttoning his revolver as he went. After a while, a single shot was heard. The story we eventually gathered was that a French woman was being raped. No one on the unit talked about the incident or asked any questions. While working in these primitive countries it's best, as they say, to keep your eyes down and mind your own business. Just get on with your own job.

Ouarzazate was then a nondescript place with just its hotel, but the vast desert encircling it had a beauty of its own and held a great fascination for me.

The film *Zulu* was made in 1964 and based upon historical fact. In 1879, King Cetewayo's warriors slaughtered a British force of 1,200 men at Isandhlwana. Cetewayo then led his army of four thousand Zulus in an attack on Rorke's Drift, a small British outpost manned by only eight officers and ninety-seven other ranks, of which thirty-six were on the sick list. The regiment involved was the 14th Foot, later the 2nd Battalion, South Wales Borderers.

The film was produced by Stanley Baker and Cy Enfield, with Stanley in the leading role of Lieutenant John Chard, Royal Engineers, and Cy as director. The whole film unit was flown out to South Africa to re-create this historic battle in which eleven Victoria Crosses were awarded. It was a movie in which three stuntmen were given acting roles. Larry Taylor was Hughes, John Sullivan played Stephenson, and I was Sergeant Windridge. I was persuaded to play the part, although I was reluctant at first because I had no acting experience. Once I got into the role, however, I really enjoyed myself. Then came some bad luck. I was bitten by a poisonous spider and my leg blew up like a balloon. I had to go to Ladysmith Hospital for an operation to remove the poison. My stay there coincided with the main part of my role, so that when I returned to the unit, it was too late to have it included.

The second unit director was Bob Porter, who had at one time worked with us as a stunt artiste. Cetewayo was played by Chief Buthelezi of the Zulus, who used to arrive for filming by helicopter. Prior to the shooting, John Sullivan and I had to train the Zulus in fight routines. As filming was in a restricted area, an encampment was built for them roughly six miles from the spot designated as Rorke's Drift. To reach our training area, the Zulus used to have a shuffling half-walk, half-run way of covering the distance, accompanied by the most wonderful chant that announced their coming long before they came into sight.

At first we carried out the instruction some distance from the main location. We formed the warriors into a half circle, and then called them out two at a time. We took one each. Initially all the Zulus eyed us with obvious suspicion, no doubt thinking that we were going to show them up in an inferior light. After a few days, however, they greeted us with huge smiles and an eagerness to participate in the rehearsals. They got so enthusiastic that they could hardly wait for their turn to rehearse. I lost count of how many we trained, but as there were only the two of us, at the end of the day we were both well knocked out.

After a while they fully entered into the spirit of things by incorporating their own traditional moves. One of these constituted a challenge, in which they jumped up, banged their shields on the ground a couple of times, then kicked the shields before coming at us and carrying out the routine we'd drilled into them. It would have been impossible to give them their own individual routines, so they all had a standard routine to follow when engaging in combat with any of the cast playing British soldiers. This eliminated any dead spots and kept things moving. And the routine was not noticeable during the shooting, as the moving camera picked up the action in different stages.

The company also placed under contract some body builders from Johannesburg, whom we trained to fight with our principal artistes. We found all the Zulus great chaps, and enjoyed working with them. One night, however, John, Bob Porter, an interpreter, and I were sent down to the Zulu camp where some trouble had been reported. We found that one of them had taken drugs and was running amok, and threatening the others. We grabbed him and took him to his bunk, to which Bob handcuffed him. As we were about to leave, I said, 'Bob, we can't leave him like that. The others will take their revenge out on him, and he'll be unable to defend himself.' We released him and took him to the hut where the body builders were housed, away from the main Zulu encampment. We asked them to look after him. As we walked away, he started to scream again, but not for long. Suddenly there was silence – he'd undoubtedly been looked after.

The following morning we learned that the last time white men entered a Zulu compound, they were never seen again. 'Thanks for telling us,' we said. Perhaps the good relations that we had established with the Zulus during our rehearsal period had stood us in good stead.

One day it had been raining, and we had been sheltering in one of the huts built as accommodation for the unit. The air was beginning to get thick with people smoking. As it had stopped raining, I decided to go out for a walk and get some fresh air. As I walked along, somebody else who had the same idea emerged from one of the other huts and came towards me. Our paths were likely to converge, but as I moved over to avoid colliding with him, so did he. As we got closer still, I again took evasive action and he did likewise, so we ended up standing face to face. As it was obvious he was doing this for a purpose, I said nothing but waited for him to say something. 'You don't remember me, do you?' he asked. I admitted that I didn't. He then added that I had given him his first job in the film industry on the film *The Steel Bayonet*. I realised then that it was none other than Michael Caine.

Before *The Steel Bayonet*, Michael had served in the Gloucester Regiment in Korea. When he was demobbed he hadn't any work to go to in Civvy Street, then he heard that our office was recruiting Equity men with Army experience for the film. It was at a time when I had laid it down that our agency would employ only Equity members.

During the battle scenes, I had to devise firing and movement to cover both advance and retreat. Just how close – or well off the mark – this was to what actually happened in the real battle of Rorke's Drift, nobody will hopefully ever find out, but the main thing was it worked. *Zulu* made Michael Caine a star, and secured Hollywood contracts for Nigel Green, who was in the role of Colour Sergeant Bourne.

One night after the day's shooting, the company put on a showing for the Zulus of scenes in which they had appeared. It was great to see their obvious delight at seeing themselves in action on film. The film ends with the Zulus having given up the fight and about to disappear over the hill. At the top they halt, turn towards Rorke's Drift and wave their shields in acknowledgement of the bravery of their enemies. It was a classic and dramatic finish to one of the most exciting engagements ever filmed.

In August 2004, I was invited to attend a show put on by the Anglo/Zulu Society, at the Artillery Museum, Woolwich Arsenal. The place was impressive. The parade ground is apparently the largest in Europe, large enough to land a plane. The walls of the main hall were covered in artillery guns covering centuries of battles around the world. One of the conference rooms was solely taken up with trophies. There was a grand ornate staircase, and the dining room had three huge tables at least sixty feet long. From the ceiling hung five huge chandeliers, and the walls were covered in portraits of past generals. The whole building wouldn't have shamed Buckingham Palace.

The show was for the public, and I was amazed at how large the crowds were. On both days there must have been 2,000 people in attendance. After forty years the popularity of the film seems to have increased. On display were the two VC medals awarded to Lt Bromhead and Lt Chard, plus other artefacts from the Zulu war. Zulu dancers entertained the crowds and got children to participate. It was a great success.

In the main hall, James Booth, who played Hook, and myself, were signing autographs. A number of the crowd said they recognised me from the film. Perhaps I have now left some of my own footprints in the sands of time.

31

A Touch of Eastern Promise

Some work came our way from the American producers the King Brothers, with the 1963 movie *Captain Sinbad*, which was shot in Munich. They didn't pay us fortunes, but we were glad to have a contracted figure for a few months' work. They did, however, pay out large sums on set design and in salaries to their art department. I found the whole way they conducted their film production strange to say the least. They phoned their mother in the States every day without fail, to keep her up to date with progress. Then, in the mornings when we were in make-up, they brought us in little packages of croissants and butter. As it seemed an unusual thing to do, I ventured to ask one of the brothers where the food came from. He told me that they considered the hotel they were staying in was charging them too much, so they were trying to get their money's worth.

They also refused to pay for the microbus I was using to transport the boys to and from the studios. They maintained that the airfares we had received covered the cost of the hire of the vehicle. Had we used the money to fly out instead of motoring to Germany, however, they would then have had to hire transport. But they knew they had us over a barrel, and as far as they were concerned that was the end of the argument.

While in Munich, I bought some skis, ski boots and ski clothing from a huge sports shop named Sports Scheck. I decided on my return to the hotel to go out into the hills to try them out. Some of the boys decided to come with me to watch the fun. We had just left our vehicle and started to walk up the hill to where this 'experiment' was to take place, when three Mercedes cars skidded to a halt by us. Out of one jumped none other than John Huston. We shook hands and had a brief chat before he hurriedly left to keep an appointment. Noticing the skis, his parting words were, 'Showing them how to do it, eh, Joe?' He obviously was under the impression that I was doing just that. I was pleased there wasn't time for me to enlighten him.

The film action work took place on Captain Sinbad's ship, in an Eastern potentate's palace and within caves, where a mythical magician was confronted who could kill people by pointing his finger, which emitted a flash of high-voltage electricity. I was one of his victims, and to create an authentic effect, the special-effects department concealed a smoke pot under my costume to be set off by the electric charge from the magician's finger. In the scene, I was filmed wading through a cave in mud up to my knees. When the time came for action and the charge was set off, I was to fall dead into the mud and remain there for the duration of the shot. I knew I had to take a deep breath if I was to lie perfectly still. Unfortunately after the charge had been set off, when I took the deep breath I inhaled the raw smoke. I had no sooner fallen under the mud than I was struggling for breath, squirming about trying to force some air into my lungs and clear them of the smoke. I thought I was about to die. It all looked realistic on camera and the crew thought I was overacting a little at the time. I just about made it to the point when the camera stopped rolling and I didn't properly recover for a week.

In the studio, filming the scene in the emir's palace involved about thirty men on horseback. When the special-effects crew turned on a fountain suddenly, the horses took fright, and in seconds we riders were all over the set trying to regain control. When we finally got the horses settled again, it was decided to do without the fountains until a later date. While the camera was turning and panning in this scene, however, huge doors were opened to a fanfare and an elephant waddled in. At the sight of the huge beast the horses panicked, and once again rampaged all over the set, scattering the crowds on foot and camera crew, and wreaking havoc with the special effects. Worse was to come. The elephant lifted its trunk and trumpeted. The sound was magnified in the confined space and this time the horses went absolutely berserk.

My horse, which had started to tremble like mad at the sight of the elephant, madly scrambled to get away when it trumpeted, its hooves skidding on the slippery floor. I was thrown, but I scrambled up quickly and knelt on the horse's neck, and stayed there until the elephant was taken off the set with all of the crowd artistes, and the horse had quietened down. The owner of the horses appeared and exploded with rage, shouting at the riders to take their mounts off the set, and the scene was cancelled.

In the first place I hadn't known about the elephant, but even if I had it probably wouldn't have occurred to me that it was going to create such mayhem. But come to think about it, isn't there a story in history about a certain Hannibal who routed a Roman army of men on foot and horsemen with his elephants...?

I thoroughly enjoyed our few weeks in Germany, with the skiing, the mountains, and Munich itself, but all good things come to an end. We returned to England to face a further quiet period for our agency.

32

More Swashbuckling

Hammer Films produced a swashbuckling pirate film, *Devil Ship Pirates*, in 1964. As to be expected from Hammer, the movie was a very imaginative production. The story was of a ship of the Spanish Armada running aground on the English coast. Christopher Lee, her captain, seals off the area to convince local people that Spain has conquered England. The Hammer ship was constructed on forty-gallon drums, and all the sea action took place on a water-filled sandpit close to Hammer Studios. How, you might ask, could this possibly be realistic enough to depict a ship aground on the English coast? I was about to find out.

I accepted a job Tony Keys, the producer, offered me as an assistant to their naval advisor, who was an ex-submarine captain. The captain and I drove to the sandpit where the ship was being constructed. As soon as we saw the mock-up we were both very impressed. The art department had done a fantastic job, assisted by two ex-naval riggers, of building a three-masted vessel with no sails, masts or rigging above the main courses. On being introduced to those involved, we congratulated them on the work they had achieved. They explained that the ship could be trimmed by means of water tanks and pumps aboard. The expertise of the ex-submariner naval advisor was needed when it came to pumping the water where needed. They had also fitted buoyancy tanks with ballast tanks above them. We queried whether they meant the other way round, with the ballast tanks below. The art department technicians were most indignant at our suggestion, and assured us that their insurance company had approved the whole plans.

As we were driving back to the studios, I said to the naval advisor, 'You know that they've not got it right. When things do go wrong it'll be on your head because you've viewed the mock-up and, having said nothing, everyone will assume that it has your approval. You must write a memo at once laying out the facts to cover yourself.' As far as I know, he took my advice.

In the film the ship is shown running aground in heavy fog, which was activated by special effects. This enabled the ship to be filmed on water with the fog obscuring the surrounding area and disguising the fact that the mock-up was only partly rigged. The ship could be seen moving through the water and eventually running aground when it reached the other side of the sandpit. Once tied up along a makeshift harbourside, the ship looked one-hundred-per-cent authentic. The whole idea and concept was fantastically ingenious.

A few days later we went down to the sandpit to see the ship craned onto the water. Cables from two heavy cranes were already attached and when everything was set, lifting commenced – or nearly did. The engines of the cranes were roaring away and the jibs were shaking under the effort, but the ship was too heavy, and a third crane was needed. After a couple of days the extra crane arrived and this time, although all three cranes were still labouring under the weight, the operation was successful and the ship was placed on the water.

We stood watching the ship, which to our amazement appeared to be totally stable and upright despite our misgivings. We were walking back to the car park and some distance from the sandpit, when we heard loud cries of alarm behind us. Turning round, we saw that the ship was at an acute angle and only prevented from capsizing because she was still held by the lifting cables. We had been right after all. There was more delay until someone hit on the idea of fitting a pontoon as an outrigger. Shooting commenced and everything worked well.

The outrigger also provided additional space for camera, sound and riggers' equipment to be stored when not required on deck during shooting. One afternoon, while the ship was being shot in the middle of the sandpit, the tea boat arrived. Everything was also being unloaded on to the pontoon. Somebody on deck shouted, 'The tea's here!', and people came over to get served. The additional weight was just too much and the whole thing turned turtle. This proved to be quite dangerous, as the sandpit was very deep. A tarpaulin had been fitted to cover all the equipment in case of rain, and when the pontoon turned turtle, the people on it were trapped underneath. Some swam to the side of the sandpit, while others were picked up by the small boat in which we ferried artistes and equipment to the ship when she was in the middle of the sandpit. After a hurried head count, much to our relief we found that everyone had got to safety.

In order to stage the shots in the film where the ship is being towed in the fog, the rowers bent to their oars with a towing line disappearing into the murk behind them. To simulate the forward movement of the ship, the director got the crew aboard to look as though they were peering ahead, while the fog was blown past them. The ship was in fact tied up and stationary.

The mock-up of the ship is an example of the ingenuity and inventiveness of Hammer productions. From the start the whole project caught the imagination of other film producers, and other contracts for the ship's use were being considered by Hammer. After the accident with the pontoon, however, all offers were withdrawn.

It's a fact that Christopher Lee was better known throughout the Far East than most American stars, and similarly the Hammer Film productions were more familiar to film fans in that part of the world than movies made in Hollywood.

The *High Wind in Jamaica* location in 1965 was, for my brother Eddie and me, an enjoyable place in which to be filming, with a lovely hotel and good beach in this beautiful country. It was also great to be working with Tony Quinn again.

Most of the filming took place on a sailing boat acting as a pirate ship, although a number of scenes, such as those in and around the pirate hideout, were shot ashore. The ship's crew was made up of sailors from the Cayman Islands. Although just as black skinned as the Jamaicans, they all spoke with a Scottish accent. Apparently donkey's years ago, a Scottish ship was sunk off the Caymans. There was no hope of the survivors returning to Scotland, so the islands became their home; hence the Scottish accents. The Cayman Islanders are renowned for their sailing skill.

As usual, when we were not required in any of the set ups, Quinn would grab me for a game of chess. We played so often, mostly with him winning, that it became hard work. Once when the unit was working ashore and neither my brother Eddie nor I were needed, I decided that I needed a break from playing chess, so we hid away from Quinn. We told nobody where we were going apart from the first assistant in case we should be needed. Our hiding place was on the top floor of one of the houses rented by the film company. We had only been there a couple of hours when the door opened – Quinn had found us.

'Oh, so that's where you are,' he said. He was clutching a chessboard, of course, which he started to set up with the pieces. There was no escape from Quinn. To say that he was a chess fanatic is an understatement.

One day when shooting ashore, the company hired a British sailor – we found out later that he had jumped ship – to assist in holding up traffic while the cameras were in action. One scene took some time, and when the traffic was at last allowed to proceed, one car stopped right in front of camera. The driver got out, furious at having been held up. Perhaps this was understandable, but he picked on this chap and really began to give him a hard time. A furious argument started and the hired man walked away to avoid further trouble. The driver, still berating him and calling him all the names under the sun, followed him. A fight started when the motorist caught up with him behind some houses. The sailor was more than capable of taking care of himself, and gave the driver a thorough thrashing.

Unfortunately local bystanders witnessed the outcome, and soon a baying mob was pursuing the sailor. All the local women started to make a shrill sound through their noses, which seemed to stir up the men. It is a weird, unsettling sound, and one that I have heard on occasion in other countries. The hired help ran straight into the house where the production office had been set up, flew up a flight of stairs, rushed into a room, bolted the door and barricaded himself inside. The premises were quickly filled with a large number of very irate men screaming for blood. The turmoil brought a Jamaican policeman, a 'special', with large red stripes on his trousers. As he entered the building he started undoing the strap on his revolver holster – it was obvious that he meant business. The crowd immediately fell silent, and backed off leaving a clear path. The policeman went up the stairs, turned around and just stood facing the mob. Moments later the local magistrate arrived and escorted the sailor out of the building. The mob made no attempt to impede their progress.

Before shooting could recommence after the incident, a huge crowd started to assemble, expressing their disappointment at being prevented from meting out their own rough justice. For some reason they focused on Quinn as someone who would listen to their woes. Quinn, who himself was of mixed race, readily identified with them and miraculously started to calm them down. He told them: 'We have to set an example, and not take the matter into our own hands, but see that he gets punished through the full process of the law. We must demonstrate that we can abide by the law.' Gradually their anger subsided, the crowd dispersed and filming continued again. The man was put in jail, and deported the following morning.

Some evenings the hotel put on a barbecue in the hotel grounds. There was a fantastic atmosphere, what with the brilliant stars in the sky and the palm trees, huge steaks and a vast amount of freshly caught fish; a large variety of locally grown vegetables; and delicious fruit. If you have never had fresh, locally picked pineapple, I can tell you it bears no relationship to the fruit you get in the UK or take out of a can. It is the most succulent thing you have ever tasted. During the meal a Jamaican band and singers serenaded us. It was all very enjoyable, all the more so because we knew that a cheque was going into the bank each week.

Before flying out to Jamaica I had bought a book on the last British–American frigate battle fought off the American coast in Chesapeake Bay. I thought that the battle and all the events leading up to it would make an excellent film. I lent the book to our make-up artist who was well known and respected on both sides of the Atlantic, to ask his opinion. After he had read the book, it was left in my hotel pigeonhole. Unfortunately someone took it and I never got it back. So I decided to forget about getting the book made into a movie and concentrated on future films that were already certainties.

One day in 1965, I was called to do two jobs at different studios. The first was on *Dick Turpin*, riding cross-country over hedges. The second was at Pinewood Studios, on *Those Magnificent Men in their Flying Machines*. For this film a sixty-foot tower had been built on the corner of the studio's exterior water tank. Between the tower and the camera there was a cut-out of a building which, from the camera angle, obscured the tower, making it appear that I was standing on the top of a very high building. The opening scenes of the film show all the mad contraptions man has come up with in attempts to fly. My role was to demonstrate how a pair of wings with a span of ten feet would enable one to take flight. Or not. The first take had what they call a 'hair in the gate', and I had to do it again. By the time I had climbed the tower again, unfortunately, the wind had increased. By now, I was being buffeted around by the wind, and it was uncertain whether my landing would be in water or on concrete. I can't remember now whether I received an additional payment for the second take. I know I should have done!

33

With General Gordon

Gordon of Khartoum, the 1966 movie, found us working with Yak Canutt's sons, Joe and Tap. Like their father, both were expert riders and stuntmen. The film was shot in Egypt and I thought Cairo a particularly fascinating place of contrasts. Here you found the most modern hotels and the latest American cars, yet at the same time Arabs were to be seen driving their camels along the capital's roads; large luxury motor yachts shared the waters of the Nile with traditional Arab dhows and feluccas. We didn't have much free time, but we did manage to make fleeting visits to the pyramids and Cairo Museum. It was a great shame that we didn't get to learn more about Arab culture. As it was, most of the time we were in the desert with Yak's sons training the horses for the movie.

I arrived late during the training period, as I had been working on another film. I had never met Joe or Tap before. Joe was a dour sort of a person, with a very dry sense of humour, which was not appreciated by our English stuntmen. He had a nauseating habit of chewing tobacco, and he constantly spat out the juice that accumulated in his mouth. Red stains appeared wherever he had been. If a rehearsed stunt was not up to his standard, he would often spit, and comment, 'Stuntmen are rarer than whale's puke in the desert.' Under Joe's tuition, we did saddle falls, horse falls and pit falls.

For pit falls, a long pit is dug about two feet deep at the start and gradually tapering up to reach ground level. The pit is filled with cardboard boxes, over which are placed mattresses. These are covered over with a tarpaulin, and finally sand, to make it appear in the film like level desert. The pit is invisible to the horse, but the rider knows exactly where it is, of course. On 'Action!' being called, the horse is ridden at a gallop straight towards the pits. When the horse encounters the pits its fore legs sink into the boxes. Arab horses are so quick, that they try to recover, but with the next

217

stride their legs hit a different level, and down they go. It's like coming down stairs in the dark and reaching for a stair which isn't there. The horses have the advantage of a soft fall, protected by the boxes and mattresses. The rider, however, is sent flying through the air to land on the unprepared desert, which at times can be like landing on concrete.

Personally I got on tremendously well with both of Yak's sons. I found Joe's humour, to which the stunt boys took exception, highly amusing. Perhaps the reason for me not coming in for Joe's sarcastic comments was partly due to Yak having favourably marked my card. As I had missed a lot of the initial training, Joe let me have one of his falling horses, which he had already trained. He was quite pleased with the way I had picked up the falling-horse stunt under his tuition. One day he said to me, 'I want you to start from here, and when I reappear over there from behind that tent, gallop over and pull the horse down immediately the other side.' When he appeared with raised hand, I put the horse into a gallop and pulled it down on the other side as instructed. Unbeknown to me, Yak was waiting there. The object of the exercise was to enable Joe to show his father how quickly I had picked up the trick.

To finish off the fall I kept the horse down and lay there with it. Yak came over to me and smiled. There was no fooling Yak. He bent down and patted the horse's neck, and remarked, 'Joe, with a little more practice, you will learn to get your leg out from under.' My leg was trapped beneath the horse which didn't matter in this instance because I happened to be on soft sand, but I took his point. On a harder surface my leg could have been crushed.

At one time during the actual filming, Joe Canutt, Jackie Cooper and I were all in the same shot doing pit falls. Neither Jackie nor I wanted to be outdone and found wanting while riding with Joe. When 'Action!' was called we got off to a good start riding three abreast, all going flat out by the time we hit the pit. Down went the horses, but the sand on the tarpaulins shot up in such a cloud that we were completely blinded. I found myself flying through the air, completely disorientated. I landed flat on my back with a tremendous crash and felt as if I had broken every bone in my body. I heard the director call 'Cut!' as I lay where I'd fallen, hardly able to move. A nurse came over to me and asked if I was all right. 'Yes,' I lied, 'I didn't hear anybody shout "cut".'

As she walked away, I started to get up looking as nonchalant as I could, all the time hoping that there would not be an immediate retake. I felt crippled. Later on in the day I heard Joe say to one of the American special-effects chaps, 'Did you see Joe and Jackie in that shot? They were really wiping them out right from under them.' Although I could hardly walk, I felt gratified that in Joe's eyes we had apparently come up to scratch.

Working long hours, six and sometimes seven days a week, in addition to travelling long journeys to and from locations, can be very tiring. Tempers can easily flare when you're on a short fuse. As an example, some harsh words were exchanged between Jackie and Ken Buckle. Ken suddenly called Jackie a crowd artiste. Although Ken was twice as big, Jackie had been a body builder and amateur wrestler. Due to the disparity in their size, Ken probably didn't consider him a threat. But Jackie just flew at Ken, and landed a beautiful right hander right on the point of his jaw. Ken went out like a light. I'm pleased to say that a couple of nights later, while I was having a drink with Ken, Jackie walked over and they shook hands; everything was forgotten over a couple of drinks.

Tension can easily arise, too, in the heat of the desert, when the hours are long and the work is really hard graft when you're riding and taking falls all day. Quite often, you suffer a lot of heavy bruising. With experience, however, you soon learn how to avoid most of these hazards, but it's impossible to eliminate all the problems. When you finish shooting, you still have to take your horse back to the stable, unsaddle it and put all the equipment away before returning to your hotel. Even under these conditions, though, fights between stuntmen were very rare. We all learned to live with each other.

The first assistant on *Gordon of Khartoum* was an Australian named Bluey Hill. He was acknowledged as one of the best assistants in the business. In the desert, the art department had constructed a fortress, which was to be attacked by thousands of Arabs. Manning the fortress were the stunt boys, and Joe had planned the falls and explosions for the battle scene. From the ramparts of the fortress, you looked out on a vast expanse of desert, with the sand dunes rising up high in the distance. All morning, Bluey had been organising huge crowds as the Arab army who, after many hours of preparation, were hidden behind the sand dunes about half a mile away.

219

A tremendous amount of work had been completed laying dozens of explosive charges between the attacking force and the fortress. The army consisted of hundreds of Arabs riding camels and horses, with thousands more on foot. It was organisation on a gigantic scale, with everyone being rehearsed for the attack. Bluey placed a large number of interpreters on the sand dunes, too far away to be seen by the naked eye and picked up on camera. Each was issued with binoculars, so that they could watch Bluey high on the ramparts organising the battle in front and behind the fortress walls. Bluey told the interpreters that when everything was set, he would wave his hat as a signal for them to start the Arab army's attack.

Now remember that we are talking about thousands that Bluey had to coordinate, including all the actors, the British crowd soldiers, and the special-effects and camera crews. Everything was in place and all set to go, when at the last minute, one of the technicians found Bluey and told him that a minor hitch had occurred and they needed another half hour to fix it. Bluey, who had been working flat out all morning in the blazing sun, went ballistic. 'You bloody idiots!' he screamed, and in exasperation took off his hat and threw it on the ground. Suddenly he became aware that the Arab army in their thousands were rushing full pelt towards the fortress screaming their war cries and firing their rifles. Thinking that they had missed their cue, the special-effects crew started setting off their explosions. By now the whole battle had started, with Bluey standing on the ramparts desperately endeavouring to stop it, rather like King Canute trying to stop the waves. Incidents like this do occur in film making, but fortunately rarely on this scale. Is it little wonder that films often run way over budget?

On another occasion, the scene being filmed was of a long line of British troops returning from a very hard-fought battle. The water in every well they come across on the march back has been poisoned. Not only are the troops exhausted and in a very bad way for lack of water, but so are their horses, which are being led, not ridden. To portray the utter weariness of the column, Yak needed a stumbling horse to drop from exhaustion and be unable to get up again. A local vet gave one horse two or three injections, but the animal failed to fall over. Yak instructed him to give it one more. At this point Dickie Graydon rode by on the only mare on the

220

location. The drugged horse instantly came to life, showing an enormous erection, and tried to reach the mare. Yak, who was getting on in years, rushed over to the vet and rolled up his sleeve. 'Doc, give me a shot of that will you?' he shouted, to the great amusement of all the crew.

34

Big Game Hunting

One of the most interesting pictures I worked on was shot in the beautiful country of Kenya. Filming on *Africa–Texas Style!* started during 1966 and went over into 1967.

I was returning to Africa to double Nigel Green, whom I first met while working on *Zulu*. One of the highlights of the movie was a fight between Nigel and Hugh O'Brian, the lead, who had become famous as Wyatt Earp in the TV series.

Several big game hunters were employed to catch wild animals for the film. During a break in filming, the principal artistes listened with great interest to their exploits, and expressed a desire to go on one of their hunts. Taking them at their word, the big game hunters lined up a night shoot on one of the days when there wouldn't be any filming. The day, however, followed a heavy drinking session the previous night, from which no one had recovered, and as a result those invited declined the offer. As the hunt had been organised, it was decided to go ahead anyway. Although none of the unit was going, I was surprised to be asked whether I would like to go along. Of course I jumped at the chance.

While big game hunters were normally hired to take clients out on hunts purely for the trophies, they often went out on their own shoots. The difference was that the latter had a definite purpose: out in the bush there are no butchers or delicatessen shops, so if you want meat, you hunt. It was a highly organised affair. They all went by Land Rovers or similar vehicles suited to the terrain, accompanied by African helpers. They killed not for trophies, but purely to stock their larders. None of the animal's carcass was wasted; the hunters took the meat they required, as did their helpers, who obtained the meat free, and the rest went to the dogs.

This was a night shoot, however, and although the hunters had a pretty good idea where the animals they required would be during the day, the game could have moved miles away by the time

223

evening came. This particular night we spent considerable time driving around trying to find the animals. Often the hunters stopped and turned off their engines to listen. The sounds from the bush at night were quite incredible. Once they had located a herd, they picked out and illuminated the beast they were to shoot with powerful lamps. I thought this gave them an advantage, because nearly all the animals stopped to stare and remained fairly still. This meant that with one good shot an animal was dead. But if a chase ensued, it would sometimes take more than one bullet to finish off an animal on the run. During the hunt I accepted an offer to shoot an antelope, which I fortunately killed with one shot. I did so knowing it was for meat. I don't think that I would be interested to kill merely for sport.

Two American cowboys featured in the film *Africa–Texas Style!* In the story they had been hired by a character named Howard Hays, played by John Mills, to lasso and round up Kenyan wild life. After the big game hunters had captured the animals, they were kept in pens until required, so the location took on the appearance of a small zoo. When required for filming, the animals were put into chutes similar to those used in rodeos. The cowboys were mounted either side of the chute, and when this was opened, they chased the released animal in an attempt to lasso it. Of course, prior to this, a shot was taken of the animal running. When the camera cut to the animal being released, the chute would not appear in the shot. The cowboys' horses were very fast and well trained; the antelopes and other animals used, however, were much faster and always escaped. The hunters then had to recapture or replace them. I was told that the only way the cowboys could catch the animals was with the help of the local vet who drugged them.

Although my doubling shots were soon completed, I was needed to stand by in case other action stunts were thought up. The location was some miles from Nairobi, but the production company had retained an office in the Stanley Hotel there. The room being used as an office was, in fact, a bedroom. I asked if I could stay there while on standby. The object of the exercise was that while I was waiting it would give me an opportunity to get some flying instruction on Cessna aircraft. The film company gave the OK, saying that all I needed to do was to make sure I would not be needed the following day. As a result I had a very enjoyable few days flying.

224

I have pleasant memories of the day we flew from Wilson Airport to the Amboseli game park. En route we passed Kilimanjaro, which I filmed with my cine camera. Unfortunately the film I sent to Kodak for developing was lost and never returned, so I didn't have the opportunity to show it to my family, and there's very little chance of doing a trip like that ever again. My work on the movie and the stay in Kenya was undoubtedly one of the highlights of my career in the film industry. As they say, it was far better than working for a living.

35

Casino Royale

Part of *Casino Royale* (1967) was directed by John Huston; I say 'part', because there were six other directors under which we worked in turn. The film was a really wacky one. Under one director, we'd have a fight scene, and under another there'd be cowboys, mounting and riding down stairways. One scene, supposedly in France, featured Mata Hari in a spy drama. Most of the scenes were shot at Shepperton in a huge studio specially built for a Bond movie.

It was a very costly film, but quite a lot of money was earned by the stuntmen, and I had never before found a film company so generous.

It was also a crazy sort of a film, part of which was shot in Ireland. In one scene, we were dressed as Scots pipers. Nothing much unusual about that, except that we were standing on the top of very high castle chimneys, about 100 feet up. The special-effects people had placed a piece of tubing in the chimney for us to lean against. The trouble was that the tube was not securely fixed, with the result that when the wind blew, we had great difficulty in retaining our balance. Added to this problem was the fact that we were wearing capes, which were flying in the wind. You would lean against the wind, but when it suddenly stopped blowing, or blew in gusts, it was more than a little hazardous. Whilst all this was happening, we were supposed to be playing a lament for the laird of the castle who had passed away. I was more than pleased to come down to earth at the end of the shot.

36

Attack on the Iron Coast

Our next movie, *Attack on the Iron Coast*, was produced in 1968. It was based on the story of the Commando raid on St Nazaire during the Second World War. The major part of the film was shot in the London Docks, which at the time were derelict. While we were shooting the film, I could envisage the tremendous possibilities for future development of the docks, and now, of course, this has happened.

In the film, the story is told of how HMS *Campbeltown*, formerly an old American destroyer, was loaded with tons of high explosive, with orders to ram the dock gates of St Nazaire. The object was to put the dock out of action and prevent it being used by the German Battleship, the *Tirpitz*, as a base for maintenance and repairs. The raid was successful and the German fleet was denied the use of the dock for the rest of the war.

The interior of HMS *Campbeltown* was set up and shot in the studios. The film showed the preparations made for the raid while she was on her way to St Nazaire, with the men priming grenades and checking their weapons. The director filmed everybody in high spirits, singing away. I pointed out that this was factually incorrect, as on the real raid the noise could easily have been picked up by the enemy's listening devices, warning them of the destroyer's presence and heading. But the director brushed my advice aside, as he thought that the singing gave a dramatic effect, filmwise.

37

Where Eagles Dare

We were once again to be favoured by working with Yakima Canutt, on the 1968 film *Where Eagles Dare*, in which Richard Burton and Clint Eastwood were the principal actors.

Most of the work was to be completed on location in Austria for this movie of a wartime action involving a parachute drop by British saboteurs, attempting to break into a castle held by the German High Command. This castle was only accessible in the winter months by cable car.

The team to assault the castle had first to be dropped by parachute, which was done by aeroplane. Then Yak had a great idea of how to simulate a parachutist dropping through the air all the way down to the actual landing.

He had a rig made, which was to be suspended beneath a helicopter, on which there was a camera platform, and seat for a cameraman. The cameraman was Ginger Gimmell, a man with vast experience and long established in the industry. The rig consisted of a metal circle, which represented the periphery of a parachute. To this, steel cables were attached to the helicopter. The rigging lines of a parachute were attached to the periphery, leading down to a parachute harness, in which I was strapped. The camera was therefore pointing down to the parachutist, showing the rigging lines stretching down to the parachutist and showing the ground below.

The plan was for the helicopter to take off, position itself over the rig, pick that up, and then hover over me and pick me up. The pilot was then to ascend to a height of roughly two thousand feet, and then head off in a direction to where the landing was to be effected, which was a couple of miles away.

When we had reached the required height, the pilot then headed off in that direction at fairly high speed. This left me and the rig trailing behind. When the pilot reached the required spot, he

231

started to hover, and we started to swing underneath him. In the swing however, we went past the point of being directly under him, and set up a pendulum effect. What happened now was quite dramatic. In trying to control the swing we were being thrown all over the sky, rather like a ship chasing the compass. We were now swinging the helicopter, which the pilot was fighting hard to control. In hindsight, I would have thought that once in the swing, when we came directly under him, if the pilot had put on full power to climb, the whole rig would have straightened out, and he would have gained control.

In the helicopter were the two German special-effects men who had constructed the rig. In the panic which followed, the pilot, I was told, shouted for the rig to be released, which fortunately the two special-effects men refused to do, thus saving my life and Ginger Gimmell's. Whilst all this was happening we were rapidly losing height. Near the ground the pilot managed to gain control, and I landed with a crash, fortunately in very soft snow. The pilot was now flying sideways in order that the rig didn't land on me, and that the helicopter didn't land on the rig and Gimmell. I was, however, being dragged through deep snow, which gave me the feeling of being drowned. As soon as we had stopped, I pulled myself out of the trough into which I had been dragged to see the rig on its side at an angle, with the rotor blade still turning and just missing the rig. Gimmell was crouched as low as he could get, but in great danger, as he had been strapped in and was having difficulty in releasing himself. I got to the rig, grabbed hold of the periphery and jerked as hard as I could, and managed to pull the whole thing level.

In order that the cameraman could communicate with the ground, a walkie-talkie had been strapped to the rig, with the on/off switch taped in the *on* position. Poor Gimmell was in a terrible position, as with each oscillation the wire supports were twanging around his head. His shouts and cries were of course all heard on the ground. They were all unprintable.

We now knew what had to be done to rectify the situation, but the pilot flatly refused to go for a second take.

In the film we played the part of German troops. Yak had us shot, blown up and generally rushing from one point to another and we were all killed a great number of times. I personally had very little to do on the cable car, as I was fitted out as a German

232

officer inside the cabin. But my brother, doubling Clint Eastwood, and Alf Joint, doubling Richard Burton, had the really hazardous jobs to do.

As I mentioned, the castle was only accessible during the winter months by cable car. Obviously with the German Army in full control of Austria, there was no way in which the saboteurs could travel inside the cable-car cabin. The method devised to complete the first part of the journey was to travel unseen on the top of the cable car. This involved first climbing to the top of the cable-car station, and then jumping onto the top of the cabin as it emerged from the station en route up the mountain. This alone was quite a dodgy job, as the top of the cabin was thick with ice. To have slipped and fallen would have meant a fall of about eighty feet onto rock.

The car would ascend to a height of over 1,800 feet. As it neared the cliff face, the angle between the top of the cabin and the cable decreased until those on the top would have been crushed between the cabin top and the steel structure carrying the cable over cable wheels. The only way to overcome this problem was to climb up the arm holding the cabin, and sit on top of the arm itself. This meant that the cable would now be running between their legs.

Having reached the top, they then had to make their way to the castle. At this time, Mary Ure, the female lead, had infiltrated the castle disguised as a servant woman. She was therefore in a position to drop a rope from a window. The height of the window was roughly sixty feet to the ground. Both Eddie and Alf had to climb. As with most films, no shot is to the director's satisfaction until he has shot the scene from different angles. The two of them were well knocked out by the time the scene was completed.

The escape scene now was to be shot. As with nearly all films, scenes were shot out of sequence. The escape also had to be made by cable car, but now of course after all the action in the castle the German troops were manning the escape route. Having disposed of the crew operating the machinery for the cable car, it meant putting the car into motion, and jumping on as it left the station. In the descent, Burton and Clint Eastwood rigged explosives to detonate on contact with the bottom cable-car station. This involved getting off the car before arrival.

To effect the escape, and to allow the men to jump off the cable car safely, Yak had an area dug out of the mountain in line with the cable. It remained quite small due to the fact that most of the ground was rock. It was only about eight feet deep and was filled with water. The cable car would arrive over this point, between seventy and eighty feet above. To hit their marks, the stunt-people had to estimate the speed of descent, and the point at which to jump. It is easy to see that the first to jump had to do so before he was over the water, as the speed of the car also had to be taken into account. It also meant that the others had to jump in quick succession as the landing area was so small. There were two obvious dangers: if the first jumped too soon, he would land on the rocks below, and this also applied to the last person to jump, as he would have overshot the water. The other danger was that, should they collide in mid-air, then they could all land on the rocks below. Under these circumstances, it was very unlikely that this stunt could be shot more than once. As it worked out, the shot was perfect. Those jumping were Tom Ditman, an American stuntman, Yak's son-in-law, Gillian Aldam, an English stunt girl, Alf Joint, and I believe the last to jump was Eddie, who had to jump backwards.

After the shot I had a few words with Eddie, who incidentally hates heights, who told me that he had asked for a very high stunt fee for his part. Whilst doing the job, he had decided that he was grossly underpaid.

The interior action inside the castle was shot at MGM Studios at Borehamwood. A lot of the scenes involving German troops, in which we were involved, took place before arrival at the castle.

All the work in the studios entailed the battles between the German troops trying to stop the escape. As the castle was a warren of tunnels and passages, the Germans were at a disadvantage as they turned corners and ran into machine-gun fire, from both Burton and Eastwood, hence there were many heavy falls and a lot of being blown up by grenades. The agency had sixty men on call.

At the conclusion of the finale shots in Austria, the snow had seriously begun to melt. An Austrian businessman had arranged a machine to create artificial snow, and it is said that during those latter scenes he made a fortune. The scenes could not have been completed without him.

234

38

The Battle of Britain

When applying for a film job, problems can occur when the film company hires the services of a so-called expert who has no knowledge of the film industry. The film company feels that the expert will add the authenticity required in their production.

In the case of the movie *The Battle of Britain* (1969), an RAF officer was hired. When I and others in the stunt world applied to do the parachuting required for the film, we were rejected. I can only conclude that our experience was considered to be in the too-distant past, as it was decided that only parachutists with modern techniques would be suitable. The reality is that the only parachuting that the Battle of Britain pilots had to do was when their plane had been hit and put out of action, so that they jumped as the only means of saving their lives. They had had no parachute training. Modern day parachutists would have used a completely different type of chute to the type used during the war, and none of them would have jumped without a reserve. The only troops which had reserves during the war were the Americans. We, on the other hand, had used the types of chute used during the war, the only difference being that most of our jumps had been by static-line. My delayed jump with a dummy on *Stop Press Girl* back in 1949 had been far more difficult than a straight parachute drop.

Some years later, a similar situation arose in the making of the film *Juggernaut*. Here again the company hired an RAF advisor. He had, I understand, lined up an RAF parachute squad for the film, so once again we were rejected.

The film was based on a true story which occurred in 1972, when a man claimed he had planted a bomb aboard the QE2 and demanded a ransom. This necessitated dropping a bomb disposal group onto the ship, in the mid-Atlantic. They were to be picked up by the ship's lifeboat, taken aboard to search and were to defuse the bomb if located. Obviously they didn't want to tie up in New

York harbour, with the likelihood of an explosion alongside. Of those who jumped on the actual day, one of the team hadn't actually done a parachute drop before. Why should we who had the experience have been excluded? One explanation might be that the company could get the RAF to do the job without payment.

I understand that eventually the RAF turned the job down because they had no experience of jumping into water. In fact this turn out to be a wise decision. What actually happened was that to get the shot the film company dropped dummies by parachute. When the dummies landed in the sea, as they were still attached to the parachute, the wind dragged them off and out of sight, with the dummies submerged in the water. This had been the fate of another man, just after the war, who did a jump into the sea for a film company. I was told later that had we done the job, we would have suffered the same fate as the dummies. During the war, however, we were trained to parachute into water. The way this is done is quite simple: when you are nearing the water, you release your harness, and by hanging onto your lift webs, you drop clear of the chute before you hit the water. I suppose you could say that the company got the shot they required. I would say that they lost the dramatic effect of being able to film the true picture close up.

Here then are two examples, of hiring experts in a particular field whose knowledge didn't extend to each particular application. In both cases we had been deprived of the opportunity not only of extending our film experience, but of earning some hard cash in an industry which hadn't yet cottoned on to the fact that professional stuntmen could greatly enhance the action of the film, and also its financial success.

39

On Her Majesty's Secret Service

On Her Majesty's Secret Service (1969) was a great production to work on, as were all the Bond movies. The location was fantastic, and due to the extreme weather you sometimes get in Switzerland, the whole unit was fitted out with the latest ski clothing, which the company allowed us to keep when production came to an end.

With George Lazenby replacing Sean Connery in the lead role in this episode, the main unit started shooting at the Piz Gloria, representing the headquarters of Bond's adversary, Ernst Blofeld, played by Telly Savalas. Piz Gloria is situated ten thousand feet up on the peak of the Schilthorn Mountain. As I was not needed in the opening shots, I took the opportunity to enjoy long walks in the mountains around us. The weather was like spring in England. I also made two trips to Blofeld's headquarters where the shooting was taking place, to make sure I was very fit when it came to being called on set.

The headquarters building was connected to the village of Mürren by a series of cable cars – the only means of getting there during the winter months. The building was in the process of completion as a revolving restaurant, which would give diners a panoramic view of the mountains and the Eiger. From Piz Gloria you could ski right back down to Mürren. The location had been chosen by Sid Cain, one of the world's top production designers. He not only dressed the interior for the film, he also built onto it a helicopter pad, beneath which he installed a generator to supply all the film's lighting requirements. No expense is spared on a Bond movie.

Once the snow did arrive, we were all fitted out with skis in order to travel from one location to the next. This suited me down to the ground, as I had some skiing experience and loved the sport. While working on this movie I met Hubert Karl, the accountant, who was a very keen and expert skier. He and the professional skiers hired by the company used to go off skiing together on their free days, and I was fortunate enough to be invited to join them. When we arrived at the ski runs, we split up. They went off on the black runs, while I went by myself on the lesser runs, but we met again for meals.

The skier doubling George Lazenby as James Bond was a chap named Luki Leitner, who from an early age was destined to become one of the world's top skiers. As a young skier, he so completely outclassed others of his age that he was granted a special dispensation to compete against seniors. There is one memorable ski-chase sequence where, doubling Bond, he is pursued by Blofeld's guards. He makes a jump, and while still in the air has one ski shot off his foot by one of his pursuers, but he lands on the other ski and continues weaving through a forest.

To obtain the height needed for this shot, a ramp was built. One of the top ski instructors working on the film stood with his back to the ramp, but to one side, so that he could see Luki's landing on each take. Lutei took a tumble on one of them. The watching skier started to shake his head. When asked why, he replied, 'That fall just shows that the man is human.'

One day while shooting was taking place on a glacier, Cubby Broccoli came out to see what progress we were making. As he walked towards us, he suddenly went down in the snow up to his groin. Nobody gave the incident a second thought after he had picked himself up and continued walking. One of our guides, however, went to the spot and started chipping away with an ice pick. Some time later, when I looked, the man had disappeared, but another guide had taken his place. He was holding a rope that ran down into the hole which the first guide had made. I walked over to see what he was doing, to find that the first guide was now standing on a ledge about fourteen feet down. Beyond him was a crevasse so deep that you couldn't see the bottom, and into which I reckon you could have dropped several London double-decker buses. Had Cubby walked in a slightly different direction and the snow had given way under his weight, he would have disappeared and probably never been seen again. It was a frightening thought. The entire unit had already been advised by the guides to always remain roped together, but they found this inconvenient and had discarded the ropes. On seeing the danger that existed, they quickly re-roped themselves.

One day we had a visit from Sir Alfred Lunn, founder of the

travel agency, who was said to be the first man to bring skiing to Switzerland. Although advanced in years, he was persuaded by the film company to put on skis again for a publicity shot. Obviously he was not about to start skiing at his age. The other Englishman who brought winter sport as a whole to the country was Lord Brabazon, who started the bobsleigh runs. It could be said that by their enterprise, both men had in a way contributed to the movie we were producing.

The skill of Willy Bogner, one of the professional skiers working on the film, was out of this world. In the film he skis backwards at the same speed as Luki Leitner, when doubling as Bond. They were really travelling – you had to see it to believe it. On another occasion, he fixed himself to the bobsleigh on skis, and filmed the whole of the run, which again was almost unbelievable.

Another innovation for the film was the car racetrack on ice. Sid Cain had the Grindlewald car park flooded and frozen, which was very effective, as the race was shot at night under arc lamps. Disappointingly for us, the company had contracted a Swiss team of drivers for this sequence. The closest we got to any driving in the race was having some of the stunt boys in one of the cars when it was turned over.

Owing to hold ups due to bad weather, the shooting was delayed, which extended the schedule into the Christmas period. All the hotels were booked and we had to get out. This meant us returning to the UK for Christmas, then coming back on location after the festive season had finished and the hotels once more became vacant. On our return, however, we found that there had been a large influx of tourists taking over some of the hotels, possibly due to the publicity generated by the film. As a result, some of us had to find our own accommodation. One of professional skiers with whom I had become friendly let me rent a flat he owned in Mürren. It was a lovely apartment with a most marvellous view, as it was perched right on the edge of the mountain. From the balcony you could look right down into the valley and Lauterbunnen. From the other side you had a full view of the Eiger and at night the moon seemed enormous and perched right on top of its peak. The air was so clear that most nights there wouldn't be a cloud in the sky. And as there was no traffic at Mürren, it remained completely silent. It was magical. Fortunately I was able to bring my wife and our youngest son out to share the beauty of the place, and to give them a fantastic holiday. The professional skier's wife occasionally looked after my son while my wife also did some skiing.

For several weeks we had fairly bad weather, but the sun always seem to shine on our one free day a week. This went on for several weeks until the company decided to change our free day. What happened? The new free day became the one day in the week that we had sun. The company began to think that the odds were stacked against them. So during the entire time we were there, not only was I able to get one complete day's skiing a week in, but I also gained experience in different locations. I began to reach an acceptable skiing standard. In addition, on the days I went with the professionals, I received some instruction from the friends of Hubert Karl.

Hubert told me of an incident that occurred when he was working on a film in Germany at the Giselle Gastag Studios. At the end of the week on a Friday night during the skiing season, he used to drive into Austria and ski over the weekend, returning Sunday night to resume work on Monday morning. One Friday the shooting had been extended, and he was waiting for the unit to stop work so that he would then be able to pay everyone and drive into Austria. While waiting, he polished his skis and adjusted the bindings on them. Unexpectedly someone with an urgent message burst into the office, causing Hubert to turn suddenly. In doing so, his skis caught under his desk and he fell over and broke both ankles. This ended his skiing season for the year.

In the film we were sometimes Blofeld's men and at other times Bond's; in between I doubled for Telly Savalas. In one scene we were attacking Blofeld's headquarters by jumping out of helicopters on to the mountain ridge and into deep snow. The danger here is that if your legs go deep into the snow, and at the same time you are thrown forward, you can break them. The solution is to bend your legs as you hit the snow.

In one of the scenes where I was doubling for Savalas, Blofeld is chased by Bond down the mountain and finishes up on a bobsleigh, which careers down the bob run. Of course we didn't go the whole distance, only a small part of it. The fight on the bobsleigh finishes up with Bond kicking Blofeld off, at which point he smashes into the overhanging branch of a tree. I had padded myself well to withstand the impact, but we were going so fast that when I hit the tree it cracked three of my ribs and nearly knocked me senseless.

Luckily I managed to get my ribs strapped up, so that I was able not only to continue working, but also to ski on my free days.

One evening while attending an evening meal with the professionals at their invitation, I was handed a box at the end of the meal by Luki Leitner, who was also present. He said that he had watched my progress in skiing, and wanted to encourage me. I was surprised and delighted to find that the box contained the latest model of ski boot in my size. I was really taken aback and deeply appreciated his gesture. In all we worked on the film for about six months and the boots improved my standard of skiing no end.

When production came to a finish, the professional skiers found that there was still quite a bit of unexpired flying time left on the helicopters which had been paid for in advance by the company. They received permission to use the several days that were left to visit other parts of Switzerland. Again to my delight and surprise I was invited to join them should I be staying on after the film. Naturally I jumped at the chance.

One of the trips planned was to ski down a glacier on the other side of the Jungfrau range, a distance of several miles, all downhill. I couldn't believe my luck. This really would be the icing on the cake, I thought, and a fantastic ending to the most enjoyable movie on which I had worked. Unfortunately the bad weather again closed in, and was forecast to continue for days ahead. By then the helicopter contract would have expired, and so to my dismay the trip was cancelled.

40

Murphy's War

If something could go wrong, it did during the making of *Murphy's War* in 1971. We flew out to Jamaica to board what we were told would be a luxury liner – which it wasn't. As far as I was concerned, however, accommodation was perfectly adequate, but it was obviously not up to the standard film crews had come to expect. The ship, whose new owners were Greek, had been formerly owned by an Irish company and, so we were told, had been a mail packet, and didn't appear to be in the best seaworthy condition. The film crew were amazed that the ship had actually completed the Atlantic crossing.

We left Jamaica to sail to Venezuela, where the ship would act as a floating hotel not more than a few hundred yards from the actual location. It was intended to be a self-contained unit and was to be a base for all the equipment and supplies needed, so that we wouldn't have to pack up again to travel to new locations.

The first thing we found on arrival at the first location was that we could only anchor between ten and fifteen miles from the first shoot. Nobody had checked whether the ship could actually navigate to that point. In fact sandbanks over which the ship couldn't pass barred our way. This meant ferrying the whole unit and equipment between the ship and the location each day, which resulted in many hours of lost shooting time. The company then decided to charter a hydrofoil from Jamaica, which could clear the sandbanks and travel at high speed to cut dramatically the travel time. The hydrofoil arrived, only for us to find that the foils would not allow the vessel to tie up close enough for the transfer of personnel and equipment. So back went the hydrofoil to Jamaica. A new location was then found on the Orinoco. The cost of this exercise must have been horrendous – and this was before we had even started shooting.

The star of the film was Peter O'Toole, playing the title role. The director was Peter Yates, who had directed *Bullet*. The film was set during the Second World War. Murphy's ship has been torpedoed, and he is the sole survivor. Murphy stays floating on the ship's wreckage until he bumps into a capped oil rig platform onto which he manages to scramble. A tugboat, piloted by a French oil engineer, played by the actor Philippe Noiret, passes the rig and rescues him. During this sequence, a Spaniard had convinced the production department that he was the man to carry out this rather tricky manoeuvre. He did not take into account the fast current that was running when he made his approach. Even when put full astern, the engines of the tug could not slow the vessel sufficiently. It hit the rig with a resounding whack, and almost knocked O'Toole into the sea. *Murphy's War* could have ended there and then with the loss of the film's principal. Of course the tug should have approached the rig steaming against the current. Things obviously were not going to plan.

After his rescue, Murphy is recovering on land when he hears that the submarine that sank his ship is lurking in the area. He also discovers an old discarded seaplane which, with the help of the oil engineer, he gets back into service. Although having never flown a plane before, he decides to use it to locate the submarine. He also decides that once he finds the submarine, somehow he will destroy it. For the flying sequences, the company employed Frank Tallman, an American stunt flyer from Hollywood, to effect the erratic flying of Murphy while he learns to fly. On a couple of occasions Tallman flew so low that he damaged the plane by hitting the forest trees and production time was lost while the plane was repaired. The flying sequences were carried out on a different location, and I was assigned to the flying unit to tow the seaplane out to midstream before take off. For this purpose I had an inflatable flat-bottomed dinghy.

One day as I was towing, the seaplane suddenly took a violent turn and headed towards the riverbank, pulling me with it. Tallman didn't seem in the least disturbed by this and I wondered why and what I had done wrong. While having a meal that night in the restaurant with Tallman's engineers, I explained what had happened. They just laughed. They told me that Tallman had a false leg which at times locked if he fully straightened it. The plane had headed for the bank, because he had full left rudder on. I

Syd Cain was an internationally acclaimed Production Designer and his credits include three Bond films, as well as *Wild Geese*, *The Sea Wolves* and Alfed Hitchcock's *Frenzy*. He did all the sketches for our brochure for The Historic Medway Seaport, many of which follow here. One of his ideas for Chatham included the building of film studios within the Listed Covered Slips, the exterior of which would have retained its historic appearance.

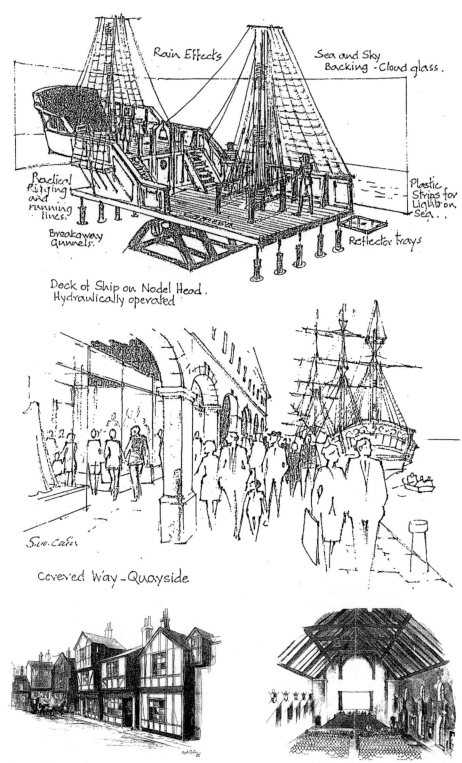

Rain Effects

Sea and Sky
Backing - Cloud glass.

Practical
Rigging
and
running
lines.

Plastic
Strips for
Light on
Sea.

Breakaway
Gunnels.

Reflector trays

Deck of Ship on Nodel Head.
Hydraulically operated

Syd.Cain

Covered Way - Quayside

Historic Medway Seaport. Chatham Docks.

Conference Room —

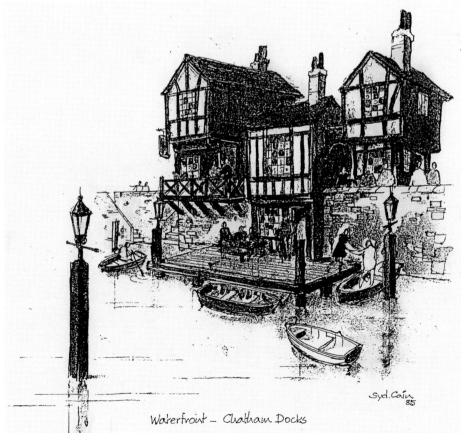

Waterfront — Chatham Docks

Syd. Cain
85

TYPICAL PERIOD SHOPS

found this amazing when you consider that he was our stunt pilot. I wondered whether his disability had something to do with the seaplane returning on two occasions with branches from tree tops protruding from the fuselage.

We then come to the part where Murphy, having located the submarine, sets out to destroy it. Here was a further problem: the submarine chartered from the Venezuelan government did not look in any way like a Second World War German submarine. For one thing, she had a very high conning tower, similar to that of a nuclear submarine. She was, however, the only submarine available, so the company had to stick with it. The tug the company had acquired as the one in which Murphy attempts to destroy the submarine was decidedly well beyond its sell-by date. Fortunately, the necessary shots aboard her had already been obtained when the tug was required to proceed up river where the encounter was to take place, because as soon as the tug reached deep water, she sank. Nobody on the production team had checked her seaworthiness. For the remaining shots, the tug was replaced by an old tank landing craft.

The village to which Murphy is taken after being rescued was an authentic replica constructed in the traditional manner, and with local natives recruited as villagers. Built on the side of the river, it consisted of a raised platform of logs from which poles extended to support a roof of reeds. The structure had no walls, and was completely exposed to the elements. Here again another problem arose. Nobody on the unit had bothered to check the rise and fall of the river. At this particular time of the year, the river was rising and the height of the water greatly increased by several feet over a very short period. This made it necessary to keep raising the huts to stop them being washed away.

All these misfortunes and the extended shooting schedule must have played havoc with the budget. In a bid to get some semblance of order in what was becoming an absolute fiasco, the existing first assistant was replaced by Bert Batt, a top first assistant and one of the best in the business. In addition, Sid Cain was brought out to use his skills as a world-ranking production designer, to re-schedule and re-design all the sets. Any success achieved by the film must have been down to those two real professionals, to whom all credit is due. Without them, it's doubtful if the movie would ever have been completed.

245

41

Young Winston

The year 1972 saw us once again working with Carl Foreman on *Young Winston*, based on Sir Winston Churchill's early life. To work on this movie was an interesting experience, with Wales and Morocco as the chosen locations. We arrived in Morocco ahead of the main unit in order to select and train falling horses. Our base was the Holiday Inn in Marrakesh.

The horses were all stallions and owned by Arab tribes, who used to put on shows known as fantasias, which are great tourist attractions. Once a year the tribes from all over Morocco met in the desert to compete among themselves in the art of fantasia – a French word which means the fantastic sport of Arab horsemen. We were invited to one of these annual get-togethers, which are attended by both contestants and their families grouped together in their respective tribes. It was a special honour to be with the tribes at their fantasia, as no other Europeans had been invited. We ate in the traditional manner of the Arabs, and I was given to understand that the eyeballs of the carcass of the traditionally slaughtered goat were given to any guest particularly favoured. I was pleased and relieved that I wasn't honoured in this way.

The fantasia is quite a simple affair, but the judging is a protracted business. Each team in turn forms up in line on horseback, and at a given signal breaks into a full gallop, with the riders standing in their stirrups screaming their war cries and brandishing their rifles. At a point marked by a straight line at the end of the course, they have to stop dead on that line and fire their rifles in unison. Points are awarded for the speed of the charge, how straight the horses have been stopped on the line, and whether the riders have all fired their rifles exactly at the same time. Also taken into account is the ornamentation of their saddles and the turn-out of horses and riders. The strange thing about fantasias is that when the Arab horsemen move to different places to give demonstrations for the benefit of tourists, they do not mount their stallions, but lead them riding on a donkey.

Later on we were taken to the government stud farm, which exists solely for the purpose of raising the high-quality horses bred throughout Morocco. Fortunately we didn't have to get involved in bargaining over the hire of the horses. Bargaining in Morocco can be a time-consuming thing. We were there to select suitable horses, and this was done by Tommy Reeves and Ken Buckle.

After the horses had been selected, they then had to be transported to our training stable a few miles from Marrakesh. Getting the stallions onto the lorries was a job in itself, as the horses had probably never before travelled in any form of transport. When we finally got them all together at the stables, there was another problem – they all started fighting. We had to station men behind the stalls with whips to stop them getting at each other. We also found that the owners had never cleaned the flies from under the horses' docks, which were crawling with them. Tommy Reeves ordered gallons of disinfectant, which was used not only on the horses but also throughout the stables. Ridding them of the infestation was instrumental in stopping them fighting and calming them. It took a couple of weeks before they settled down.

The doubles' horses were chosen, and here Ken hit upon what turned out to be a great success. He named one horse Carl, after Carl Foreman, and called other horses after members of the cast. This proved so popular that during the period we were training the horses a few miles from Marrakesh, everyone had to come and see the horse bearing their name. As there were so many horses, the names of members of the production unit as a whole were used. Sid, the accountant, arrived one day and asked why a particular horse had been named after him. Ken's reply wasn't exactly diplomatic: 'Because he's such a mean bastard.' Everybody else seemed pleased with the arrangement, though, and everything went along swimmingly until a dog turned up.

Arabs will never allow dogs to come close to them, especially strays, because most dogs carry rabies. A little bitch arrived on the scene to which Tommy took a fancy and started feeding. She became part and parcel of the unit and the stable hands soon got the message that the bitch was not to be ill-treated, certainly not in front of Tommy. She had previously been badly treated, because her front teeth had been kicked out. Like the horses, the bitch was also given

248

a female name. Unfortunately it happened to be the same name as that of our production secretary. We never did find out for sure why from then on there was a definite lack of cooperation from the production department – although we could hazard a guess.

We were all hard at it six days a week on this production, with hardly any let up in the very hot weather. The evenings brought some relief though, because we could enjoy French cuisine at one of the excellent local restaurants. The hotel also laid on some form of entertainment.

One Sunday, there was work to be done filming on the local railway, as it was the only day on which the station and a train were available. As Sunday was normally our free day, we were offered double pay and another day off in lieu. To my amazement the unions refused to let their members accept the offer. Although the unions were aware of the necessity to work on a Sunday, they wouldn't budge. I am, and have always been, a union member, but I could not understand this pig-headed attitude.

Towards the end of the location, time was running out and there was still an amount of work left to complete. This invariably leads to the 'hurry up' situation and results in the lack of adequate precautions in stunt work. In one scene, while a battle was being filmed, I was sitting on a horse out of camera shot. As the battle progressed, the camera was going to pan round to where I waited. When I actually came within shot, I was to pull the horse down as if it was shot from under me. The trouble was that the ground hadn't been prepared and it was just like concrete. Though horses are readily trained to fall, you have to make sure that they do not get hurt in the process, otherwise they will not readily perform afterwards. The horse and I had already done this particular shot four times, and I refused to do the shot again with the same animal, for this reason. There was only one other horse available, and it was one which had injured one of the other stuntmen.

I decided that only one more take was possible for safety reasons. I considered that as I was sitting quietly prior to coming into shot, the horse was unlikely to do anything dangerous on the spur of the moment. But then after the fifth take, the director insisted on yet another. This time the horse reacted with such speed that I was caught completely unaware. He rolled over in a flash and landed right on top of me. I ended up in hospital with both hips damaged.

We found out later that the poor horse had a bad tooth which, when touched by the bit, must have caused the animal terrible agony and resulted in him falling so violently. If everyone hadn't been in such a rush to complete the shooting, there would have been time to prepare the ground properly so that I could have continued using my own horse for the fall.

While I was recovering, I heard that the American manager of the hotel had gone missing. They eventually found him in hospital, where he'd been taken after being hit by a car. It was discovered, however, that he hadn't received any treatment for his injuries. The reason for this, it was said, was that the hospital staff didn't know who was going to pick up the bill. The owners of the hotel promptly chartered a private plane and flew him back to the States. The film was finished while I was in hospital, so I was able to return to England with the unit and not lose any work as a result.

Unfortunately, as a result of the stunt, an X-ray in England showed damage to both hips. Not realising the extent of the problem, I embarked on a long period of jogging to regain fitness. This aggravated the situation and in time I ended up in hospital for the total replacement of both hips. Then, thinking that I could continue as before, I caused further damage, eventually leading to a second total hip-replacement and, subsequently, the end of my career.

42

The Man Who Would Be King

Filmed in Morocco in 1975, *The Man Who Would Be King* was the fourth film directed by John Huston on which I worked. The two principals were Sean Connery and Michael Caine, playing two British NCOs released from duty in India during the days of the Empire. The story goes that these two ex-Army men decide to search for mythical treasure in the hills of the Himalayas. During a battle with tribesmen wielding bows and arrows Sean is hit by an arrow which penetrates his jacket and lodges in his bandolier underneath. The tribesmen see this man carry on fighting with an arrow still sticking out of him and think that he must be a God, as any man would have been killed. He is then treated as a king and spends many months ruling his kingdom and figuring out a way to remove the fantastic treasure, which does in fact exist. His lie is discovered when he decides, against the advice of his friend, to take a wife. During the marriage ceremony, his bride bites his cheek and draws blood, revealing that he is a mere mortal. As punishment, they decide to kill him by making him walk to the middle of the rope bridge spanning a tremendous ravine which he had made them construct. They then cut the ropes leaving him to fall to his death. This is where I came in.

The bridge was 85 feet high, but for the fall it was ratcheted up to 100 feet in order to give it more spring. At that height, however, another 15 or 20 feet is neither here nor there.

My position on the bridge had to match that of Sean's prior to the ropes being cut. The professionalism of Sean was immediately apparent; before moving into his final position, he asked me exactly how I wanted him to stand. This was in order to allow me the best chance of making it spectacular, but as safe as possible, as it would be his final position from which I would start my fall. A great number of artists would not have thought of that.

This was without doubt the most difficult fall I have ever been asked to perform. When I looked down, the sides of the ravine narrowed to a ledge where the bed onto which I had to fall had been built, beyond which the drop continued for a further 2,000 feet. This left no room for error of judgement.

There is always adrenaline before each stunt and one is keyed up. The best way to overcome and control your nerves is to concentrate on what you have to do and remain relaxed. Every stunt is different from the last; in effect you are experiencing it for the first time. With this one, there was the question of how far, or where, the tightened bridge might throw me. Prior to the fall, Jack Martin, the first assistant, radioed all crew with the command for radio silence until after I had finished my stunt, so that he would be able to call for emergency assistance, if necessary. Michael Caine started to walk away, saying, 'I'm not going to watch this one.'

I walked out onto the bridge with only the thoughts of what I had to do in mind. My two objectives were, first, to hit the target ledge with the boxes to break my fall, and second, to land on my back in order to spread the effect of the fall over as great an area as possible. Should I not achieve the correct position on landing then there was the possibility of serious injury from hitting the sides of the ravine, or even worse, missing the landing stage completely and continuing my fall for a further 2,000 feet.

The bridge was about approximately 90 feet across and about four feet wide. Despite the extra tension, it swayed slightly in the wind, adding another unknown factor into the equation. I walked out to the middle of the bridge and adopted the position that Sean had finished with. The whole crew was at this time focused on me. When I was ready, I shouted to Dick, the special-effects man, 'Are you ready Dick?' He replied, 'Yes,' and then I gave the command 'Go' and the ropes were immediately released. There was no way of controlling my initial trajectory, but luckily I was flung in a somersault clear of the bridge. I was now falling in an uncontrolled way, but at the last moment I managed to gain enough control to throw one arm around and turn my body over, and I landed bang in the middle of the landing stage. I lifted one arm up in the air to signal that I was OK and was met with a huge cheer.

Later, John Huston said to Michael Caine, 'That was the darnedest stunt I ever saw.'

Two American stuntmen joined the unit from the States, bringing with them two stunt horses. For some reason the British stuntmen were given mules to ride, as apparently there were no other horses available – although it could have been that they were more in keeping with the location. Mules have a mind of their own, which resulted in many extra takes. Thanks to the Americans being on the payroll and commanding higher rates of pay, this resulted in some of the best pay packets we had ever received.

It was a great pleasure to be working again for John Huston and Michael Caine, in a place of such magnificent scenic beauty. It also gave me great satisfaction to learn that the film was a great success at the box office.

43

Creating a New Future from the Historic Past

My interest in the last British–American sea battle which I read about while filming in Jamaica was re-awakened some years later during a reunion of the *Mayflower II* crew in London. While chatting with fellow ex-crew member Peter Padfield, by then a well-established author, I discovered that one of his novels, *Broke and the Shannon*, was based on that very battle of 1812 which had caught my imagination. The two frigates involved were the British Navy's the *Shannon* and the American ship the *Chesapeake*.

When I came to read Peter's novel, I realised what a good movie the story would make and asked him if he would let me promote it around the studios, to see if I could find a backer. His book had been meticulously researched, and was far superior to the one I had read while in Jamaica. I learned, too, that as a result of the expert historical and technical knowledge he had displayed in his story of the conflict, the American naval authorities had acclaimed Peter as the leading UK authority on the gunnery of period ships. He would therefore be an ideal technical advisor for the film I had in mind.

By now I had become well enough known in the film industry to gain admittance to the offices of the major movie makers and was able to place my idea before some of the most important producers of the moment. Their response, however, disappointed and dismayed me. I was unsuccessful in convincing any one of them that a film based on this story was one that would be a sure-fire winner in both the UK and America. They didn't take into account my experience as a crewman aboard square-rigged ships on several movies and the fact that I was well aware of the problems involved in shooting a film at sea.

Of course the problems are enormous. First you have to find a hull suitable for conversion, and then there's the construction of the superstructure and rigging plan to be considered. For the movie *Moby Dick* only one ship was involved, as the vessel doubled for both the *Pequod* and the *Rachael*. For the film I had in mind, however, two ships would be required to depict the *Shannon* and the *Chesapeake*.

Working on *Moby Dick* gave me a good insight into the problems of shooting sea sequences. A tremendous amount of structural alteration had to be made to the *Rylands*, a ship formerly trading between the UK, Ireland and North Africa, to turn her into the *Pequod*. From the planning stage onwards insurance was granted, but certain safety conditions were imposed. One of these was that there had to be a tug always in attendance, because the ship's engine had sufficient power to make headway only in the calmest sea conditions. The insurers also stipulated that the ship was never to operate outside a ten-mile radius of the shore. These restrictions caused production costs to escalate.

When shooting a sea scene the first requirement is to ensure that the ship, with her engine running, is positioned correctly in relation to the land or any other vessel required in the shot and the prevailing light conditions. While the engine holds her in position, rehearsals then take place. However, when the actual filming is about to begin, the order is given to cut the engine so that it will not intrude on the sound track. Now comes the tricky part: how can the shot be completed before the tide or wind alters this critical position? Once she starts to drift, getting a vessel back to her original position at sea takes time and in the meantime cloud may have obscured the sun. To overcome this problem with the *Pequod*, a diesel generator was installed on the tug, with a cable running between the two ships. Obviously this posed all manner of difficulties when repositioning of the ship was required. It also meant shooting time was lost, which cost a fortune. In the UK the vagaries of the weather can be an added complication. Therefore with the problems that are involved, it's not hard to see why so many scripts for sea productions are shelved. Having been rebuffed by a number of companies, it became obvious to me that if I was to succeed in my venture, a new approach was needed.

My thoughts turned to the USA where, due to the vast number of Western movies made, American stuntmen had an advantage over their British counterparts. A young stuntman in the States could enter the business knowing that he had a whole career before him, working on nothing but cowboy movies. We had nothing like this in the UK – or had we? My interest in sea productions had increased over the years with each sea movie on which I worked. The more I thought about it, the more I became convinced that our wealth of seafaring history and tradition spanning hundreds of years could provide us with similar opportunities.

Not only were there the great sea battles against the French, Spanish and Dutch, but what about the exploration and trade which the enterprising British carried on all over the globe? Two examples spring immediately to mind: the Hudson Bay Company, with its fur trading in Canada, and the British East India Company, which dominated trade on the sub-continent and led to India becoming part of the old British Empire.

A great step forward would be to build replicas of classic historical ships capable of sailing to film locations around the world where sun could be almost guaranteed, and which could be actually filmed in rough weather. Silent power was essential to hold a vessel in position without affecting the soundtrack while the cameras were rolling. For principal artistes the conditions on board and at sea could be simulated in a studio.

Here, then, was my latest challenge. For the *Broke and the Shannon* movie I needed to find:

- a means of building replica square-rigged ships economically;
- silent engine power for the ship (to allow maximum shooting time);
- a ship fully classified and able to sail to any port in the world;
- a purpose-built ship containing every department necessary for filming at sea;
- a full professional crew.

I began by looking into building costs using steel, wood, fibreglass and ferro-cement. The last was undoubtedly the cheapest of materials, but involved a labour-intensive method. Once built, there was also the question of cladding to replicate period hulls; the hull also had to need minimum maintenance and have proven longevity.

My first port of call was to speak to Peter Wood, a film scenic painter, and recognised around the world as a painter of square-rigged ships. Drawing upon his phenomenal knowledge of these vessels and their development over hundreds of years, I asked him to produce plans of several types of square-riggers which could be replicated using the same hull shape. We took this even further by devising superstructures and rigging plans which could be bolted onto the one basic hull. In his plan of the hull, Peter incorporated the cabins and other necessary accommodation all film departments would need when filming at sea. We called the finished design 'The Multi-Purpose Film Ship' (MPFS), and I formed a company called Cinemarine Ltd.

I visited Captain Alan Villiers of *Mayflower II* fame at his home in Oxford to show him the drawings. I fully expected to be sent away with a flea in my ear for even daring to suggest to the great seaman the use of ferro-cement for the hull of a traditional square-rigged sailing ship. To my delight he showed great interest and approved of the concept of an all-purpose motion-pictures sailing ship which could be converted at no great cost to a ship of the type needed for a particular film. Following our meeting, he wrote me an enthusiastic letter giving his blessing to what he described as 'an entirely feasible idea' and giving me permission to use his name if it would be of use in persuading 'possible doubters of your imaginative enterprise'.

After I had researched the ferro-cement system, I showed Harry Turner, an architect employed by British Gas, my plans. He told me to come back and see him in a week's time. When I returned, he came out of his office and held out his hand. 'It's a great idea. This will help to bring the ferro-cement system to world notice,' he enthused. Obviously with the planned ship not only appearing around the film circuits, but eventually on TV as well, it could prove to be a great advertising opportunity for obtaining ship-building orders for a variety of shipping needs.

It was now up to me to find the finance. I had heard of grants being given for innovative ideas, so I suggested to Harry that this might be the starting point. The first approach would be to the Ship & Marine Technology Requirements Board (SMTRB). Harry poured cold water on this suggestion by saying that the board had already rejected his own project. It would just be a waste of time, he said. Nevertheless, I decided to give it a go and Harry agreed to come to any meeting if I managed to obtain an interview. After some weeks had passed with no response, I concluded that perhaps Harry was right. One day, however, I received a phone call from the SMTRB arranging an interview. Harry couldn't believe it.

Harry and I were joined on the day by David Hudson, our naval architect, and Michael Franks, who was lending his experience as a director of several companies. I was rather taken aback by the size of the conference room and its table, and the number of SMTRB directors facing us. As I had called the conference, I was expected to open the proceedings. I began by outlining the problems which to date had deterred film producers from making sea movies. I explained that should the project prove successful, then it would attract American finance to the British film industry. Harry then went over the technical details of his revolutionary hull construction.

The hard-faced men sitting opposite us seemed unimpressed, but then the chairman turned to me, and started to take an interest in the filming side of the proposal. It was amazing how this aspect of our application stirred their imagination, and they all gradually became more relaxed and attentive. When the meeting drew to a close, they told us that due consideration would be given to our application and we would be informed of the board's decision.

A week later, the board awarded us a small sum for research purposes. The money was enough to enable Harry to canvass help from a number of commercial companies. Harry's method was called the variable geometry mould system. From one mould it was possible to obtain different shaped panels by altering the configuration. These, after being bolted together, were pre-tensioned and assembled into the hull form.

Harry demonstrated that his method worked by constructing a fourteen-foot model using money from the SMTRB grant and imput from some of the companies he had persuaded to join in the experiment. The whole concept had to be rethought several times, and I ended up taking the final project to Smiths Dock at Middlesbrough, Cleveland, where I could rely on substantial financial backing.

On my return from Cleveland I contacted the American Bureau of Shipping. I thought that with their backing, it would be easier to sell the project to American film production companies. The bureau turned it down, pointing out that in a collision at sea the ribs could cut into the hull surface. So once again it meant a rethink.

I then heard of a firm in Australia that was producing a new reinforcing material. I got in touch with them, and they airmailed a sufficient quantity to produce a number of test panels. I built and welded the steelwork for the test panels myself, and a concrete spraying firm did the necessary plastering over before we took them to MacAlpine's laboratories for testing. When I phoned them up for the results, the laboratory technician started to give me a lot of technical jargon that meant absolutely nothing to me. I asked him to give me the answer in layman's terms, to which he replied that it was 'fucking strong'.

Armed with this latest information, I presented the results to the American Bureau of Shipping, Lloyds of London, and Bureau Veritas. All agreed that the results could be the basis for classification – their classification, of course, conditional upon their surveying each stage of construction.

This, then, was the concept: a purpose-built ship for the film industry constructed to the highest specifications including first-rate seaworthiness. The hull was to provide accommodation for every department necessary for filming at sea from cast, production, camera and sound through to wardrobe, make-up, special effects and property. There would be catering facilities for two hundred people aboard. Externally, the superstructure was to be capable of being altered, the masts re-stepped, and the sail plan changed to depict any type of craft, spanning centuries of maritime history. It would have the added advantage of taking on the role, if required, of more than one ship in the same film. Whatever guise the MPFS appeared in, she was to comply with A1 specification for ship insurance, and be capable of sailing to any port in the world where she was needed on location.

She was to be constructed using a new method of shipbuilding, which had been backed by some of the UK's leading technical societies, and backed with grants from the Ship Marine Technology Requirements Board and the Design Council. The plans had been backed up by a highly successful research and development programme. As a further guarantee of quality, a classification company was to supervise the hull's construction at each stage of building. Fitted with a noiseless means of propulsion in the form of two silenced engines, the MPFS would be able to hold station at sea during the total period of shooting whatever the effects of tide and wind, resulting in a saving in production time and costs when making seafaring movies.

260

Quentin Falk of *Cinema and TV Today* said of the project: 'The outlet could do for the home industry what the Western has done for the American Cinema.' Gregory Peck commented that I appeared to have overcome most problems that arose on sea pictures. He said he would see that the *Hornblower* series used my ship, if he were in the series.

44

Chatham Dreams

Some time later a new and attractive possibility arose when I read that the Royal Navy was pulling out of Chatham, and that the whole dockyard was to be sold off. The more I saw of the dockyard, the more the possibilities it offered grew far beyond what I had originally envisaged.

The dockyard was huge. It had fourteen miles of steam railway, which was a potential tourist attraction on its own, and sixty listed buildings, some of which had served as accommodation for Nelson's officers. Everywhere there was a sense of Britain's centuries-old maritime history. There was even the original pay office in which Charles Dickens's father once worked as paymaster. The dock where Nelson's flagship, HMS *Victory*, was built remained intact, and still in original working order was the Ropery, one of the longest buildings in Europe, where all the cordage for the men-of-war was produced. There were also several covered slips, some of which must have been there even before Nelson's time. No.7 slip, with its working mobile gantry, was ideal for building our ship.

Just when I thought that I was beginning to make some headway, the dockyard was handed over to an organisation called English Estates, which seemed more interested in building luxury housing than utilising these wonderful facilities as a magnificent tourist attraction.

Still, I was not going to give up trying to fulfil my dream. With its period listed buildings and historical atmosphere, I could visualise the dockyard as an ideal location for filming. If a leading writer like Dudley Pope, author of the number of popular seafaring novels featuring a character named Ramage, were to lend his support, years of filming could be set up. I could already see the possibility of several frigates being built for a film series based on his work. Meanwhile, of course, there was Peter Padfield's *Broke and the Shannon*.

When not being used for movie making, the ships could form part of the tourist attraction at the dockyard. Remember, too, that we are talking about classified ships able to sail to any port in the world, so there was also the prospect of them taking part in the tall-ship and transatlantic races, or perhaps employed for sail training cruises. This meant that when not hired by film companies the ships would be self-financing. However, I was getting nowhere with English Estates in trying to convince them of the fantastic possibilities of this wonderful site which, to my mind, was an historic treasure. Setting up this facility would ensure work on sea films for years.

As I was making no headway, I decided to approach Peggy Fenner, the local MP, who gave an enthusiastic reception to my idea. She arranged for me to meet Geoffrey Pattie, Parliamentary Under Secretary of State for Defence Procurement at the Ministry of Defence. Here I also received great encouragement. I felt that at last I was beginning to make progress.

About this time I had been meeting people at BAFTA, and it was there that I met Gerry O'Halloran, an ex-Merchant Navy officer turned film producer. It appeared that he had been working along similar lines to me. He was attempting to set up a studio in St George's Dock on the north side of the Thames. He hadn't, however, made any plans for the construction of square-rigged ships. When he found out about my project, he asked me to join his group.

After weighing up the prospects, I considered that Chatham was the better bet. My assessment turned out to be correct and Gerry O'Halloran's project was rejected.

One day at BAFTA, Gerry and his group were considering their next move, when Gerry saw me at the bar and invited me over to join them. We looked into the possibility of combining our plans at Chatham, as this seemed to be advantageous to us both. By now Gerry had by now been joined by Douglas Reeman, the author who wrote contemporary stories under this name but who also had several historical seafaring novels published under the pen name of Alexander Kent. Featuring the adventures of Captain Bolitho in the heyday of square-rigged ships, these books are widely read in Britain and in the States. After a couple of meetings, Gerry and I decided to pool our efforts.

As we were formed to set up our operation at Chatham, we

registered the company as the Historic Medway Seaport Ltd – or H.M.S Ltd for short. We now had to submit a business plan for Chatham. Around this time I met up with a man by the name of Kelly Dow, who for two years running had been voted top UK salesman. Kelly had an extraordinarily imaginative mind, and he could see a fantastic future for the shipbuilding throughout the world using the new method of construction. Kelly soon found an additional market for the ship building system, it was for *Ships' Hotels*.

His company Global Leisure Ltd was well placed to enquire into the possibilities for this market. He and his co-director John Miller soon identified a number of potential sites for their use, places with wonderful beaches and scenery but without the hotel-building expertise, or the materials to build luxury hotels, or the staff to run them. A number of these sites were also in areas that were politically unstable. They reasoned that a ship hotel, in the event of political unrest, could up anchor and move to another location. It could also move if dictated by the seasons. The building of the film ship, appearing on screens around the world would present fantastic opportunities for obtaining further orders. Kelly saw no problems in obtaining orders within the first year.

Once again disaster struck, as Kelly sadly died before his plans could be activated.

Having been given the brief to turn Chatham dockyard into a profit-making concern, English Estates divided the site into two parts. The first was earmarked for luxury housing, and the second was to be developed as a museum. Major General Sir Stuart Pringle was placed in charge of the museum. Sir Stuart, formerly a Marine Commando, had suffered serious leg injuries when he was blown up by the IRA. When we met it so happened that we were both wearing our Commando ties. I said 'Snap!' to which he replied very haughtily, 'Not quite' – the inference being that Army Commandos were inferior to Marines. I remembered my mother saying that at times it pays to keep your tongue between your teeth. This was one of those times ... He was a very courteous man, however, and very easy to talk to, but unfortunately the real authority was in the hands of English Estates, whose interests lay in luxury housing.

With the people we had lined up through Gerry, plans became more grandiose. They had started to veer away from the historic past towards a theme park, and they included space travel, which is a form of exploration and would have fitted in well with the square-rigged ships that had opened up routes around the world. The theme park ideas were beginning to take preference, and my original plan for a film-making centre seemed to be of less significance. How could I object, however, when things seemed to be going well? We met with Sir Stuart Pringle on several occasions, but as no decisions were made at these meetings, we had nothing concrete on which to raise capital. The plans were now running into millions, and after literally years of striving the whole project was grinding to a halt. To my way of thinking, a sea museum without seagoing ships was a dead museum. Although I had secured the interest of the UK representative of a major Hollywood production company, I was told that until there was a positive response for an agreement from Chatham, I could not use their name, and they would not enter into negotiations.

Without the backing of the film industry, I found that I was knocking my head against a brick wall. While there had been lots of encouragement, none had offered financial backing. It was like the old saying: all wanted to jump on a moving vehicle, but none wished to get out and push.

Even with all this information and research already completed, I still couldn't generate enough interest within the British film industry to convince them of the value to the industry of an historic Medway seaport. The Government had spent millions of pounds refurbishing listed buildings, which would provide a backcloth for historic films – a film set always ready to be used over the years. Additionally, square-rigged ships, along with studio facilities, would generate their own finance and profit in the tourist industry. There was also ample evidence that rail links with the Victoria, Charing Cross and Cannon Street stations, plus the planned roads, a new Thames bridge and tunnel, and the Channel Tunnel to the Continent would make Chatham one of the most accessible sites in Europe – a gift to the film industry if ever there was one.

I had based the idea on the successful Disneyland complexes, which are a complete spin-off from Walt Disney's films. Props constructed for his films have become exhibits and tourist attractions. The Bond films, too, are classic examples of the way in which props and storylines from the movies can provide additional dividends for their shareholders. If the same facilities obtainable at

Chatham had been available in the States, the Americans would surely have capitalised on them.

Here was our opportunity to capitalise and exploit centuries of sea history in the ideal setting. The themes of exploration, endeavour, trade and merchant adventurers and overseas settlement would be represented in both the museum section and the complex as a whole. Allied to this would be the introduction of the world of film and television to re-create this past, both helping to revitalise the British film industry and communicate instantaneously through the multi-communication outlets of the media.

As with any leisure complex, we planned to have something for everyone and for all ages, from archaeology and history to the spaceship age, with special effects similar to those in Stanley Kubrick's film production of Arthur C. Clarke's *2001: A Space Odyssey*. With an accelerated approach it should have been possible to open as a major tourist attraction for the season of 1986. This would also have coincided with the completion of the M25 ring road round London, and the opening of other approach roads.

While negotiations for Chatham were still going on, instead of halting progress we decided to build a ship to act as a catalyst for financial backing. It was reported that a New Zealand naval architect by the name of Connor Mulvey had built a model of HMS *Lutine*, whose ship's bell hangs in the underwriting room of Lloyds of London and is rung to signal when a vessel has been lost at sea. The model had been presented to Lloyds and adorned the chairman's office. Chatham needed something as a tourist draw, I thought, and what better than the building of the *Lutine* in one of the historic dockyards? Lloyds gave me permission to photograph the model. As far as they were concerned, it was all good publicity for them if a replica of this historic ship was built and featured in a series of films around the world. After all, if they had to pay for such good advertising the cost would be prohibitive.

Our replica of HMS *Lutine* could portray the *Shannon* in the film I planned to make of Peter Padfield's novel. A second ship could be built to act as the American ship, the *Chesapeake*, when needed. Between films the *Lutine* could be used for visiting foreign ports promoting Lloyds, and entertaining business guests during the Cannes Film Festival once a year. She would bear Lloyds' name on the sails, ensuring them good publicity when she participated in transatlantic and tall-ship races.

267

I now more than ever believed that Alexander Kent's best-selling novels would be ideal material for Historic Medway Seaport film productions. They offered a wealth of action involving the hero, Richard Bolitho, and followed his career from entry into the King's service as a midshipman in 1768 to attaining the rank of admiral in 1812 against the backdrop of the most colourful period of naval history embracing the American War of Independence and the Napoleonic wars.

While the Chatham proposal was stalling due to not finding a film backer for the Bolitho film stories, another possibility presented itself. There was talk of the BBC planning to make a TV series of *Hornblower* from the novels by C. S. Forrester.

After several phone calls to the BBC, I finally made contact with Michael Ferguson, the producer of the series. I ran over what we were trying to achieve at Chatham and explained our method of ship construction was not only fast, but also an economical method of building replica ships. After a couple of meetings, Mr Ferguson introduced us to his technical advisor, Fred M. Walker, a naval architect from the National Maritime Museum. After discussions with Mr Walker and Mr Ferguson's assistant producer we were invited to produce specifications for three ships to feature in the *Hornblower* series.

The first, a third-rate ship of the line, we based on the Belona class of 1797, complete with armament of the period. She was to be authentic in appearance above the waterline, together with a full period interior from the lower gun deck up. A modern 'service module' incorporating ship's heads, galley, back-up generator and rest room was to be built into the structure. We stressed that the vessel would be fully seaworthy, complete with sails and rigging and fitted with additional silenced out propulsion, and would meet all current maritime safety regulations. The figurehead and stern decorations would be made easily replaceable if the film company design team wished to provide their own.

Similar features were incorporated in our specification for the second ship, a frigate along the lines of the Apollo and Euryalus classes of the same period. An extra feature, however, was that the internal period cabins were to have an open structure to allow for the fitting of several differing cabin arrangements by the design team.

The last ship was the most versatile of all three, a multi-purpose vessel for use as a three-masted brig or two-masted sloop. As a sloop it would be resemble the Laurel class of 1806, while in the brig mode it would be a typical example of the cruiser class. Multiple mast positions, variable gunports and a removable poop deck and stern galleries made transformation easy from one type of craft to the other.

It now seemed that we had at last found the catalyst needed to reopen serious negotiations for Chatham. If used as a set for the *Hornblower* series which would be seen all over the world, Chatham dockyard and its three square-rigged replica ships berthed there would undoubtedly constitute a major tourist attraction. You couldn't wish for better publicity. If you had to pay for it, the cost would be prohibitive.

There was further good news. I had managed to make contact with the director of a heritage and leisure group, who immediately saw the possibilities and benefits if we combined our efforts. His group was already well established in the heritage and leisure market, added to which he had access to financial backers. His particular interests were in setting up an undersea technology and exploration centre, and an exhibition on the history of piracy, all of which dovetailed into our own plans.

It now seemed that the last piece of the jigsaw had fallen into place. An added bonus was that the government was considering making Chatham an Enterprise Zone with numerous tax incentives, which undoubtedly would encourage international film companies into the docks. As a film base what more could you want? The *Hornblower* series, if successful, could develop like the Bond movies. The ships, when not used for filming, could act as tourist attractions, and even participate in sail training cruises, transatlantic and tall-ship races, fitting in with trade exhibitions around the world.

Eventually it might be possible to build replicas of some of the sailing ships which opened up trade routes around the world and which also transported immigrants to countries such as Canada, America, Australia, New Zealand and South Africa. These vessels, too, could earn their keep by plying the original sea routes while also remaining available for future films over the foreseeable future.

Another cause for optimism was that Kelly Dow had used his know-how as an acknowledged tourism expert with international contacts to identify opportunities for our method of construction for maritime structures around the world, and in particular in the Pacific.

But my optimism was short lived. suddenly everything started to fall apart. The BBC dropped the proposed *Hornblower* series, and the final nail was hammered in the coffin when members of Gerry O'Halloran's group into which I had tied myself held a meeting with Sir Stuart Pringle without my knowledge. Negotiations failed and their proposals were rejected. So the outcome of that meeting to which I had not been invited sounded the death knell of my Chatham dream.

45

More Ambitious Ideas – The £5,900 Million Project

During this period, various commercial concerns had submitted plans for the building of the Channel Tunnel. Among them was the Eurobridge Consortium which submitted a tremendously ambitious scheme to build a two-level tubular suspension bridge over the Channel, supported by six pairs of seabed piers. What caught my attention was that a new cementicious material was to be used for the surface of the road. The material was one quarter the weight of traditional material. I decided to find out more about this new material from the company making it, to see if there was a chance that there was some way in which it could be used in our ship construction.

Their office turned out to be at Waterloo Bridge. I tried several times to phone them, but the line was always engaged. Late one night just before I was about to leave my office, I decided to have one more go and this time I got through. I explained who I was and the reason for the call. The person who answered asked me to wait a moment while he passed on my message, and covered the mouthpiece with his hand. However, I could still hear him giving my name and the reason for the call to someone in the room. He then said, 'I'm passing you over to our chairman.' I was completely taken aback to be greeted with 'Hello, Joe, how are you?'

'Who's that?' I asked. It was John Lowe, the partner of Warwick Charlton of the *Mayflower II* project. What a stroke of luck! We met several times, and I helped in making several test panels in his office for his own project. As a result, John Lowe introduced me to a fellow company director quoting for their company's materials to be used by Eurobridge. Better still, the director joined my company. The Eurobridge project was not accepted.

Out of the blue came an entirely different approach. My work in ferro-cement shipbuilding had come to the notice of groups in the commercial world of shipbuilding. One day Anthony Harvey,

271

Secretary of the British Maritime Charitable Foundation, phoned me and invited me to lunch with him and Admiral Sir Anthony Griffin GCB, to discuss my building methods. A couple of weeks later, I again lunched with Sir Anthony and Professor Sir Alan Harris, CBE, at the Army and Navy Club Piccadilly.

Their plans were more than just ambitious; they had wanted to extend the scope of the British maritime industry. First on the list was the building of a United Nations relief ship which was to be enabled to proceed at high speed to any area in the world where a disaster had occurred, whether it was the result of flood or earthquake.

Within the hull were to be flat-bottomed boats able to reach flooded areas with relief supplies. Also on board were to be freshwater supplies, a desalination plant, a hospital with an operating theatre and stores for famine relief. The hull was to contain a second deck with space devoted to accommodation, emergency stores, victuals, a diving facility and further workshops. The whole vessel could be beached to allow ro-ro (roll on/roll off) vehicles to be off loaded. The top deck was to house helicopters able to reach areas out of reach of the flatbottomed boats.

Their second project was a cargo-carrying submarine. The advantages of the submarine over surface craft included being unaffected by bad weather such as high seas, storms and fog, and being able to shorten dramatically the distances between ports around the world. Operating at depth, a submarine would require less power for speeds above 20 knots; they reckoned estimated cruising speeds would be between 30 and 60 knots. With the ability to operate under ice, the submarine would be able to use very much shorter trade routes. Her size would be about 500k tonnes.

Both projects were based upon the extensive use of ferro-cement, as recent advances in ferro-cement technology provided opportunities to reduce considerably the capital costs of all kinds of ships, including submarines, for which ferro-cement was especially suited. In addition, significant claims had been made, and are actively being investigated for a revolutionary means of extracting hydrogen energy safely from any kind of water, including salt. Should such a claim be proven, both the material and the power would be available to build and operate cargo submarines to commercial advantage.

Subsequent to our meetings, Admiral Sir Anthony Griffin kept in touch with me by letter and phone, but sadly he died before anything could be put into motion.

Following the collapse of my Chatham dream, where do I go from here? What can be my goal in the future? My thoughts have turned back to when I developed an idea for a silent steam engine for use within the film industry.

After many years of trial and error, with the help of a professional draughtsman, my plans have been submitted by a patent agent to the patent office, and is now patent pending. I am about to build a prototype. Should this prototype prove to be successful, then my ambition is to build a seagoing boat powered by my engine. Perhaps then I can sail to all those countries I have read about, but which to date I have not yet visited – even during my earlier life as a soldier or as part of my international career as a movie stuntman.

Appendix

Here are some of the better known productions on which I personally worked, not taking into account additional films contracted through our agency, on which other stunt artistes were employed:

Production	Locations filmed
Miranda (1948)	Studio
The Small Voice (1948)	Studio
Cardboard Cavalier (1949)	Studio
Stop Press Girl (1949)	UK
The Spider and the Fly (1949)	Studio
Captain Horatio Hornblower (1951)	Studio
The Crimson Pirate (1952)	Italy
Knights of the Round Table (1953)	UK
Quentin Durward (1955)	Studio
Helen of Troy (1956)	Italy
Moby Dick (1956)	Ireland, Wales, Studio, Las Palmas
Zarak Khan (1956)	Morocco
True as a Turtle (1956)	Channel Islands, UK
The Steel Bayonet (1957)	UK
The Inn of the Sixth Happiness (1958)	Studio, Wales
Camp on Blood Island (1958)	Studio
The Key (1958)	UK
A Night to Remember (1958)	UK
Exodus (1960)	Israel
The World of Suzie Wong (1960)	UK
The Stranglers of Bombay (1960)	Studio
The Challenge (1960)	UK
The Guns of Navarone (1961)	Greece, Studio
The Green Helmet (1961)	Silverstone, UK
Billy Budd (1962)	Spain
Lawrence of Arabia (1962)	Morocco

The Longest Day (1962)	France
Captain Sinbad (1963)	Germany
Cleopatra (1963)	Spain
Zulu (1964)	South Africa, Studio
Devil Ship Pirates (1964)	UK
633 Squadron (1964)	UK
High Wind in Jamaica (1965)	Jamaica
Those Magnificent Men in their Flying Machines (1965)	Studio
The Brigand of Khandahar (1965)	UK, Studio
The Heroes of Telemark (1965)	Norway
Mr Moses (1965)	Kenya
Cast a Giant Shadow (1966)	Israel
Gordon of Khartoum (1966)	Egypt
Fahrenheit 451 (1966)	Studio
The Dirty Dozen (1967)	Studio
Africa–Texas Style! (1967)	Kenya
Casino Royale (1967)	Ireland, Studio
You Only Live Twice (1967)	Studio
The Great Catherine (1968)	Studio
Attack on the Iron Coast (1968)	Studio, London Docks
Where Eagles Dare (1968)	Austria, Studio
Submarine X-1 (1968)	Scotland, Studio
On Her Majesty's Secret Service (1969)	Switzerland
Mosquito Squadron (1969)	UK, Studio
Hell Boats (1970)	Malta
The Last Grenade (1970)	Spain
Murphy's War (1971)	Venezuela
The Last Valley (1971)	Austria
Young Winston (1972)	Morocco
Fear is the Key (1972)	Studio
Warm December (1973)	UK
The Macintosh Man (1973)	Ireland, Studio
11 Harrow House (1974)	UK, Studio
The Odessa File (1974)	Germany
The Land That Time Forgot (1975)	Studio
The Man Who Would Be King (1975)	Morocco
At the Earth's Core (1976)	Studio
The Pink Panther Strikes Again (1976)	Germany
The Squeeze (1977)	UK

Golden Rendezvous (1977)	South Africa
The Man in the Iron Mask (1977)	UK
Caravans (1978)	Iran
Death on the Nile (1978)	Egypt
The Passage (1979)	France
North Sea Hijack (1980)	Ireland, Malta
Flash Gordon (1980)	UK
Who Dares Wins (1982)	London
Top Secret (1984)	Studio
A View to a Kill (1985)	Studio
Half Moon Street (1986)	UK, Studio

Index

279

280

282

Index prepared by Indexing Specialists (UK) Ltd